G000150860

Scribe Publications
IN CONVERSATION

Ben Naparstek was born in Melbourne in 1986, and gained degrees in arts and law from the University of Melbourne before taking up a graduate fellowship at the Johns Hopkins University in Baltimore. He returned to Melbourne to become editor of *The Monthly* in May 2009, after eight years of writing about books and ideas for more than 40 newspapers and magazines. He is co-editor with Justin Clemens of *The Jacqueline Rose Reader*, forthcoming from Duke University Press. *In Conversation* is his first book.

To my editors

IN CONVERSATION
encounters with 39 great writers

Ben Naparstek

SCRIBE
Melbourne

Scribe Publications Pty Ltd
PO Box 523
Carlton North, Victoria, Australia 3054
Email: info@scribepub.com.au

First published by Scribe 2009

Typeset in 12/17 pt Granjon by the publishers
Printed and bound in Australia by Griffin Press
Only wood grown from sustainable regrowth forests is used
in the manufacture of paper found in this book.

National Library of Australia
Cataloguing-in-Publication data

Naparstek, Ben

In conversation : encounters with 39 great writers

9781921640117 (pbk.)

Authors–Anecdotes.

809

www.scribepublications.com.au

Contents

Part II: Non-fiction

Preface

The legendary British profile writer Lynn Barber once advised that an interviewer should start 'from a position of really disliking people and then compel them to win you over'. There are few comments about the interviewing craft that I find more instructive. It's not that I dislike the people I interview — usually I do like them, and when they irritate me from the outset that rarely changes as I spend more time with them. But I always endeavour to maintain a sceptical eye when asking questions of people much more distinguished than myself. I try to avoid being won over by their intelligence or charm so as to understand the idiosyncrasies and emotional background that gives rise to their intellectual and creative obsessions. Thinking of Barber can set my mind at ease when I fear that I'm being too harsh.

Interviewers, according to *The New Yorker*'s Janet Malcolm, are untrustworthy by definition. As she opens her classic study of the profession, *The Journalist and the Murderer* (1990): 'Every journalist who is not too stupid or too full of himself to notice what is going on knows that what he does is morally indefensible.' Hyperbole, for sure. But Malcolm is right that no matter how much an interviewer appears to attentively listen to or even befriend their quarry, they will inevitably have their own agenda and will construct a narrative at odds with the subject's fuller conception of herself. It was perhaps only to be expected that Malcolm, who time and again in her books dissects the nuances of the journalist–subject relationship, would be the most wary and reticent interviewee I've encountered. She was also possibly the most knowing, recognising that whatever I wrote would be a deeply subjective telling — like all profiles, an account of a life and its relationship to a body of writing, synthesised from one or two hours of conversation into just 1500–2000 words.

This collection pulls together 39 profiles of international writers from the more than 100 interviews I've published in newspapers and magazines since 2001, and are very partial constructions of lives based on brief encounters. The interviews that I wrote while living in my home city of Melbourne were generally based on telephone conversations. Others were conducted in person while I lived in the United States from 2007 to 2009, studying first at Columbia University in New York and then the Johns Hopkins University in Baltimore. Five of the authors represented here — namely, Michel Houellebecq Elfriede Jelinek, Catherine Millet, José Saramago, and Ismail Kadare — responded to questions by email through translators.

While the facts have been updated — so that the writers' ages, for example, are current as this book goes to press — the articles were always written with an eye to a particular new book or author tour, and therefore should be read with the time of writing in mind. Mostly, I've left the interviews as originally published, only ironing out occasional stylistic oddities and including longer versions of pieces where they were originally published in shorter form due to space constraints.

This book is organised into two parts, 'fiction' and 'non-fiction', although many of the authors are almost equally renowned for their work in both areas. Over the years, I've constantly returned in my mind to my conversations with these remarkable writers, which hopefully reveal the interview to be a genre more evolved than John Updike's description of it as 'a form to be loathed: a half-form like maggots'.

Part I
Fiction

Paul Auster

Paul Auster can't help picking up the phone. It's an understandable habit for a writer obsessed with the vagaries of fate — how a random phone call or chance encounter can alter the course of a life.

The first person to call during our chat is Frances Coady, Auster's editor and the partner of his close friend Peter Carey. In the kind of uncanny coincidence that structures Auster's novels, my attempt to reach Carey the previous day elicited the reply: 'Can't talk now. With Paul.'

The phone rings a second time and Auster answers. From upstairs, his novelist-wife Siri Hustvedt calls out: 'Honey, you don't have to pick up the phone.' The couple both used to work from home, but Auster now rents a nearby studio where few people have his number. 'He gets more work done,' Hustvedt says.

'It was a wrong number which started it.' So begins Auster's *City of Glass* (1985), the first in a triptych of metaphysical detective novels published together as *The New York Trilogy* in 1987. The narrator, Daniel Quinn, a solitary novelist, receives three misdirected calls for a private detective named Paul Auster. With the third call, Quinn pretends that he is Auster and starts investigating.

The Paul Auster sitting before me explains that the novel was triggered by two misdialled calls asking for the Pinkerton National Detective Agency. After setting the caller straight and hanging up for the second time, Auster regretted not playing along.

Auster is an intense and dark-complexioned man, dressed in black. He's good-humoured despite a strep throat, which doesn't stop him puffing on his trademark Dutch cigarillos. In the immaculate sitting room of their four-storey Brooklyn brownstone — with its polished floorboards, paintings and chic furniture — nothing is left to chance. 'Siri is imbued with a Scandinavian spirit of cleanliness and order,' he says. 'If I were living alone it would look like a shambles.'

On the wall are three paintings of his Olympia typewriter by the artist Sam Messer, with whom he collaborated on *The Story of My Typewriter* (2002). Auster writes in longhand but types up his paragraphs immediately, before he's unable to decipher his crabbed handwriting.

His novels combine compulsive plots with philosophical ruminations on the alienated self and the elusiveness of truth. But he bristles at reductive labels such as 'postmodern', 'Beckettian', and 'European'.

Now 61, Auster observes that his work has become preoccupied with ageing and mortality. He describes *Timbuktu* (1999), *The Book of Illusions* (2002), *Oracle Night* (2004), *The Brooklyn Follies* (2005), and *Travels in the Scriptorium* (2007) as 'books of wounded men — books about people in various stages of falling apart'.

His 2008 novel, *Man in the Dark*, finds a septuagenarian protagonist recuperating from a car accident. A few years earlier, Auster's car collided with a speeding van that smashed into the passenger side where Hustvedt was sitting. 'I thought Siri was going to die,' he recalls. 'I thought her neck was broken. I can still feel the impact just talking about it.'

Man in the Dark takes place over just one night and imagines a parallel universe in which various American states have proclaimed independence from the federation following the 2000 election of George W. Bush.

It's Auster's most political outing since *Leviathan* (1992), about a novelist named Peter Aaron (observe those initials) writing a book titled *Leviathan*. Aaron's book documents the life of his late friend Benjamin Sachs, a novelist turned terrorist who toured the country exploding replicas of the Statue of Liberty before accidentally blowing himself up.

Auster's novels frequently focus on writers and depict stories within stories, fudging the line between reality and invention. He sees an overlap in his concerns with J. M. Coetzee's later novels — 'that borderline between reality and imagination that he seems to be exploring now'.

Fiction and fact merge in the names of Auster's characters. The private eye Paul Auster in *City of Glass* is married to Siri; Peter Aaron in *Leviathan* marries Iris ('Siri' in reverse); *Oracle Night* features a writer named John Trause whose surname is an anagram of Auster.

But his characters are not autobiographical. In *City of Glass*, he explains, 'I was poking fun at myself. The Auster character is a bit of a pompous oaf. Nearly everything he says is basically the opposite of what I believe.'

Critics who dismiss the improbable occurrences in Auster's work as contrived should read *True Tales of American Life* (1999), which emerged out of Auster's collaboration with National Public Radio on *The National Story Project*. Auster called for submissions of short true-life stories to broadcast on the radio, receiving more than 4000 stories that comprise 'a museum of American reality'. 'How can you think about the world without factoring in the unforeseen, the unknowable, the fluke event?' he says. 'Sometimes we are able to fulfill our plans. But often we're not. Something intervenes. This is where stories begins.'

In his twenties and early thirties, Auster made himself especially vulnerable to chance, leading a 'reckless, stupid life without any planning or real way of earning a living'. After graduating from Columbia University in 1969, he worked on an oil tanker and moved to France for four years to eke out an existence as a translator and pursue his literary ambition: 'I thought I could learn more working on an oil tanker than in an office. These were tough days during the Vietnam War — the noise, the politicisation of everything — and I needed to be alone and look at my country from a distance.'

In *Hand to Mouth: a chronicle of early failure* (1997), Auster writes of having suffered a 'constant, grinding, almost suffocating lack of money that poisoned my soul and kept me in a state of never-ending panic'. In 1978, after publishing a few volumes of poetry, Auster hit his lowest point. His marriage to his first wife, the writer Lydia Davis, collapsed, just one year after their son, Daniel, was born. 'I went for about a year without writing anything. I didn't have the time or the focus.'

Desperate for money, he tried to market a card game based on the rules of baseball, and published a baseball thriller, *Squeeze Play* (1982), under the pseudonym Paul Benjamin. Auster's father died unexpectedly in 1979, precipitating the memoir *The Invention of Solitude* (1982) in which Auster grappled with the absence of the passionless man who, even in life, hadn't really been present. 'He did not seem to be a man occupying space, but rather a block of impenetrable space in the form of a man,' Auster writes.

Auster's father was perplexed by his literary aspirations. 'He was bewildered that a boy with what he considered to be my gifts was so inept at earning a living. Now that I'm a parent, I totally understand why he would have been worried.' Auster was shaken by his death because 'there were so many unanswered questions, so many conversations we hadn't had'.

With his father's death came the modest inheritance that enabled him to write full-time for the next six years. Fortune also arrived in the form of Hustvedt, then 26, whom he met at a poetry reading in 1981. Being eight years older than her eliminated the possibility of rivalry, he says, 'because I had already been publishing things for years'. Their daughter, Sophie, now a successful singer and film actor, was born six years later.

Peter Carey seems shocked when I ask whether Auster shows him his works in progress: 'You decide in your life who you might listen to, and Paul reads to Siri as he works. He doesn't need me.'

Another fortuitous intervention in Auster's life came at Christmas 1990, when the film director Wayne Wang read Auster's story *Auggie Wren's Christmas Story* in *The New York Times* and decided to make a film about the eponymous tobacconist. Auster subsequently wrote the script for *Smoke* (1995), a quiet and whimsical depiction of various lives that intersect around Auggie's Brooklyn cigar store, and became a de facto co-director. 'Wayne Wang said, "I think we should just make the film together." That was my film education. We worked together for two years.' Auster was credited as co-director of the sequel *Blue in the Face* (1995).

Auster made his solo directorial debut with *Lulu on the Bridge* (1998), a dreamy film starring Harvey Keitel and Mira Sorvino about a cynical saxophonist who discovers a magical stone and love after being accidentally shot. Auster's friend Salman Rushdie was set to have a minor role as a sinister anthropologist in pursuit of the precious stone. But Willem Dafoe replaced him after the teamsters, fearing that their lives would be risked by having the then fatwa-threatened Rushdie on the set, demanded exorbitant compensation payment.

Auster's 2007 film, *The Inner Life of Martin Frost*, germinated for almost a decade. He wrote a short version of the script after being approached in 1999 to contribute a film to a sequence of 12 'Erotic Tales'. But when his friend, the filmmaker Hal Hartley, warned Auster that the contract gave him little control over the project, he pulled out and used the idea in *The Book of Illusions* instead.

The novel describes a film about a novelist named Martin Frost, who retreats to a country house to rest in solitude, only to find his muse disguised as a beautiful woman in his bed. 'A few more years went by, and the idea of filming it just kept coming back to me,' Auster says.

Martin Frost is typical Auster, exploring the slipperiness of truth, the blurring of reality and fantasy, and the power of the written word. There's even a floating typewriter. His daughter, Sophie Auster, features in the cast of just four actors, which also includes David Thewlis, Irène Jacob, and Michael Imperioli.

Though set in the US, the film was shot in Portugal to save money. Peter Carey notes the paradox that 'Paul, who won't even use a computer, and gets a look of panic on his face when you use a word like "Google", is highly technically accomplished in making a movie.'

Film doesn't influence his fiction, Auster says, noting: 'I don't think my novels are cinematic at all. They're not structured like films.' Yet extraordinary chance happenings pervade his work in both mediums, as well as his life.

Auster recalls how his Polish publisher gave him a Polish telephone book from 1938 — 'a book of the dead'. He subsequently named the protagonist of *Oracle Night* Sidney Orr (an abbreviation of the family name Orlowski) after some Orlowskis that he found in the phone book. Auster included a photocopy of the page from the phone book in the novel, and arranged an interview with a Polish journalist. 'The man walks in trembling and sweating. He said, "I just finished the book. The Orlowskis, the people in your book, were my grandparents."'

— *January 2008*

Russell Banks

In New York's fabled Algonquin Hotel, where literary giants traded gossip in the early half of last century, Russell Banks is drinking red wine. Leftist writers like Ernest Hemingway and John Dos Passos — mentioned in Banks' Depression-era novel *The Reserve*, published in 2008 — mixed in affluent circles far from the working-class sympathies of their fiction. 'Insofar as they were financially successful and famous, they found themselves associating with a very different class to the people they came from or wrote about,' Banks says. 'It's also true of me.'

A thickset man of 68, with close-cropped hair and a white beard, Banks resembles Hemingway physically as well as politically. He's best-known for two novels that became Oscar-buzzed films: *Affliction* (1989), about a small-town cop driven to a violent showdown with his abusive father, and *The Sweet Hereafter* (1991), a portrait of a hardscrabble community that loses 14 children in a schoolbus accident.

He is, in short, a fixture of the American literary and film firmaments.

Yet Banks was raised in an impoverished New Hampshire backwater, and his 11 novels are fired by a commitment to the lower classes. His measured tones betray nothing of his violence as a younger man — violence he stopped inflicting physically on others in his early twenties, but which manifested as internal rage until his thirties. He suspects if he hadn't become a writer he would have faced a life of petty crime and barroom brawling — repeating the pattern of alcoholism and abuse that Banks' plumber father, Earl, inherited from his own father.

Banks' left eyelid droops slightly from a blow inflicted by Earl when he was two. He doesn't remember seeing his father sober ever again after Earl abandoned the family when Banks was 12. His mother, Florence, was a bookkeeper and also a heavy drinker — a beautiful but emotionally unstable narcissist. The eldest of four siblings, Banks became a surrogate father: 'I did the weekly and the monthly budget, and organised the children. I had to chase my father down to get the child support he wasn't paying. I didn't really have a childhood after about the age of ten.'

Banks stole a car at 16, spending three months on the road before the police caught up with him in Los Angeles. His experiences of adolescent homelessness fed into his portrayal of Chappie, a drug-abusing school dropout, who narrates *Rule of the Bone* (1995). 'I was a turbulent and angry kid,' Banks says, 'so it wasn't hard for me to get into his head. He's a seeker, a boy on a quest, and he wants to be decent and good.'

While Banks' trajectory is a classic story of white trash made good, his novels are sceptical about the American Dream. His characters often try to make clean starts, only to find themselves imprisoned by economic circumstances and re-enacting their damaged pasts.

At 18, Banks won a scholarship for underprivileged students to Colgate University, but felt so out of place among the offspring of captains of industry that he dropped out after eight weeks. 'I wasn't emotionally mature enough to handle that kind of difference I was made to feel.' He hightailed it to Miami, Florida, hoping to travel on to Cuba to enlist with Fidel Castro's insurgents. 'My politics, love of the underdog — everything could be easily transferred to Castro and his men.'

Without enough money to get to Cuba, Banks stayed in Florida, where he worked as a mannequin-dresser in a department store. 'I ended up working and living for the first time in a segregated society. Florida had an *apartheid* established. I was poor enough that I could see this.'

By 19, Banks was married, and had a daughter, Lea, the following year. But at 21, like his father before him, he deserted his family. 'Of the few things I regret, that's one of them. But I hadn't a clue. I was stuck with a job I was not capable of performing.' Lea re-entered Banks' life in her mid-teens after she fell out with her mother — just as Banks was reunited with his father when he returned to New Hampshire, at various points, to work alongside Earl as a plumber and pipe-fitter.

Banks got married again at 23, to a southerner with whom he had three more daughters. The couple moved to Chapel Hill, where Banks attended the University of North Carolina — the only southern university of its calibre that was racially integrated and co-ed. Immediately swept up in anti-segregation demonstrations, he was jailed a day after arriving in the city. 'What am I going to do? Drive by and wave? No, you end up picking up a sign and walking along with it.'

He explains his involvement with the civil-rights movement as 'a displacement of anger from my own personal and familial dynamic onto a political context. But it was also a way of expressing that big, romantic identification with the underdog — the early longing to run off and join Castro — and giving it a more coherent and useful shape.'

When Jack Kerouac, then 45, passed through Chapel Hill, Banks hosted a party for the Beat writer at his home that lasted a week. 'He was a hero for many of us, and here he was slightly mad and certainly physically ill, alcoholic and dying. Every now and then, he'd have great presence and great memory and articulation — then the next minute he'd be spewing this anti-Semitic, racist stuff.'

The rebellious Beats inspired him. 'The 1950s was a very buttoned-up time in the US — sexually repressed, socially conformist, politically still under the cloud of McCarthyism. And here came these free-wheeling spirits, breaking down all those barriers.'

At 33, Banks stopped working in blue-collar jobs, finally able to support himself through teaching and writing. Writing wasn't cathartic, he insists, but the rigour helped stabilise him. 'It could have been Zen Buddhism or psychoanalysis. Any ongoing discipline which required my special attention would have been sufficient.'

Though indifferent to his writing career, Earl was proud of his son becoming a professor. 'He'd never met a professor in his life. I don't think he read anything of mine ever.' Banks recalls his mother visiting him at Princeton, where he taught for 16 years; seeing two bearded, pipe-smoking men dressed in tweeds, Florence said, 'Quick, quick, look, Russell. I think they're professors.' Banks replied, 'Mother, I'm a professor.'

By his late twenties, Banks viewed Earl more sympathetically: 'I could begin to see what he had come out of, and how he had tried and failed to be someone other than who he was. He was a right-wing Republican, a man who voted against his self-interest his whole life. But he was very bright. He wasn't literary in any sense, but he had a photographic memory.'

The outrage at racial discrimination first experienced in Florida remained with Banks, who sees race as 'the central story in America — in the American imagination and mythology'. A year and a half spent with his family in Jamaica spawned *The Book of Jamaica* (1980), about a white American professor who travels to Jamaica to complete a novel. 'It was very important for me — getting out of the country and looking back. Very few white people were there then. It made me understand much better the whole history of race in the Western hemisphere.'

Continental Drift (1985) follows an oil-burner repairman from New Hampshire who becomes involved in the plight of a Haitian refugee. In *Cloudsplitter*, published in 1998, Banks re-imagines the life of abolitionist John Brown, whose role in attacking Harpers Ferry in 1859 is sometimes credited with starting the Civil War. 'Most African-Americans regard John Brown as a hero of the first magnitude who gave his life to free the slaves, and most white Americans regard him as a terrorist and madman.'

With *Cloudsplitter*, Banks' fictional terrain expanded to become preoccupied with history. Both *The Darling* and *The Reserve* have female protagonists, and Banks remarks that his concerns are no longer exclusively male. 'I don't want to do a father-and-son story or a conflicted working guy's life again. I want to explore other mysteries.' His next novel will investigate Internet pornography and the Iraq War.

Hollywood will surely snaffle film rights to his novel *The Reserve* — a *noir* thriller set in 1936, which makes nods to flicks like the Bette Davis vehicle *The Petrified Forest* (1936) and James M. Cain's novel *Double Indemnity* (1943). Banks transplants *noir* conventions from their typical urban setting into the Adirondack Mountains of upstate New York, where he's lived for two decades with his fourth wife, poet Chase Twitchell.

The Reserve unfolds over one summer on a private resort for old-moneyed vacationers, revolving around the affair between left-wing artist Jordan Groves and *femme fatale* Vanessa Cole. The philandering Groves, who resents the plutocratic world that made him famous, was partly modelled on the radical artist and adventurer Rockwell Kent. Vanessa, a beautiful but unstable heiress, was loosely based on one of Hemingway's paramours — a married woman who inspired his 1937 novel *To Have and Have Not*.

Creating Vanessa was technically and emotionally challenging, for Banks: 'Trying to portray a full-blown narcissist in fiction is very difficult. There's no interior to a narcissistic consciousness. Everything is reflected. For her, the question of lying or not lying, truth or falsehood, is non-existent; you can't be a liar unless you know what the truth is. It was a little scary.' Scary, perhaps, because of how Vanessa recalls his description of his own mother? Banks says he'd prefer not to answer the question.

The social stratification described in *The Reserve* persists in the Adirondacks today. The locals, sometimes living in trailers, often scramble to make ends meet; the wealthy outsiders visit for their summer holidays before returning home, leaving widespread joblessness in their wake. Unemployment in the winter is 20 per cent.

After emptying his second wineglass, he gets up. And Banks — man of the people and literary titan — leaves the historic haunt of intellectual New York's great and good to return to his hotelroom to watch the football.

— *February 2008*

Carlos Fuentes

Carlos Fuentes, novelist, essayist, ex-diplomat, and Mexico's roving international mouthpiece, is many things — including, he will have it, an exorcist. His novels imagine nightmarish scenarios to ward off imminent dangers. 'I try to do the witch-doctor thing of, "If I mention this, it won't happen",' he says. But, time and again, his exorcisms become prophecies.

In his 1999 novel, *The Years With Laura Diaz*, Fuentes wrote about a young writer's death, hoping to prevent his haemophiliac son, Carlos Fuentes Lemus, from dying. The younger Carlos, an emerging poet, filmmaker, painter, and photographer, succumbed later that year, aged 25. 'He knew he would die young, but he therefore created a lot,' Fuentes says.

In his 1987 novel, *Christopher Unborn*, Fuentes invoked Mexico in the near future disfigured by severe pollution, crime, and corruption. He hoped time would prove him wrong, but his vision was accurate.

With the ascent of Sarah Palin, Fuentes feared that America would soon have a right-wing female president and he'd become an unwitting prophet again — his 2002 novel, *The Eagle's Throne*, is set in 2020 when Condoleezza Rice is the first female president of the United States. 'Condoleezza Rice is a genius compared to Sarah Palin!' he exclaims.

The 16 interlocking short stories of his 2008 book *Happy Families* are political 'in the Greek sense of the word because they happen in the city, in the *polis*', according to Fuentes. The stories are united by Greek Chorus-like interludes that recall the incantatory prose of William Faulkner. To Fuentes, Faulkner was 'the most Latin American writer of the United States — a very baroque writer, very close to our own style'.

The title is an ironic reference to the opener of Leo Tolstoy's *Anna Karenina*: 'Happy families are all alike; every unhappy family is unhappy in its own way.' Like Tolstoy, Fuentes never won the Nobel Prize ('good company, eh?') that many people believe is his due.

By phone from London, Fuentes, 80, has the breathless energy and didactic tone of someone accustomed to holding forth at podiums. He divides the year between homes in London and Mexico City, where the custom of four-hour lunches and his vast social network leaves little time for writing.

In London, he has a relatively quiet life with his wife of 37 years, Mexican television presenter Sylvia Lemus. But he maintains an exacting travel schedule. This month, he returned to Mexico City for a ten-day conference to mark his 80th birthday on 11 November. 'I'll be sitting in the first row trying to look intelligent,' he quips.

A month before we talked, he was in Spain to collect the new Don Quixote prize, awarded jointly to Fuentes and Brazilian President Luiz Inácio da Silva. Fuentes rereads *Don Quixote* every year and believes that Cervantes was one of the few writers ever to create a compelling fictional character who is also a good person: 'My characters are rather nasty, most of them.'

With a new 600-page novel recently out in Spanish, the author of more than 30 books feels at the top of his game. 'I have more energy than ever,' he says. 'I think death will finally slow me down forever, but before that I don't think I will.'

Born in Panama City, he spent most of his childhood in Washington DC, where his father was legal counsellor of the Mexican embassy. When Mexico nationalised its oil industry in

1938, Fuentes ceased to be popular at school and 'became the alien, the bad guy, the foreigner, the Mexican'.

President Roosevelt responded with a policy of negotiation rather than confrontation, launching what Fuentes still sees as a breakthrough in Mexican–US relations. As a child, he once shook hands with FDR, and jokes that he hasn't washed them since: 'Listen, Roosevelt came to power the same year that Hitler came to power in Germany, and look at the difference — the social commitment of Roosevelt, his confidence that civil society could solve the problems of the United States!'

Aged 21, while studying international law in Switzerland, he saw Thomas Mann dining in a restaurant. Fuentes didn't approach him, 'dumbstruck with admiration', but resolved at that moment to become a writer. For income, he served in the Mexican foreign service throughout the 1950s, and later spent four years as Mexico's ambassador to France. Yet he lacked the tact of a career diplomat.

Along with fellow 'Boom' writers such as Mario Vargas Llosa, Julio Cortázar, and Gabriel García Márquez, Fuentes led the renaissance of Latin American writing in the 1960s. Briefly, he collaborated with García Márquez on film screenplays, but their literary eyes hindered their efforts: 'We spent a lot of time worrying about commas in the script.'

For many years, his left-wing politics barred him from entering the United States. Fuentes backed the 1979 Sandinista Revolution in Nicaragua, and was an early supporter of Fidel Castro's Cuba. His sympathy for Castro waned in 1965, however, when the Cuban authorities branded him and Pablo Neruda traitors for attending a PEN International ceremony in New York.

Feminist critics sometimes object that his female characters are either Madonnas or whores, but Fuentes will not be drawn into feuding with his detractors: 'I don't read them, I don't answer them, I don't care about it.'

Yet when Mexican Nobel laureate Octavio Paz published a polemic against him by author Enrique Krauze in his literary journal *Vuelta*, Fuentes ended a friendship of nearly four decades. When Paz died in 1998, Fuentes didn't attend his funeral. 'I did not provoke that feud,' says Fuentes, 'therefore I had no reason to heal or unheal it.'

Krauze's essay became a *New Republic* cover story in 1988. Under the headline 'Guerrilla Dandy', Krauze charged Fuentes with being a foreigner in his own country: 'For Fuentes, Mexico is a script committed to memory, not an enigma or a problem, not anything really living, not a personal experience.'

In *Myself With Others*, his 1988 collection of autobiographical essays, Fuentes writes about his early decision to be 'a wanderer in search of perspective', knowing that 'no matter where I went, Spanish would be the language of my writing and Latin America the culture of my language'.

His first marriage, to Mexican screen icon Rita Macedo, lasted for 14 years, despite affairs with the likes of actors Jean Seberg and Jeanne Moreau. The daughter he had with Macedo, Cecilia, is now his only surviving progeny. In 2005, Fuentes and Lemus lost their second child, Natasha, aged 30.

The Mexican media reported different versions of Natasha's death. One paper said she collapsed in Mexico City's infamous 'Tepito' district, apparently from a drug overdose; another alleged that her body was found beneath an overpass. Rumour also has it that she was kidnapped and stabbed to death by gang members. Pressed, Fuentes will say only, 'Tragedy', and demands the next question.

In Mariana Cook's 1994 book of photographs, *Fathers and Daughters*, there's a haunting black-and-white portrait of Carlos and Natasha Fuentes. The author has his arm around Natasha, less in affection as restraint, as she defiantly faces away.

In a commentary accompanying the photo, Fuentes writes about how, aged 11, Natasha was sent to French boarding school: 'She cried for a return to the security of what she called "my beautiful house". Discipline, culture, learning languages: the reasons prevailed over the emotions.'

Fuentes described her precocious intelligence, in what now reads like a premature obituary: 'She knew too much, shielded herself in knowledge both brilliant and evil, did not find the way to invent herself on the stage, on a piece of paper, instead acting out the night, writing on the pavement.'

Novelist Chloe Aridjis was one of Natasha's closest friends, and suggests that the truth about her death was suppressed. Her next novel, *Oaxaca*, will be dedicated to Natasha's memory. 'So much of what she did in her life was a cry for attention,' she says. 'She felt somewhat abandoned.'

Natasha and her brother left school early, and moved between cities and countries, sometimes every few months. 'They both tasted freedom very, very early on in their lives ... and as a result felt quite autonomous and were quite free to do whatever they wanted,' Aridjis says.

She remembers Natasha as 'always slightly detached from reality, but in a very beautiful and moving way'. Natasha wanted to become an actress, and mused about collaborating with her brother to act in one of his films: 'I think she would have been a very talented actress had she had more constants in her life.'

Natasha's parents, proud of her beauty and charm, bought her expensive clothes and hoped she would become a glittering society girl. Instead, she styled herself variously as a Goth, a punk-rock waif, and a Hispanic gangster. 'Her boyfriends were usually rock stars or ...' Aridjis trails off: 'Well, later it got a little darker.' Drugs began to destroy Natasha by her mid-twenties, when she 'fell into a dark hole and never really got out of it'.

Aged 15, after her best friend died from a drug overdose, Natasha rented a flat near Harvard where Aridjis was a college student. Aridjis says Natasha wanted to be near her, and also lacked 'anywhere else to go, really — something that happened often'.

Jenny Davidson, an English academic at Columbia, also studied at Harvard and befriended Natasha when she had recently shaved her head in mourning for her dead friend. 'One of the first conversations Natasha and I ever had was her saying, "You admire my father's writing. My father is a great writer. But he is a terrible father",' Davidson recalls. 'It was amazing to me that a 15- or 16-year-old girl would just be allowed, or even encouraged, to roam the world staying with random people.'

Despite his silence about Natasha's death, Carlos Fuentes calls drug-related crime 'the paramount issue facing my country right now'. He hopes Barack Obama and Mexican President Felipe Calderon join forces to address it: 'The USA has refused to commit to any responsibility. But Mexico would not export drugs if there weren't buyers in the USA.' Asked how one survives the deaths of two children, he says: 'You don't. I have them with me when I write. They're present.'

— *November 2008*

David Guterson

When David Guterson was a child, his disturbed mother, Shirley, warned him that people aren't who they appear to be. 'She'd say things like, "The mechanic at the gas station working on the car — it's not really him, he's wearing a mask,"' he says. Shirley was herself a Jekyll-and-Hyde personality who could prepare dinner one night and be hospitalised the next.

Her paranoia about the identities people assume contained some truth, however. In his latest novel, *The Other* (2008), Guterson considers how people are shaped by their repressed other selves. 'We're all inhabited by shadow figures,' he says, 'other permutations of ourself that are unconscious and yet impact our lives.' The epigraph quotes French poet Arthur Rimbaud: 'I am an other.'

The Other tells of two friends, seemingly opposites, who bond as teenagers through their passion for the outdoors. The narrator, Neil Countryman, is a public high school student of working-class stock who follows the path of Guterson's life — graduating from college, marrying young, and becoming a high school English teacher.

Neil's friend, John William, is a brooding heir to wealth, so outraged at society that he drops out of college and disappears into the wilderness to live hermetically in a cave. Only Neil knows John's whereabouts, and he brings his friend supplies and nurses their secret, even as the hermit deteriorates.

The Other is Guterson's most autobiographical novel, drawing on his experiences trekking through the mountains near Seattle as an adolescent in the early 1970s, which he recalls as a time of cultural limbo. According to the 53-year-old novelist: 'We were the generation that was after the zeal of the Sixties and slightly early for disco.'

North America's Pacific Northwest was also the setting of his debut novel, *Snow Falling On Cedars* (1994), about the murder trial of a Japanese–American fisherman in 1954 when anti-Japanese sentiments remained prevalent. Winning the prestigious PEN-Faulkner Award for Fiction in 1995, *Cedars* sold nearly five million copies and became a film by Australian director Scott Hicks in 1999.

Guterson's subsequent novels, *East Of The Mountains* (1999) and *Our Lady Of The Forest* (2003), returned to his native landscape but earned less critical acclaim. *East Of The Mountains* charts the spiritual journey of a retired surgeon diagnosed with terminal cancer; *Our Lady Of The Forest* is a dark fairytale about a teenage runaway who claims to see the Virgin Mary.

In *The Other*, Guterson asks whether it is possible — or desirable — to lead a life of uncompromising principle. 'Neil projects his own alienation onto somebody else so he doesn't have to carry it in his conscious life,' Guterson says. 'John is projecting his own will towards conventionality onto Neil.'

The novel is narrated in flashback decades after John's demise, as Neil considers how his friend developed the hatred of civilisation that drove him to choose death over life in what he termed 'the hamburger world'. 'I started with the question floating around after 9/11 — "Why do they hate us?"' Guterson says. 'This book is a look at somebody who has a devastating critique of Western society.'

Neil wonders about the role of John's parents in fostering his rage — particularly his mentally ill mother, Virginia, whose idea of disciplining her infant son was to ignore his cries. Guterson admits that Virginia's condition is similar to Shirley's undiagnosed illness, which lasted for ten years and disappeared once her children grew up. He suggests his mother's condition was probably a reaction to the pressures of child-rearing.

Guterson's father, Murray, remains, at 79, a noted criminal defence lawyer, but he was largely absent in Guterson's childhood. Murray was the model for Nels Gudmundsson, the defence lawyer of *Cedars*, and Guterson says his father and Nels share the 'distance from which they view events and the sadness with which they view human nature'. John's workaholic father, Rand, wonders guiltily whether he contributed to his son's fate by being passive about his wife's neglect.

As a child, Guterson accepted that his father needed to work long hours; such were the norms of the day. But it felt odd that his mother, a perennial student who never worked, was rarely home: 'You were more likely as a kid then to be mad at your mum, and say, "Hey, all the other mums are making breakfast. What are you doing?" She'd say: "Well, I'm off. Make your own breakfast."'

Fortunately, Guterson wasn't an only child like John, and he and his four siblings took care of each other: 'We got up in the morning and worked together to get breakfast.' Guterson remembers visiting Shirley in hospital when she was heavily medicated: 'They make them do things like draw pictures or make little clay figurines or play shuffleboard, and it's like your mum's in *One Flew Over The Cuckoo's Nest*. You'd come out of the hospital and think, "God, I wish I'd never visited. I don't want to see this."'

As an adult, by sticking to the conventional, Guterson seems to have gained the stability he once lacked. He has spent nearly all of his life close to his Seattle birthplace, only once moving interstate for a masters in creative writing program at Brown University, Rhode Island. He quit after two months, finding the program overly experimental, and frustrated by the seminar environment. 'It was one of those writing programs where you sit at a seminar table with ten other people and you go over people's manuscripts, and they all yell and get mad at each other,' he says.

What Guterson likes most about the mountain terrain, which surrounds his 10.9-hectare property on an island in Puget Sound, near Seattle, is its familiarity. 'It's great to really know some place well and know what you're looking at in all directions.' He cannot imagine returning to the city, since 'you spend all your time on logistics; everything is too much trouble'.

His four children — now 16, 24, 25 and 28, — could never say they were abandoned: Guterson's wife, Robin, his high-school flame, home-schooled them until their teenage years. Last year, the couple adopted a girl, Yerusalem, seven, from Ethiopia.

Guterson made the case for home-schooling in *Family Matters: why homeschooling makes sense* (1992), and doesn't think parents' emotional involvement with their children precludes them from being effective teachers. Nor does he believe it's important for children to socialise every day with their peers: 'In many institutionalised educational settings, there's a kind of neurotic social engagement that's competitive and clique-ish. It's not normal to take a whole lot of people of their own age and force them to be together all day.'

His friend the novelist Charles Johnson remembers him talking fondly about the values he acquired during his years as a Boy Scout, when he rose to the rank of Eagle. 'He's always been solid as a rock,' says Johnson, who taught Guterson at the University of Washington, where he earned a graduate degree in creative writing after leaving Brown. 'He has none of the childish and irresponsible traits that we in the West often associate with creative people — drunkenness, sexual promiscuity, or drug use.'

Guterson acknowledges that he remains a scout in spirit: 'If there's an old lady who needs help to cross the street, I'm not embarrassed to help her. I don't think it's corny.' But he still has peccadilloes. For years, he shot birds and ate them. 'I did it without giving it a lot of thought,' he says, 'but at a certain point I started thinking, "I just don't want to knock another bird down." '

His good deeds are many. As an undergraduate at the University of Washington, he volunteered as a firefighter during his summer holidays, and the smoke gave his voice its permanently raspy quality. With the windfall from *Cedars*, he co-founded a local writers' centre, Field's End, and endowed a scholarship for creative writing students.

Guterson wrote *Cedars* over eight years while working as a teacher and struggling to raise four children in a dilapidated shack on an annual income of less than $US30,000. After the book became a bestseller, he built a comfortable home and became a full-time writer. But he continued to live modestly — with no holiday houses, lavish cars, boats, or expensive travel — and mentions the teachings of Buddha as an important influence.

Raised Jewish and now an agnostic, he finds himself increasingly preoccupied with spiritual questions. 'Just by virtue of getting older, I think everybody becomes more spiritual. Coming to grips with the absolute, undeniable reality of your death forces you to start asking yourself, "What am I going to do right now that matters? Is there anything that matters?" ' He adds: 'The general trend over time in my life with regard to these questions is towards a much greater calmness about them.'

He also appears calm about his childhood, despite what *The Other* suggests, and refuses to pass judgment on his mother. 'Nowadays I think people would say it shouldn't be just her responsibility to make breakfast,' he says. 'I mean, she had every bit as much right to go out and study as my dad had to do what he did.' The forgiving words of a polite and loyal Eagle Scout perhaps mask an angry child underneath.

— June 2008

Peter Handke

The town of Chaville, outside Paris, has a sleepy, almost pastoral, air. It is here that Peter Handke, the fallen man of German letters, lives secluded behind high fences and trees. Once Austria's most venerated living writer, Handke fell from favour, with the disintegration of the former Yugoslavia, for his pro-Serb polemics. In his home beside the forest, Handke lives without a computer, beyond the reach of the consumerist and media culture that his neo-Romantic novels, calling for communion with nature, seek to remedy.

The gate opens, and Handke greets me bare-footed, his trademark shoulder-length hair blowing turbulently in the wind. A black sportscoat lends a faintly chic air to his rugged outdoor attire. He's been walking in the forest, gathering wild mushrooms and berries, piled high on the outside table where we sit. 'Don't be hard on me,' says Handke, 66, nursing an arthritic hand. 'I'm not feeling well.' Serving mushroom soup for lunch, he tells me not to fear; he can, he promises, identify the poisonous varieties.

No contemporary European writer has ex perienced such extremes of praise and ignominy as Handke. He achieved fame in his early twenties as an *enfant terrible* associated with the so-called Gruppe 67, which sought to free literature from the politically engaged realism of post-war German literature. In a historic symposium at Princeton University in 1966, he laid into Günter Grass and Heinrich Böll for reducing fiction to social criticism. Handke argued that language itself was the only reality which art was capable of representing.

His early plays were *succès de scandales* that attacked the artifice of the theatre. Doing away with theatrical conventions of character and plot, his debut anti-play, *Offending the Audience* (1966), consisted of anonymous actors assailing the paying public. But his international reputation rests predominately on his novels; most notably *A Sorrow Beyond Dreams* (1972), an affectless yet strangely powerful novella about his mother's suicide at 51; and *Repetition* (1986), which follows a writer from Handke's native province of Carinthia, who journeys to Slovenia in pursuit of a brother who vanished during World War II.

When fellow Austrian writer Elfriede Jelinek won the Nobel Prize in 2004, she declared Handke more deserving. Most people agreed, but Handke's partisanship for Milošević's regime was surely anathema to the controversy-shy Swedish Academy.

International opinion rounded on Handke in 1996 when he published *A Journey to the Rivers: justice for Serbia*. Fusing travelogue with political tract, Handke portrayed the Serbs as 'an entire, great people, Volk, that knows itself to be scorned apparently throughout Europe, and experiences that as insanely unjust'. Handke found in Serbia a pre-capitalist idyll of people drinking water from their hands. In a manner patronising to the Serbs impoverished by Western economic sanctions, Handke hoped the country would remain untarnished by consumerism.

On encountering a man who 'literally screamed at how guilty the Serb leaders were for the present suffering of the people', Handke writes: 'I did not want to hear his damnation of his leaders; not here, in this space, nor in the city or the country.' His distrust of journalistic language made him elevate his intimate encounters with ordinary Serbs over the reported facts of Serb brutality. He argued that Bosnia's Muslims massacred their own people in Sarajevo and then held the Serb forces responsible.

Using scare quotes to invoke the Srebrenica 'massacre', he questioned 'the naked, lascivious, market-driven facts and supposed facts'. *A Journey to the Rivers* makes it seem as if foreign journalists were the main culprits of the Yugoslav wars. 'The journalists committed real crimes with language,' Handke reflects now. 'You can kill a lot of people with language.'

Handke continues his assault on the media in *Crossing the Sierra de Gredos* (2007), his latest work to appear in English. A 500-page philosophical novel, originally titled *The Loss of the Image*, it features a wealthy female banker who credits her success to the inspiration of invigorating 'images'. 'When I was young, images came to me involuntarily,' says Handke. 'They meant everything to me. Then as life went on, the images became weaker and weaker.' Predictably, Handke blames the decline of authentic images on the media.

As the unnamed celebrity banker journeys to Spain's La Mancha region to meet her biographer, she is joined by a reporter, who Handke lampoons for his imperviousness to subjective experience. They encounter a secluded population known as the Hondarederos, which the reporter dismisses as 'refugees from the world'. But for the banker, whose romantic outlook parallels Handke's sentimental vision of the Serbs, the primitive people lead Eden-like existences, with an intimate relationship to the land uncorrupted by Western capitalism.

There are traces of polemic here, but Handke describes his long, elliptical sentences as a battle against opinion: 'I have a lot of anger, but I have to avoid it when I write. But you can't avoid it because the fury is a material thing in you. So your sentences become very complicated.' What he aims for is Brechtian detachment: 'I have to be moved, but a moment before I get profoundly moved there's a kind of light that moves me in a direction other than emotion.'

Clarity for Handke entails the tyranny of meaning; thus, he dismisses the Austrian filmmaker Michael Haneke as 'an ideologist

who says, "This is how people are." ' Equally disdained by Handke
are French writers Alain Finkielkraut, André Glucksmann,
and Bernard-Henri Lévy, who 'are not intellectuals, they're not
searching, because they know where good and bad is'.

Like his prose, Handke's speech is often fragmentary and
elusive, but he bristles at attempts to pin him down: 'When you ask
a question and start with "why", it's a fake. You can't answer that.
There are so many "whys", so many non-reasons.'

The heroine of the novel was inspired by Handke's encounters
with female bankers. 'They had to be cruel, but at the same time
they were very sensitive. Each one looked hurt and in danger. I told
myself, "This is a controversial person." '

I ask about the perplexing subplot involving the banker's
brother, a terrorist, who dreams of an unspecified utopian country.
Handke says that the brother's story remains a fragment because
it was too painful to complete; presumably because it echoes the
author's blighted romance with Greater Serbia: 'For a lot of us
there's a country which suggests a brighter life — a life with more
soul. That never could be Yugoslavia now.'

The romantic sensibility of Handke's novels comes through in
his recollections of growing up near the Slovenian border, 'a very
authentic and dignified life — the forest, the apples, strawberries,
blackberries, mushrooms; looking, hiding, smelling'. His mother, an
ethnic Slovene, was traumatised by the deaths of her two brothers in
World War II: 'They were Yugoslavians in their minds and souls,
but they were obliged to fight in Russia for Hitler — something
they wanted to fight against. My mother was in love with her dead
brothers all her life. This was the myth of my family. What she told
me about them was the beginning of me as a writer.'

It was at age 12, during one of his six years at a Catholic boarding
school, that Handke started to read in earnest. Finally expelled for
reading a sexually explicit Graham Greene novel, he eventually

studied law, while remaining determined, he says, 'to save myself through writing.'

What vague interest in the law Handke had, he attributes to the hatred he felt towards his stepfather, Bruno Handke — a tram driver whom his mother married before he was born: 'Sometimes I told myself that I wanted to become a defence lawyer to defend murderers. I myself could imagine killing someone — my stepfather when he was drunk. He became very violent and would hit my mother. For us children, it was unbearable. I always fantasised about taking an axe and killing him during his sleep. In my imagination, I killed him every night.'

When he delivered a eulogy at Milošević's funeral in 2006, Handke fulfilled his youthful fantasy of defending a murderer. 'His death symbolised the end of Yugoslavia. Yugoslavia for me was the most beautiful, free, and utopian republic in Europe.' France's flagship theatre company, the Comédie-Française, subsequently withdrew a scheduled performance of Handke's play *Voyage to the Sonorous Land, or the Art of Asking*. Soon after, when Handke was awarded the prestigious Heinrich Heine Prize, the politicians of Düsseldorf threatened to veto the jury's decision. Handke preemptively renounced the award in a letter to the mayor headed *Je refuse!*' 'My last book received almost no reviews in France,' he says with a laugh. 'They boycott my writing because of my erotic attraction to funerals.'

Dubbing my voice-recorder 'the hostile machine', he takes visible delight in using the presence of a journalist to vent his contempt for the profession. 'Journalists, they hate literature. Journalists write and write, and travel and travel, and drink whisky and drink whisky, but they never become heroes like writers — only when they're killed. They now have even more power than the government, but they're not grateful. They are mean people. They hate writers.'

Evening has fallen by the time I leave, and Chaville has taken on a more desolate air. I remember what Handke said earlier: 'In Paris, people think they're not alone, but they are. Here, they know they are alone. There are a lot of drunks — a lot of lost people. I like that.'

Handke's wife, German actress Katja Flint, now lives in Paris to afford him the solitude to write. Perhaps no contemporary writer evokes the elation and despair of loneliness better than Handke. Like Ezra Pound, Louis-Ferdinand Céline, and Knut Hamsun, whose literary masterworks remain admired despite their fascist politics, Handke deserves a permanent place in literary history. But his idiosyncratic aesthetics and cynicism about the media can no longer be sidelined as merely the innocent excesses of an eccentric mind.

— November 2007

Seamus Heaney

It is often said that few Nobel Prize winners produce anything of note after receiving the accolade. The burden of expectation and the ambassadorial demands on laureates are fatal for creative energies. When the 56-year-old Seamus Heaney was decorated in 1995, it was feared that he might fall victim to Stockholm syndrome. Extra-literary concerns clearly contributed to the Nobel committee's choice of an Irish writer on the heels of historic strides towards peace in Northern Ireland. Yet the decision was rare in recent Nobel history in attracting scant opposition.

A decade and three books later, Heaney has proved immune to the Nobel curse. After the death of his friend Ted Hughes in 1998, he is surely the most celebrated living poet writing in English. Eschewing the opacity of modernists such as Eliot and Pound, his books are as popular as they are critically praised. They sell in hundreds of thousands — almost unheard of for poetry.

His often-remarked-upon humility was similarly unaffected by 'the Stockholm thing' or 'the N-word' (as Heaney euphemistically calls it). He continued to shoulder a full teaching load at Harvard University, where he was poet-in-residence. 'I didn't want to seek special status because I was a poet — didn't want to confuse my calling with my profession.' Rather than just conduct poetry workshops, Heaney lectured in British and Irish poetry because, he says, 'I didn't want to swan about in the robes of my creativity.'

Heaney writes in the attic of his Dublin home, ascetically fitted out with just desk, photocopier, single bed, and books. 'I don't want to don the armour of ego or the costume of the stage poet, with my special set of pencils and handmade paper,' he says. 'I want a hand-to-hand engagement with myself — self-forgetfulness rather than self-consciousness.'

Commenting on the process by which a poem emerges, he quotes, approvingly, Frost's sketch: 'Sight, excite, insight.' 'By the time you start to compose, more than half the work has been done. The crucial part of the business is what happens before you face the empty page — the moment of first connection, when an image or a memory comes suddenly to mind and you feel the lure of the poem-life in it.'

Born in 1939, the eldest of nine children, he was raised in a three-bedroom thatched house on a farm in County Londonderry. He absorbed the mandatory Catholic litany and the cadences of the BBC shipping forecast, overlaid with the background rhythms of the potato drill.

At 12, he won a scholarship to study in Derry. 'One part of me can still sit at the head of a farmhouse table, be the man I might have been had I not won a scholarship to St Columb's College, and look from that distance at the person I've become as at a stranger,' he says.

While still a student, he met Hughes, nine years his senior, who encouraged him to submit poems to local publications. Reading Hughes' 'View of a Pig', Heaney realised that his rural background needn't be an albatross, but instead could serve as a wellspring for poetry.

His 1966 debut, *Death of a Naturalist*, was swampy with the puddles and peat of his boyhood. Heaney contrasted his writing with his spade-wielding ancestors: 'Between my finger and my thumb/The squat pen rests./I'll dig with it.' Heaney was critically anointed as heir to Yeats, who died in the year of his literary son's birth. But a minority of critics dismissed his poems as conventionally pastoral, criticising Heaney for skirting the sectarian clash bloodying his country. One reviewer carped: 'Put on your wellies, here comes Heaney.'

Teaching at Berkeley College, California, in 1970, Heaney observed how black writers compromised their independence by pouring themselves into the civil-rights movement. He was determined that the pressures to become a political mouthpiece in Ireland would not lead him to do the same. In *The Flight Path*, an IRA militant assails Heaney: 'When, for fuck's sake, are you going to write/Something for us?' He responds: 'If I do write something … I'll be writing for myself.'

Yet with the publication of *North* in 1975, the Troubles started to bleed into his poems. 'I needed to do so in order to breathe more freely,' he says. Some, who previously felt that he shirked his obligations as an Ulster Catholic poet, were satisfied by the political turn. But Heaney also outraged partisans who felt let down by the ambiguity of his political stance.

For the *North* poems are less about the Northern conflict than the artistic dilemmas it presents. The tension between the prettifying effect of poetry and the cruelty of political violence surfaces in poems such as 'Station Island', where Heaney stands accused by the ghost of a dead cousin for sanitising his death: 'You confused evasion and artistic tact/The Protestant who shot me through the head/I accuse directly, but indirectly, you.'

In 1972, when Heaney moved his family to a rural cottage in the Irish Republic, some felt that he was betraying his tribe. Whether his heading south was politically motivated depends on which journalist he's talking to. Now he stresses that the shift was non-political: 'I got a letter from a woman offering me the use of a gate lodge on an old estate in County Wicklow. I went there for two weeks with my family, loved the place — its stone and slate fabric, its seclusion, the rightness of it as a retreat — and came home to resign and relocate.'

Heaney's 1991 book, *Seeing Things*, marked his biggest shift of key since *North*. Heaney felt that sectarianism was exhausted as a theme. He also wanted to show that the richness of experience could not be killed off by the bloodletting. So he returned to the more introspective tenor of his early work.

Yet where he'd previously recoiled from visionary tones — words such as 'spirit' and 'soul', which his early mentors taught him to avoid — Heaney here 'exalt[ed] everyday miracles' (as the Swedish Academy put it). The earthy imagery of his early bogland poems gave ground to transcendent descriptions of water and air. As Heaney writes in 'Fosterling': 'I wait[ed] until I was nearly fifty/To credit marvels.' The recent deaths of his parents freed him to develop this ecstatic edge. 'Call it the flight of the soul or the spirit,' he offers. 'It helped me to lose my shyness of the vocabulary of eternity.'

Heaney returned to an ominous political backcloth with his most recent book *District and Circle*, which won the 2006 T. S. Eliot Prize and examines 'the post-9/11, post-Iraq invasion world of violent polarisation, crack-down and reprisal'. Memory remains the springboard for the poems, but it is infused with a piercing sense of threat.

'The underground train journey which is the motif of the title sequence really starts,' he explains, 'in 1962, when I had a holiday job in London and rode either the District or the Circle line every day. What's different is the level of awareness. An underground journey now is shadowed with a certain menace. Not only do you have the archetype of the journey to the land of the dead, but you have the actuality of the bombings of the London tube train in July 2005.'

In 'Polish Sleepers', Heaney's tactile descriptions are overhung by the shadow of the Nazi death camps: 'The physical reality of railway sleepers is something I'd always have enjoyed writing about — the textures and bulk and reliability of them. But when sleepers from old railway tracks in Poland were supplied by a landscape gardener as curbs for a new lawn, I couldn't help thinking of what trains might have rolled over them in the 1940s.'

The title *District and Circle* evokes Heaney's enduring preoccupation with the tension between the English and Irish facets of his identity. He made his anti-assimilationist sentiments clear in the early 1980s by refusing to be anthologised in *The Penguin Anthology of British Verse*. Yet, while calling himself Irish, he has long resisted being conscripted into the nationalist cause. He never forgets that he's working within an English literary tradition, nor that his calling was nurtured by London publishers.

'Its associations are primarily with London rather than Ireland or the countryside,' he says of *District and Circle*. 'I liked it because it's somewhat unexpected. But on second thoughts a reader might realise, "Ah, yes, in spite of the London poem, in most of the others, he's circling his own district." '

In 1997, Bill Clinton toured Ulster and quoted Heaney's poetry in nearly all of his speeches. He treated Heaney's lines like a blueprint for peaceable cohabitation: 'History says: don't hope/On this side of the grave./But then, once in a lifetime/The longed-for tidal wave/Of justice can rise up,/And hope and history rhyme.'

Given his reticence about public matters, one might imagine Heaney's discomfort at being treated like a living peace emblem. But his telling is subtler: 'The opposite of war is not peace but civilisation, so I'd like to be considered a representative of Yeats' hope: "That civilisation not sink,/Its great battle lost." '

What, in Heaney's view, is poetry's power? 'To give pleasure. To draw the mind, as Eliot says, 'to afterthought and forethought'. To create a shared culture of inwardness and tenderness, conscience and scepticism. To help us recognise ourselves and how we are in the world.'

— *February 2006*

Peter Høeg

When Peter Høeg's *Miss Smilla's Feeling For Snow* was published in an English translation in 1993, critics celebrated its haunting mix of Arctic conspiracy and moral outrage at colonial Denmark's dispossession of Greenland's native Inuit population. It was an unlikely book to sell two million copies. A melancholic whodunit with provocatively loose ends, *Miss Smilla* had more in common with a European novel of ideas than a typical blockbuster thriller.

Narrated by icy, half-Inuit glaciologist Smilla Jasperson, it was filled with dense metaphysical speculations and detailed accounts of ice formations and numerology. By Høeg's own admission, Bille August's 1997 film version failed because it adhered too closely to the book; Høeg warned August that the novel's ambiguities wouldn't transfer successfully to celluloid.

With his most recent novel, *The Quiet Girl* (2006), Høeg returns to the thriller genre, telling of Kaspar Krone, a world-famous circus clown with passions for Bach and poker, on the run from the authorities after amassing exorbitant debts. Kaspar's preternatural hearing gives him access to people's acoustic core — the musical key in which 'SheAlmighty' tunes everyone. When a ten-year-old former student who shares his mystical gift is abducted, Kaspar is lured by an offer of immunity from his arrears to track her down.

The Quiet Girl has drawn comparisons to postmodern writers John and Thomas Pynchon for its play with trivia and disjointed narrative. Its pages teem with *aperçus* about theology, music, philosophy, pop culture, and science. Yet, despite the novel's rambunctiousness, *The Quiet Girl* is not an entirely inappropriate title, given Høeg's silence over the ten years of its writing. The studiously reclusive author agreed to just this one interview for the book's English-language publication.

Høeg only bought a telephone and television when his three daughters — the offspring of his former relationship with a Kenyan dancer — became old enough to make demands. 'I prefer the quiet life,' says Høeg, 52, in his publisher's Copenhagen office.

Slender and youthful, Høeg moves with the poise of a dancer (his one-time profession), and his arms vibrate with tension as he speaks: 'I think the level of stress and information is generally higher than is healthy.' The high-voltage pace and informational overload of *The Quiet Girl* counterpoint the search for higher consciousness at its centre.

When *The Quiet Girl* was published in Denmark last year, many critics were disappointed that the faint spiritual undertow of *Miss Smilla* had developed into bald, esoteric mysticism. The *Dagbladet Information* (newspaper) argued that the novel 'doesn't want the authenticity of art, but that of faith'.

Critics also complained that they couldn't follow the plot. 'If you don't understand something, it's a psychological reaction to feel that there must be something wrong with what you're reading,' says Høeg. 'It's much harder to feel, "Maybe I should read the book more times?"'

He attributes the novel's labyrinthine plot to its ten years of development: 'I had a lot of time to work it together into something very condensed. I felt I was taking the reader to the edge; I might have gone further than I completely realised.'

Pre-empting reviewers who criticised the incessant cultural references, one character assails Kaspar for flaunting knowledge that's 'Borrowed. Stolen. Patchwork! Your feelings have no depth. You live and talk as if you're performing in the ring all the time.'

The Norwegian novelist Jan Kjærstad leapt to Høeg's defence, asking: 'How could such a rollicking, generous, open book be greeted with so much gravity and severity, such closed minds, in broad-minded old Denmark?'

Høeg expected some resistance from the Protestant Danes, but was surprised by the degree of hostility: 'The idea of training the mind and heart — the possibility of experiencing the world differently — feels strange to the Danish public. Since the Reformation, several hundred years ago, all mystic training has been banished.'

Every day before work, Høeg meditates for an hour, 'to be more compassionate and less distracted'. He does most of his writing while living away from his family in a rural retreat — he refuses to say where — for periods ranging from one week to three months. 'The important thing is to close the container and not get too much information from the outside.'

After completing a book, he rests for a year while monitoring its reception: 'I feel moved, both if it is positive and negative, like grass moves when the wind blows; it moves this way, it moves that way, but it straightens up.'

He identifies the central question of *The Quiet Girl* as whether 'it is possible to be more awake than we are normally — to sense the world more intensely and completely than we do now'. Høeg tried to make his exploration of spiritual awakening accessible through focusing on the power of music. 'I needed something that conveyed the message in a plausible way, and everybody relates to music.'

Like his protagonist, Høeg venerates the music of Bach, which he listens to every day. 'When the mind becomes very quiet, Bach is the only music I like to hear again and again, because it is unemotional. It is not without heart, but it is without rough emotions.' Høeg could be describing his own unsentimental and austere but also deeply heartfelt prose, which made *Miss Smilla* as much an elegiac study of loneliness as a page-turner.

That novel drew on Høeg's memories of growing up in an underprivileged suburb of Copenhagen, heavily populated by impoverished Inuit. Although his father was a lawyer and his family comfortably placed, Høeg's surroundings meant that he couldn't take their affluence for granted. 'I saw the last poverty in Denmark,' he says.

Destitution vanished from Denmark with the rise of the welfare state, but in its place arose new problems associated with the crushing of individualism by social engineering. Høeg explored the chilling underside of Danish inclusiveness in his 1993 novel *Borderliners*, a polemic against the education system, based on the controversial experiment of 54 schools in the 1960s to assimilate wayward children by bringing them into contact with gifted students.

Writing about children gives him shorthand access to human nature, he says, because children express the unconscious of adults: 'Adults always have a child inside them.'

The theme of child abuse remains in *The Quiet Girl*, but the anger of *Borderliners* has gone, he says. 'Confucius said: "Better even the tiniest light or candle, than wasting your life with abusing the darkness." I wasted some time in *Borderliners* attacking the darkness rather than making the light shine. I went to a very strict private school and I was carrying anger from my childhood. Human development has a lot to do with forgiving.'

In 2007, Høeg joined a group of 12 people from different professions committed to devising new models of learning, seeking to fill what Høeg sees as the void created by the breakdown of the traditional authoritarian relationship between teacher and student.

At the end of *Borderliners*, the narrator, Peter, casually reveals that, after escaping from his sinister experimental school, he was adopted by a couple named Eric and Karen Høeg (the author's parents). Høeg says that by giving the novel's narrator his name he wasn't implying that the book was autobiographical, but merely having a joke with his then-small readership. *Borderliners* was published a year after *Miss Smilla*, but completed just before he became an international celebrity. 'I had 5000 Danish readers. I felt that I knew them all, because I met them travelling in Denmark and performing. One day, I just let the "I" who is speaking take my name, because I felt I was only provoking 5000 people. They might be shaken, but they know me. But when that book appeared, it was a question of millions of readers.'

Before winning fame with *Miss Smilla*, Høeg toured Denmark once a year performing a one-man comedy show, inspired by the *commedia dell'arte* tradition — 'a medieval clown way of acting' — popularised by Italian Nobel laureate Dario Fo. Høeg wrote about circus performers in his collection of short stories, *Tales of the Night* (1990), and in *The History of Danish Dreams* (1998) — a baggy, magic-realist saga that traced 450 years of Danish history. Marginal figures recur in Høeg's fiction — gypsies, artists, disabled people, children, Inuit — but circus clowns particularly interest him because he sees them as embodying the essence of art. 'Even writers can be supported by the Danish state, but not the circus artists. They are beyond being refined or trendy. People will sit in a theatre because it is polite and it's high class. It doesn't work like that in the streets. You either grasp their attention or you lose it. Their livelihood depends on that. That kind of directness and honesty I admire a lot. I never had the courage myself to do anything on the streets.'

Like a circus clown, Høeg is both intensely engaged — fixing his interlocutor with a commanding gaze — yet also masked and elusive, smiling shyly whenever pressed for personal details. He became a performer after feeling underwhelmed by his undergraduate studies in comparative literature. 'A stable science of texts and meaning has not developed. One trend comes after another. That made it boring for me.' Trained as a fencer, he shifted to dance when the dance boom of the late Seventies hit Europe. 'They took everybody, especially boys who could move. I was never a good dancer. I had an inner certainty that it would not be my way of life in the longer period.' Throughout his twenties, he wrote short stories, before finally, aged 30, resigning his teaching position at a performing-arts college to write full time.

He began writing his first novel, *The History of Danish Dreams*, drawing heavily on his literary idols — Gabriel García Márquez, Jorge Luis Borges, Karen Blixen, and Per Olov Enquist. These literary lodestars continued to guide Høeg's work up until his 1996 eco-fable, *The Woman and the Ape*, about the love affair between an alcoholic British aristocrat and a chimpanzee. 'When I was around 40, the models dropped away and I became aware of writing from a deeper level — the collective mound of language and ideas.' He stopped reading fiction around the same time. 'You get in contact with a deeper level of yourself, where you are less dependent on stimulation from outside. With *The Quiet Girl*, I had a distinct feeling of making a trail where no one has trodden before, with the sense of danger and freedom there is when you make such a trail.'

At university, Høeg was taught by the pioneering structuralist linguist Peter Brask, who introduced him to the human potential for risky intellectual endeavour. 'I saw for the first time how it's possible to go out to where all knowledge until now is, and take a great step into empty space. You collect, slowly, the courage to take those great steps in your life or marriage or work by seeing somebody who has that kind of courage. There are not many people who are free. Most of us are caged or closed up somehow.'

He counts the Dalai Lama, Desmond Tutu, and Nelson Mandela as living avatars of freedom — 'people who have no fear, who speak their heart and mind, who are not closed by conventions but propelled by a greatness of heart and clarity of mind'. Yet while Høeg obviously regards *The Quiet Girl* as his most trail-blazing work, he demurs at the suggestion that he has attained the freedom of his role models: 'When I write, I'm somehow worried that I won't reach the reader, that they will not like it completely. I'm worried for my own standing, my position. Maybe before I die I will have obtained some level of freedom, but I'm not free towards the reactions of the outside world.'

— *October 2007*

Michel Houellebecq

Ever since Michel Houellebecq unleashed *Atomised* in 1998, and became the most talked-about French novelist since Albert Camus, opinion has been divided. To his champions, Houellebecq's broadsides against left orthodoxies have single-handedly rejuvenated French literature, making him the pre-eminent voice of contemporary ennui. To his detractors, he's a racist misanthrope who throws out splenetic provocations to the media to cynically drum up publicity.

Atomised was a vengeful assault on the '68 generation, who buried religion and unmoored society from its moral foundations. For Houellebecq — who was abandoned by his hippy parents at six and thereafter raised by his grandparents — his parent's generation reduced sex to a commodity, making an underclass of the aged and the physically undesirable.

His next novel, *Platform* (2000), sparked outrage for promoting sexual tourism as an antidote to developing world poverty. It also confirmed his reputation as a prophetic genius, depicting an Islamic terrorist attack on a Thai resort only months before the Bali bombings. Houellebecq now regrets having used Thailand as a paradigm of sex tourism. 'The archetypal sex tourist is the rich, aged Westerner who comes to enlist the sexual services of poor girls,' he says by email. 'Thailand is more complex. A large portion of the clientele is itself Asian. Thailand is not really a poor country.'

In anticipation of his latest novel, *The Possibility of an Island* (2005), five studies of Houellebecq were published in France in 2005.

They range from a literary polemic, *Help, Houellebecq's Back!,* to an unauthorised biography, which argues that Houellebecq monkeys with the facts of his life just as freely as he toys with the pieties of the liberal left. His biographer, Denis Demonpion, revealed that he was born in 1956 — not 1958, as Houellebecq claims. Demonpion discovered that, contrary to what Houellebecq told the press, his mother is neither dead nor a born-again Muslim. 'The spirit in which I made the statement made it clear that the conversion of my mother wasn't to be taken seriously,' Houellebecq says. 'It was just an eccentricity — a pose.'

In *Island*, as with Houellebecq's earlier novels, the identity of the protagonist fades into the author. The narrator, Daniel, is a depressed stand-up comedian, celebrated and loathed for shows such as 'We Prefer the Palestinian Orgy Sluts' and 'Munch on my Gaza Strip'. As with his author, Daniel's humour is unapologetically racist and sexist (think: 'What do you call the fat stuff around the vagina?'. 'Woman'). And like Houellebecq, Daniel has a son who he neither sees nor cares about, and loves his corgi with a devotion he never feels towards people.

Daniel describes his style as 'light Islamophobe burlesque'. Houellebecq might have used the same terms to explain his remark, in a typically alcohol-fuelled interview in 2002, that Islam is the 'stupidest religion'. He was subsequently hauled before court, although acquitted, for inciting racial hatred.

Daniel would have you believe that sexual love is the only genuine joy available to humankind: 'It was in truth the sole pleasure, the sole objective of human existence, and all other pleasures — whether associated with rich food, tobacco, alcohol or drugs — were only derisory and desperate compensation, mini-suicides that did not have the courage to speak their name.'

But can the views of Houellebecq's narrators necessarily be pinned on their author? 'When my characters express their artistic tastes — on literature and, occasionally, music and cinema — these tastes are mine,' he says. 'Apart from that, I feel capable of giving almost any opinion to a character, as long as it's presented convincingly.'

Yet Houellebecq undermines his claim when pressed, at separate points, about his attitudes towards women and cloning (which he's previously described as 'well-adapted to modern times, to our leisure-based civilisation'.) He replies, dismissively, that his opinions are clear enough in his books. What's more, in *Island*, Houellebecq appears to mock those who resist identifying him with the assault on human rights that runs through his oeuvre. Daniel jeers at critics who read his satire as the work of a liberal humanist: 'I had found myself cast in the role of a hero of free speech. Though personally, as regards freedom, I was rather against.'

British newspaper *The Observer* has described Houellebecq's work as 'literary Le Penism' in its nostalgia for pre-1968 certainties. Yet Houellebecq denies that he's a reactionary: 'A reactionary is someone who wants to return to a former state of society. My books are suffused with the idea that all evolution is irreversible. One could more accurately describe me as a conservative, being someone who prefers to conserve a functioning system rather than embark on risky transformations.'

Island swings between the present and a dystopian future, where the narrator's cloned descendants, Daniel 24 and Daniel 25, observe the human past from a world devoid of emotion or lust, liberated from sexuality. Houellebecq's interest in cloning grew from observing the demise of religion in Ireland, where he's lived since 1999. He wondered whether a new belief system would take its place. 'Ireland, which was the most Catholic country in Europe, stopped being it in the space of a few years as soon as prosperity arrived,' he says. 'It was stupefying to me that a religion could collapse so quickly.'

While sometimes hailed as an heir to the French nihilist Louis-Ferdinand Céline, Houellebecq insists that he's a moral writer. In his novels, he suggests, 'good and evil are always clearly delineated. There's no ambiguity'. That he's regarded as a pessimist is indicative of our age, he says. 'I don't think of myself as pessimistic or optimistic. I think of myself as a realist, as did the majority of novelists of the past centuries. People are looking for more reassurance today, because the world is more disturbing and unstable, so they demand an elevated level of optimism.'

Houellebecq's aggressive smoking habit and alcoholism suggest that his jaundiced vision may have less to do with the times than with the depressive lens through which he views them. He was regularly hospitalised for depression in the 1970s and 1980s. 'At first, I felt like these were unlivable places, where I was a prisoner. And then, insidiously — and this is what frightened me — I'd start to feel good, as though these asylums had been made for me, as if they were my real home, and probably my destiny at the end,' he says.

Even fame is a source of anxiety for Houellebecq. 'The excessive giving of interviews gradually leads people to consider me a sort of virtual creature of pure spirit. Recently,' he adds 'I began to feel anguish at the idea that I would gradually be cut off from all human contact, because everyone would be afraid of disturbing me, and also afraid of feeling inferior.'

— November 2005

Elfriede Jelinek

When Austrian writer Elfriede Jelinek heard she was nominated for the Nobel prize for literature in 2004, she responded — true to her dim view of humanity — with gloom. She told the *Berliner Zeitung* that she desperately hoped the Swedish Academy would prefer fellow Austrian novelist Peter Handke. 'I prayed that he wouldn't die or get sick,' she said. He didn't, but she still won. There was no question in Jelinek's mind that she was chosen over Handke because she is a woman.

Today, Jelinek recoils from those remarks. In a rare email interview, on the eve of the English-language publication of *Greed*, the agoraphobic novelist explains that she merely feared the fishbowl of a laureate's life. 'Of course I'm very happy and proud to have received it,' she says. 'My problem is that because of my anxiety disorder, publicity is close to torture.' Her phobia barred her from attending the ceremony; Jelinek delivered her acceptance speech by telecast.

A renegade anti-patriot in her homeland, Jelinek came to international attention in 2001 through Michael Haneke's screen version of her 1983 novel, *The Piano Teacher*. Her novels and plays attack what she sees as the fascism latent within Austria's proud celebrations of high culture, natural beauty, and folk traditions. 'Cruelty, the lack of consideration of the strong for the weak, and the master-servant relationship, in the Hegelian sense; these are my themes,' she says.

Reviled by the right, Jelinek polarises the left. She specialises in satirical critiques of patriarchy, yet her masochistic heroines are the opposite of feminist role-models. She was a member of the Austrian Communist Party from 1974 to 1991, but her sarcastic portrayals of the working class are far from empathetic. Despite her trenchant criticism of the objectification of women, she is a legendary style-queen who loves Yves Saint Laurent.

Jelinek's shrill anti-capitalism and feminism mean that her novels are often dismissed as sermons. *The New Criterion* pronounced the Nobel committee a 'laughing stock' for lavishing prestige on Jelinek's 'shameless wallowing in clichés'. The Nobel citation put it differently, applauding her 'musical flow of voices and counter-voices in novels and plays that with extraordinary linguistic zeal reveal the absurdity of society's cliches and their subjugating power'.

Jelinek's experimental prose plays with everyday scenes from popular culture, lampooning the electronic media, fashion magazines, pulp fiction, pornography, political slogans, press releases, and tourist brochures. 'For me, reality appears more clearly in clichés than in the most subtle psychological description,' she says. 'The balance of power in society is wrapped up in them.'

Greed follows a sadistic country policeman, Kurt Janisch, who treats sex as an instrument for accumulating property. Janisch embarks on an extra-marital affair with the middle-aged narrator, Gerti, and forces her to surrender her villa as a trade-off for his affections. Gerti's plight parodies the popular view of romance. As Jelinek writes in *Greed*: 'Love doesn't pull down barriers, as is often said, it builds them up, so that behind them people learn to wait and are not always pointlessly kicking the iron banisters.'

Jelinek's characters are agents of ideology, more caricatures than personalities. Thus Gabi, the 16-year-old minx who fatally falls prey to Janisch's charm, is described as: 'Golden haired. Good as gold to get used to the inevitable, that is: gold makes the world go around.'

As Jelinek explains it: 'The characters are marionettes of their social conditions ... for me, the psychology of a character is deduced retrospectively — that is, from their involvement in the plot, not the other way around.'

Her novels evoke a hyper-reality, where authentic experience is eclipsed by the recycled images of the mass media. As Jelinek observes in *Greed*: 'Nature doesn't exist any more, so why should it suddenly come back?' She mimics and undermines tourist-industry commonplaces: 'Come right in, you cute comparison of mountain lake with diamond set among the mountains, how well I know you, just lie down there! no, but not on my toes!' Jelinek says: 'I cannot view the landscape from a naive perspective, as though nobody has ever seen it like I have before.' *Greed* inverts the storybook picture of an alpine paradise. 'The beauty of Austria — under which the corpses of the Nazi period are buried — has covered up much of its history,' says Jelinek.

Her 1980 novel, *Wonderful, Wonderful Times*, traces the transmission of Nazism to the children of perpetrators, as four disaffected adolescents commit random violent acts in the late 1950s. 'In post-war Germany the crimes were worked through, letter by letter,' says Jelinek. 'But in Austria, because we wanted to be viewed positively by the Allies, we needed to deny our complicity with the Nazis and portray ourselves as 'little innocents'. One mustn't forget that Hitler learnt his anti-Semitism from trashy magazines in Austria and was exported to Germany as a complete political mind. Anti-Semitism was once our great export, so to speak.'

Jelinek's critique of Austria's historical blindness makes her the *bête noire* of conservative pundits. When *The Piano Teacher* was first published, *Die Welt* likened her writing to spit: 'She hates music, she hates Vienna, she hates people. And above all, she hates herself.' *The Piano Teacher* remains her most powerful work because Jelinek reins in her avant-garde excesses and allows her characters a measure of psychological realism. The novel autobiographically explores the disturbed sexuality of Erika, a 36-year-old pianist who has lived alone with her cruelly authoritarian mother since her father was interned in a mental asylum when she was a child.

Also an only child, Jelinek was born in 1946, when her mother was 43. Her father was a Jew who saved himself by working for the Nazis as a chemist. He went mad while she was still at school, dying in an asylum in 1969. 'He was certainly not made to be a father to a small child,' says Jelinek. Her mother was a paranoid psychotic, who forbade her daughter from leaving the house to play or have friends. She imposed a strenuous daily program of piano practice, composition, and ballet lessons, convinced that her daughter was a genius. Any form of pleasure was prohibited. 'My mother wasn't just neurotic, she was extremely neurotic — a terrorist of normality,' says Jelinek. 'I have had the strange fate of having two crazy parents, but seeing as the whole world is crazy, maybe this is normal! People are, without exception, neurotic. I cannot cope with people and therefore avoid them. This is certainly a result of my extremely unhappy childhood.'

Jelinek turned to writing aged 18, after she suffered a mental breakdown that derailed her university studies in art history and theatre. After a year spent recuperating at home, she earned a diploma as an organist from the Vienna Conservatory, and fell in with the 'Vienna Group' of surrealist poets. 'I then pursued these techniques into the realm of realism and tried to combine them,' she says. 'I work with phonetics — with the sounds of language. I would not have followed this method without my music background. The disadvantage of this is that it is difficult to translate my work.'

Aged 28, she married film composer Gottfried Hüngsberg, who collaborated with the German director Rainer Werner Fassbinder. Jelinek and her husband maintained a long-distance marriage: she visited him in Munich while continuing to live with her mother in Vienna most of the time. The arrangement remained until her mother's death in 2000, aged 96. Nowadays, Jelinek splits her time between both cities. 'My mother was completely mad, though not demented — she was very intelligent until her end,' she says. 'Of course I had to stay. I couldn't leave her in this state. It was mere blank horror. Still today, unfortunately, I feel culpable. I am happy every day that she is finally dead, otherwise I surely would be.'

Jelinek's treatment of her characters is so pitiless that it might seem to mimic the tyranny of her mother. Yet Jelinek insists she is not parodying the suffering of her characters, but rather the ideologies that reduce them to playthings: 'I see myself as a kind of scientist who looks in the Petri dish of society without enthusiasm and without anger. You can always see more if you look at the bigger picture, despite a seeming lack of sympathy, than if you just look at things up close. But if you read between the lines, you can see much enthusiasm, anger and confusion.'

Jelinek is drawn to write about murder because, through violent death, 'the brutality of society hisses out in a surge, as though it were the vent of a pressure cooker'. She attributes the superiority of female crime writers — Dorothy L. Sayers, Ruth Rendell, and P. D. James — to their subordinate status: 'The underdog, which in a patriarchal society is the woman, must study power in order to overcome it, as the slaves did in Rome. This is why women write such good crime novels; they know the mechanisms of power.'

Greed is billed as a thriller, despite its bare-bones plot and absence of tension. The murderous Janisch resembles the late far-right politician Jörg Haider — also a passionate alpine sportsman — who posed bare-chested in publicity shots, in chilling deference to Aryan body culture. During the 1999 National Council elections, Haider launched a poster campaign against 'degenerate' artists, with billboards posing the question: 'Do you want Jelinek or do you want Art?'

From 2000 to 2002, when Haider's Freedom Party was a partner in the governing coalition, Jelinek protested against the country's far-right lurch by prohibiting the performance of her plays in state theatres. But surely Austria's right-wing elements would have welcomed her boycott? 'It was certainly the wrong decision, but hindsight is a wonderful thing,' she says. 'When the atrocity of the formation of the government occurred, I tried despairingly to do something. Of all countries, it was Austria which was the first to reinstall an extreme right-wing government postwar.' Jelinek had supported the Communist Party as a counterweight to Austria's right-wing consensus: 'In genuine socialist countries I would certainly have been a member of the opposition. Unfortunately, I never really believed in the history-making power of the working class.'

She was wounded by the Austrian reception to *Greed*. 'I just don't understand why so much hate is brought against me,' she says. 'I don't mean negative reviews, which are of course acceptable, but contemptuous and hate-filled writings, which have destroyed me personally.'

Winning the Nobel prize may not have made her less vulnerable, but she is certain that it has diminished her sexual status. 'A man can increase his erotic value through success, regardless of whether he is 30 or 80,' she says. 'A woman is erotically devalued by achievement because she becomes intimidating. She is forever chained to her biological being.'

— *September 2006*

Ismail Kadare

In 2005, the judges of the inaugural Man Booker International Prize assembled a shortlist of 18 luminaries, including Gabriel García Márquez, Philip Roth, Günter Grass, Milan Kundera, and Kenzaburo Oe. When the £60,000 prize for an author's body of work was won by Albanian writer Ismail Kadare, the choice seemed eccentric. He had once been nominated for the Nobel Prize but, until he was awarded the Booker, the émigré writer was little read outside his native country and France, his adoptive home.

Since winning the Booker, there has been a surge in interest in Kadare and his more than 30 books. *The Successor* had already been translated, and was published after the award was announced. Since then, Princeton academic David Bellos has translated a number of others, including, most recently, *The Siege*. Set in the early-15th century, it tells of the Ottoman army's attempted capture of an Albanian citadel. Written in 1969, the book was translated into French in 1972, and was widely applauded.

Though the Anglophone world is only just realising the strength of Kadare's fiction, he has long been a spokesperson for the Balkan nation. Kadare was born in 1936 in the southern fortress city of Gjirokastër, near the Greek border. As a child he saw the arrival, and equally abrupt departure, of the Italian, Greek, and then German occupying forces — experiences reflected in his autobiographical novel *Chronicle in Stone* (1971).

Kadare wrote under the 40-year rule of Albania's Stalinist dictator Enver Hoxha, who presided over Europe's most brutal and isolated communist regime until he died in 1985. After earning his first degree at Tirana University, Kadare went to Moscow to study at the Maxim Gorky Literature Institute — an institution aimed at producing socialist-realist writers who conformed to the system. 'I enjoyed student life in Moscow a lot,' Kadare explains in an email interview, 'but I was entirely refractory to the teaching doled out. The courses constituted a negative education — one of the most effective forms of learning that exist. Whenever I heard a piece of advice, I said to myself: "Never do that!"'

Other writers have flourished creatively in repressive regimes. But, of all Albanian authors, only Kadare is known beyond the country's borders. For Kadare, the very constraints of living and writing under a repressive regime spurred his creative spirit. His fiction offers invaluable insights into life under tyranny — his historical allegories point both to the grand themes and small details that make up daily life in a restrictive environment. But his books are more than just political statements — at his best he is a great writer, by any nation's standards.

So few English-language scholars speak Albanian that Kadare's work is translated first into French and then retranslated into English. 'Theirs is a strange dialect,' says a Turkish character in *The Siege*. 'It's as if Allah had cast on it a cloak of fog to make it impossible to separate one word from the other.' His novels weather their double translations surprisingly well. His limpid prose loses less in translation than do more elaborate and poetic stylists.

Despite his Stalinist prose training, Kadare did not make his novelistic debut with a depiction of peasants toiling cheerfully in sunny wheatfields. Instead, in 1963, at the age of 27, he did something much more risky. *The General of the Dead Army* is a brooding tale following an Italian general on a mission to Albania to repatriate the remains of his countrymen killed in World War II. The novel won Kadare acclaim in France when it was published there in 1970, and in 1983 it became a film starring Marcello Mastroianni and Michel Piccoli.

This earned Kadare an international profile that helped shield him from the Albanian regime's worst excesses, and he went on to write his best novels, which include *The Three-Arched Bridge* (1978), *The Palace of Dreams* (1981), and *Broken April* (1978). 'International acclaim was a two-edged sword for me,' Kadare says. 'On balance, I think it's fair to say that it did more to protect me than to put me at risk, but it also gave rise to potentially very dangerous suspicions.'

Having enjoyed the protection of Hoxha, Kadare received threats after the autocrat's death. He sought political asylum in France in 1990, and now splits his time between Paris and the Albanian capital, Tirana. 'All through the Hoxha era, escaping from Albania prompted terrible reprisals on your whole family,' he says. 'All your relatives and friends would suffer demotion, banishment to the countryside, imprisonment, or worse. Flight, assuming you could get away with it, was not something any decent human being could undertake with a clear conscience.'

There had been calls for him to follow the example of Czech writer-turned-politician Václav Havel, and stand for Albania's presidency. But, says Kadare, 'I'm a perfectionist by nature, and when you go into politics the first thing you abandon is any pretence of perfection. Also, Albania is not Czechoslovakia. Albania is a difficult country and Albanians are difficult people.'

So what's the real story — did Kadare flout his principles or did he stay just within the bounds of acceptability to offer criticism from within? Although his writing divides opinion, the answer is probably both. Other Albanian writers were banished to labour camps or executed for producing work that wasn't considered to be in line with the official Marxist ethic. But Kadare's career flourished. One of the few Albanians allowed to travel abroad, he was a member of Hoxha's parliament and the regime-sponsored Writers' Union. Yet when the Booker was announced in 2005, some Albanians criticised the award judges for commending a collaborator.

'I have never claimed to be a "dissident" in the proper meaning of the term,' retorts Kadare. 'Open opposition to Hoxha's regime, like open opposition to Stalin during Stalin's reign in Russia, was simply impossible. Dissidence was a position no one could occupy even for a few days without facing the firing squad. On the other hand, my books themselves constitute a very obvious form of resistance to the regime.' Kadare survived precisely because his work could be read both ways. In *The Winter of Great Solitude* (1973), his novel about the 1961 Soviet–Albanian split, Kadare portrayed Hoxha as a heroic maverick refusing to kowtow to Khrushchev. Kadare admits that he wrote the novel to ingratiate himself with Hoxha and to preserve his chances of survival. 'I came under constant criticism throughout the 1960s for writing about myth and legend and for setting my stories in the past,' he says. 'Eventually I was presented with a kind of ultimatum — unless I wrote a novel about the present, I would be finished. I would have to give up writing for ever, or else cook up a bowl of Socialist Realist soup.'

In *The Concert*, a sequel written 15 years later, Kadare charted the dissolution of Albania's alliance with China, and cast Hoxha in a less flattering light. It was banned in Albania for five years. 'I feel very proud of the fact that those of my books which criticise the dictatorship most harshly — *The Palace of Dreams* and *The Concert* — were written under the Hoxha regime and not after it collapsed. I've not grown any more courageous since the fall.'

Hoxha's Albania had no pre-publication censorship, which forced writers and publishers to become their own harshest censors. In 1975, the regime exiled Kadare to a remote town for several months, and barred him from publishing for three years. His offence was to write a poem, 'The Red Pashas', which opened by satirising the paranoia of the regime: 'At midnight did the

Politburo gather/What's new at the northern border?/What's up at the southern border?' Kadare then depicted communist officials raiding the graves of Albania's formal rulers and trying on their bloodstained clothes.

Kadare certainly camouflaged his political critiques by using allegory and historical settings — Mao's China in *The Concert*, 1930s Albania in *The File on H* (1981), or ancient Egypt in *The Pyramid* (1992). But these visions of societies gripped by terror and mistrust also had a clear subtext.

The Siege, his fifth novel, is set in the fifth century, but alludes to Albania in 1968: when the Soviets invaded Czechoslovakia, Hoxha fuelled anxiety that Albania would be next. By focusing on the Turks, Albania's enemies, Kadare created a portrait of tyranny with parallels to Hoxha's reign.

A commander, sensing that his soldiers are losing motivation from defeat, stages public executions, sows dissent among the generals, and invokes phantom threats. At the novel's centre is Mevla Çelebi, an army historian charged with immortalising the battle, but actually a dim-witted functionary. As Çelebi sculpts events into an aggrandising epic, Kadare mocks the construction of official history. It is definitely not a novel that glorifies Hoxha.

Kadare parodies the provincialism of a closed society isolated from the world. He is depicting Albania's historical enemies, which is perhaps why the few sympathetic characters have limited stage-time. But characterisation is not Kadare's métier. The characters in his novels principally serve to advance themes. In his short fables this isn't necessarily a problem, but in *The Siege* — unusually long for Kadare at more than 300 pages — the lack of sustained characters makes it difficult to stay absorbed.

When Kadare finally balances pathos with polemic drive, the result is what many consider his masterpiece, *The Palace of Dreams*. Kadare depicts an imaginary Ottoman Empire that sorts and interprets the dreams of its subjects to control their collective subconscious and intercept subversive impulses. After it went on sale, the state authorities withdrew the book. Kadare poignantly portrays the conflicted loyalties of his protagonist, who is caught between his flourishing new career as a functionary of the state dream-reading apparatus and the Albanian heritage of his family — a centuries-old dynasty. Kadare describes an ancient Albania of legend and superstition, which eludes the stranglehold of Hoxha's rule.

Despite the dark subjects he often covers, Kadare's strength as a writer is to maintain a light touch without trivialising the content. His most playful novel, *The File on H*, unfolds in pre-World War II Albania under the rule of King Zog. It follows two Irish–American scholars who travel to Albania to research the composition of Homeric epics. The scholars are immediately taken for spies — a conceit that enables Kadare to parody the bureaucratic madness of Hoxha's state machinery. Meanwhile, Kadare comments slyly on his own predicament. Was Homer, the novel asks, 'a conformist, a troublemaker, or an establishment figure'?

For Kadare the very constraints of Hoxha's regime seem to have unleashed a creativity and freedom that results in his strongest work. By contrast, *The Pyramid*, completed shortly after communism fell, is less successful. It showcases Kadare's talent for absurdist black comedy. But, freed from the restrictions of the communist period, the message about the human sacrifices on which tyranny is predicated lacks subtlety.

When the regime collapsed, the breakdown of law and order fuelled a resurgence of vendetta killings. In *Spring Flowers, Spring Frost* (2000), Kadare portrays the anarchic mix of medieval and modern forces in post-communist Albania. Boldly interweaving ancient myth and contemporary events, Kadare shows traditional blood debts vying with the Mafia for the lives of townsfolk. But with the indignant edge of his communist-era novels gone, it's hard to see what Kadare is driving at. The plot ambles, and this time Kadare's symbolism is not too obvious but obscure.

Kadare returned to Hoxha's Albania with his 2003 novel *The Successor*, which reopens the mystery surrounding the demise of Mehmet Shehu — the heir apparent to the ailing despot, found dead from a bullet wound in 1981. With a burlesque tone not seen since *The File on H*, Kadare skillfully portrays a society where truth is buried and gossip prevails.

Kadare's novels suggest that it's impossible to live under totalitarianism without being somehow implicated in it. The hero of *The Palace of Dreams* inadvertently brings tragedy upon his family by misreading a dream. In *Broken April*, Kadare's most moving work, a writer is assailed for his interest in blood feuds: 'Instead of doing something for these unfortunate mountaineers, you help death, you look for exalted themes, you look here for beauty so as to feed your art.' An architect in *The Successor* believes that by lavishly renovating the leader-in-waiting's villa, he provoked the envy of the dictator and thereby caused his employer's murder.

That Kadare survived under Hoxha is extraordinary. His novels provided imaginative nourishment to a people starved of cultural life. Some necessary complicity with the regime should hardly be seen as a hanging offence. That, surely, would be the logic of tyranny.

— *April 2008*

Peter Matthiessen

On a bleak day in New York's Hamptons, the roads are deserted, and torrential rain floods the salt ponds near Peter Matthiessen's home. In summer, the region is a playground for the holidaying rich, and Matthiessen lives in perhaps the most expensive postal code in the United States. But today, the area resembles the unassuming landscape, populated by potato farmers, that drew him there more than five decades ago.

Did he prefer the Hamptons then? 'Oh yeah,' Matthiessen sighs, driving back from the tip, where the agile 82-year-old hauled boxes of waste through sheets of rain. He surely didn't think to wait for the weather to clear, having spent much of his life exposed to the elements. A tall man with a furrowed and gaunt face, he looks weather-beaten but healthy.

Across an oeuvre of 30 books, including eight novels, he's established himself as one of the foremost living wilderness writers. His commitment to preserving the natural world and native populations against capitalist greed has yielded books on New Guinea, Africa, South America, Antarctica, Alaska, Siberia, Nepal, and the Caribbean. Nearer to home, he's championed the rights of native Americans, indigenous Long Island fishermen, and migrant farm-labourers. He's also ventured out on spiritual quests, as a pioneering advocate of hallucinogenic drugs and an exponent of Zen Buddhism.

We pass the graveyard where his second wife, poet Deborah Love, is buried. Matthiessen mourned her death from cancer through the Himalayan journey recounted in *The Snow Leopard* (1978), in which he travelled with zoologist George Schaller to observe *bharal*, or blue sheep, and the elusive wild cat of the book's title. It won the National Book Award for non-fiction in 1979, but Matthiessen got labelled a nature writer when he saw fiction as his major work. While he writes non-fiction quickly, his novels are vast undertakings. His trilogy about swampland outlaw Edgar Watson — *Killing Mister Watson* (1990), *Lost Man's River* (1997) and *Bone by Bone* (1999), revised and published in 2008 as a single 900-page novel, *Shadow Country* — was a 30-year endeavour.

On his front porch sits the 1.5-metre-tall whale skull that he found while walking on the beach the day he finished *Men's Lives* (1986), a non-fiction elegy to the dying traditions of Long Island baymen. Inside the door is a model of Charles Darwin's ship, the Beagle, which Matthiessen's late neighbour Kurt Vonnegut gave him just weeks before he died: 'He just walked in and he said, "Here, this is my present for you." I said, "Kurt, stay for lunch", and he turned around and went out. He got kind of cranky as an old guy.'

A stone fireplace stands in the middle of his living room — cluttered with ornaments, photographs, and souvenirs from his travels — in implicit rebuke to the toney estates of the present-day Hamptons. The irony is that he purchased the property as a young man rebelling against his patrician origins. His father was a wealthy military architect and friend of the Bush family, whom he recalls as 'rather dull, ordinary, moneyed people'.

Although born in New York City, Matthiessen grew up mostly in wild areas of New York State and Connecticut, where he kept copperhead snakes in cages. Aged 13, he volunteered to assist at a charity camp for children from the Connecticut slums. The indignity of economic inequality first hit him the night he helped put on a banquet for the kids: 'They were looking over their shoulder every two seconds, which would suggest that they never had enough, that they always had some bigger brother or uncle who took their food away. They all violently overate and violently were sick.'

After learning his family was listed in the *Social Register* (an annual directory of elite society), Matthiessen removed his name at age 15. His emerging social conscience led to him being thrown out of his home at 17, after which he spent a year in the navy — an experience drawn on for his third novel, *Raditz*er (1961). Depicting the friendship between the scion of a rich family and an orphan in the navy, it was the novel in which Matthiessen feels he was 'starting to come into my own'.

Moving to Paris after college to study at the Sorbonne, he co-founded the *Paris Review* in 1952. His first novel, *Race Rock*, appeared in 1954, but upon returning to America he worked as a commercial fisherman to support his young family. 'It was extremely hard work, but it was interesting. I loved the fish and the sea birds. And it kept me in very, very, good shape. The better shape I'm in, the better I write.'

By the late 1950s, regular commissions from *The New Yorker* magazine enabled him to write full-time. 'I wanted to go explore the last wild places before they were ruined. In those days, they didn't cover anything wild. The furthest afield they would go was to Europe.' His itinerant lifestyle meant he was rarely home, which he admits was 'tough on my family'.

Matthiessen suggests his novels are 'too demanding for the general reader' and offer little to 'your average woman reader who wants a romance or something', so his critical acclaim was never quite matched by mass sales. He had high hopes for *The Snow Leopard* when his editor phoned to congratulate him on a rave review scheduled for the cover of *The New York Times* literary supplement. 'My editor said, "You've struck it rich this time!" Well, the day before it was supposed to appear they had a huge strike at *The New York Times*, and nobody ever saw that review.'

East coast reviewers have been cool to his fiction, he says. 'My kind of people just don't interest them very much — very tough, hardy people. Of course, people in the city have the same problems — the same heartbreak, the same grief, and the same love. But their lives have been so well chronicled by practically all our modern writers.'

Published in 1965, *At Play in the Fields of the Lord* was his 'first real novel', depicting the collision between Amazon Indians and missionaries. Made into a film by Hector Babenco in 1991, the novel inspired psychedelic drug culture icon Timothy Leary to send Matthiessen a letter saying it was the best account of tripping he'd read.

Matthiessen turned to Zen in 1969 for a way of seeing holistically without chemicals — a journey chronicled in *Nine-Headed Dragon River* (1986). But he feels he greatly benefited from LSD. 'Every patient has some block, and it takes them sometimes years to ferret that out through conventional therapy. LSD goes right to the heart of the trouble. It really does bust through to what your hang-up is.'

A 'roshi', or Zen teacher, Matthiessen leads a group of meditators every morning in the converted stable adjacent to his house. His fifth novel, *Far Tortuga* (1975), a paean to Caribbean green turtle fishermen, was the novel he most enjoyed writing because he experimented with a minimalist style that mirrored Zen teachings: 'I cut out all the adjectives and adverbs. I just give the bare facts. So you have the "hereness" of everything.'

Throughout his interior journeys, social advocacy continued to drive him. From his commitment to native Americans came *In the Spirit of Crazy Horse* (1983) — a 650-page polemic about a shoot-out in 1975 between American Indian Movement activists and the FBI. Matthiessen argued that Leonard Peltier, a native American given two life sentences for allegedly murdering two FBI agents, was convicted on trumped-up charges.

A former FBI agent and the one-time governor of South Dakota sued Matthiessen and his publisher, Viking, for US$50 million in libel damages. Though ultimately decided in Matthiessen's favour, the suits lasted for nine years. 'The lawyers said, "If they get us into court, you're going to lose everything." We were going up against all the government, and they had unlimited bucks.'

Then president Bill Clinton read the book and in 2000 was reportedly planning to pardon Peltier, but demurred under FBI pressure. 'We thought we had nailed it down. I was very angry at the time.' Matthiessen remains in contact with Peltier and says: 'He's a very brave man. I've never heard a whine out of him. He's supposed to be a cop killer, but even his guards like him.'

There's little question about the guilt of Edgar Watson, the buccaneering entrepreneur at the centre of *Shadow Country*. The epic work, which won the National Book Award for Fiction in 2008, recreates the harsh world of farmers and fishermen in backcountry Florida around the turn of last century.

Matthiessen's fascination with Watson dates to the 1940s, when his father took him on a boat trip up the west coast of the Florida Everglades labyrinth of ten thousand — mostly mangrove — islands. 'He showed me this river that came down into the Gulf of Mexico, and he said that about three miles up that river there's the only house in the Everglades, and it belonged to a man named Watson who was killed by his neighbours. That detail of the man killed by his neighbours in this very lonely river stuck in my brain. They would have been very small-time farmers or fishermen. They're not murderers. So what happened? What did this guy do? It was either a lynching or self-defence — they said he shot first.'

Matthiessen planned to write a novel mostly about the devastation of the Florida environment and wildlife, and the dispossession of its native tribes, but as he immersed himself in research the Watson saga took over. 'I interviewed everybody over 90 years old in south-west Florida. This whole incredible American legend opened up. He was supposed to have killed over 50 people — not true at all. He probably did kill seven or eight people — workers in his fields. The rumour was that when payday came around he shot them instead.'

Watson's several children from his three marriages initially ignored Matthiessen's approaches. 'He was a disgrace to the family. His daughter was married to the head of a big bank in Florida — socially very well established — and had a father who was shot down in a hail of bullets! He already had a very dark reputation before that. He'd been in murder trials in northern Florida.' Eventually, Watson's children caved in; one of his granddaughters sounded Matthiessen out in short letters, then other family members expressed curiosity about his research.

As Matthiessen probed deeper into Watson's life, the bogeyman sugar-cane baron of myth became more complex: 'The wives all admired him. His kids did, too, with the exception of one. He was very likeable, very personable, very charming, very smart, a very good farmer — he just had a murderous temper, and he drank too much. He had children with other ladies, too, unofficially. He was a rascal. I had great fun with Watson. I gave him a very, very quick wit, and a sardonic take on life.'

Though originally written as a single novel of over 1500 pages, Matthiessen cut it into three volumes, much to his later regret. 'The three parts were like movements of a symphony,' he says. 'When you separate it you lose that architecture of the whole novel.' After the triptych was published, he decided to rework it as a single novel. He expected it to be a one-year project, but it ended up taking six years: 'My first notes went back to 1978. This was my fiction over the whole period, except two novellas. That's half my writing life on this project.'

If the author partly admires Watson, that's probably because his idols are people that stoically endure life's trials. The eldest of

Matthiessen's four children, Luke, became blind after developing a congenital eye disease when he graduated from college. Luke's eldest son was run over by a bus and killed; a reformed alcoholic, Luke now runs clinics for alcoholics and drug addicts. 'This guy's had every bad blow you can get in life and he never whines. He's my hero, really.'

Tacked to the wall of his office — a weatherboard cottage across from his house — are photos of his British-born wife, Maria Eckhart, from her modelling years, and a picture of art critic Robert Hughes, his former travel-mate and deep-sea fishing companion. Matthiessen enthuses about Tasmanian novelist and environmentalist Richard Flanagan, describing him as 'a very bold, original writer'.

Despite a lifetime of battling political treacheries, Matthiessen says he's 'past bitter'. As he pulls out of his driveway to take me to the bus, he points to an old giant willow that fell in the storm a few nights earlier. The tree collapsed with geometric precision in the narrow space between his house and meditation garden, even missing the surrounding wires. On the turf of this environmentalist visionary, it seems like no accident.

— March 2008

Jay McInerney

There was a time, after the publication of his debut novel *Bright Lights, Big City* in 1984, when it seemed that Jay McInerney might go to seed. The autobiographical work recounted the coke-fuelled nightlife of a *New Yorker* fact-checker, sold more than a million copies, and defined the spirit of the exuberant 1980s.

But what does an epoch-definer do once his epoch has been defined? Await the backlash, in McInerney's case. His follow-up novels *Ransom* (1985) and *Story of My Life* (1988) were received tepidly in the US. The 1988 film of *Bright Lights*, starring a miscast Michael J. Fox, was a monumental flop.

Nor did it bode well to be compared constantly with his hero, F. Scott Fitzgerald, who was anointed the voice of the jazz age on the publication of *This Side of Paradise* in 1920. Like McInerney, Fitzgerald was known as much for his carousing as for his novels about the hedonistic rich, and he died an alcoholic at the age of 44.

What gin was to Fitzgerald, Bolivian marching powder became to McInerney and his contemporaries. There was a risk that McInerney's hard-partying ways would catch up with him, too, as the go-go years gave way to the jaded 1990s, and left their literary spokesman behind.

But of all the literary brat-pack — the label applied to writers such as Bret Easton Ellis and Tama Janowitz, who satirised their generation's mores — McInerney maintained the highest profile, partly due to his star-studded social life and his willingness to indulge gossip columnists. But it was also because foreign critics kept trumpeting his work. 'There's a less hysterical reaction to my books in Europe,' McInerney explains. 'They're treated more as literary events and less as new instalments in Jay McInerney's autobiography.'

We're chatting in the spacious sitting room of his Lower East Side penthouse, to which I've been escorted via the wood-panelled elevator by a surly doorman who calls him Mr Jay. 'I've always wanted to live in a penthouse,' McInerney says. He is 54 and his waist has thickened, but he remains boyish and is smartly dressed in a blue shirt and black suede loafers.

It's been said that every time McInerney writes a book, he gets a new girlfriend and a new apartment. He moved here three years ago, about the time he married his fourth wife, publishing heiress Anne Hearst, and released his seventh novel, *The Good Life* (2006). 'For the first time almost that I can remember, I'm pretty serene,' he says. It's clear that McInerney won't be changing his home or his wife with the publication of his second collection of stories, *The Last Bachelor* (2009; the first was 2000's *How It Ended*).

Writing a novel is analogous to the long-term commitment of marriage, he says; short stories are like one-night stands. 'It's scary to sit down at your computer and think about spending the next 18 months of your life doing something you're not sure you can commit to,' he says, smiling. 'But with the short story, you can just experiment because it will be over in a few hours.'

McInerney kicked the illicit drugs years ago, but the bad-boy persona sticks. In 2005, Ellis, his close friend, published *Lunar Park*, featuring a designer drug-consuming, social-climbing character named Jay McInerney as his 'toxic twin'. 'I thought it was funny,' says the McInerney before me. 'But the Jay McInerney that appears in it wasn't the Jay McInerney of the present.' He continues to go out most nights, however, and occasionally visits clubs with younger friends, but admits that now he finds the club scene 'a little repetitious and boring'.

His charm seems spontaneous, but it didn't come easily to a child forever forced to fit into new environments. The son of a paper company sales executive, McInerney moved frequently between cities in the US, Canada, and Britain. 'I was a very awkward kid,' he recalls, 'so I went to some lengths to create a persona more sophisticated and polished than my real self.' He attended 18 schools, his longest stay at a single institution ending when he was expelled for exploding a lavatory. So he craved the limelight as a child, too? He laughs easily: 'Yeah, I suppose there's a continuity there.'

It seemed natural that he'd end up in New York, 'the home town of restless transients and ambitious provincials'. He moved here at 22, a year before his mother succumbed to cancer. That sent McInerney into a tailspin like that experienced by the hero of *Bright Lights*, whose mother's death gives the novel its melancholic undertow. Writing in *The New Yorker* after his father died, McInerney recounted his mother's deathbed confession to her son about an extra-marital affair. His brother was initially furious but has since forgiven him, a fraternal feud echoed in one of the dozen stories in *The Last Bachelor*.

While working as a fact-checker at *The New Yorker*, McInerney became friendly with the writer Raymond Carver, who encouraged him to apply for a graduate writing fellowship rather than working full-time to support himself. In any event, *The New Yorker* fired him, so he headed to Syracuse University, where he studied under Carver and Tobias Wolff, and wrote *Bright Lights*.

There he met philosophy doctoral student Merry Reymond, who became his second wife. His first wife, a half-Japanese runway model whom he met during a year teaching English in Japan, ditched him for a Milanese photographer after four months. His marriage to Reymond lasted seven years, but fractures began to emerge after he became a celebrity. 'She was tired of all the attention that I was getting,' he says.

They separated in 1987, after McInerney two-timed her with Marla Hanson, a high-profile model whose career had been destroyed when a razor-wielding attacker slashed her cheek. Reymond attempted suicide. 'I'd been ill-equipped to understand her bipolar condition from the beginning because I'd never encountered anything like it,' he says. 'I used to think she was just moody.' McInerney spent US$200,000 on her psychiatric treatment; Reymond returned the favour by writing an excoriating novel about him and an article for *Spy* magazine in which she described him as 'dangerous and not very nice'.

His obsessive affair with Hanson, complete with mutual cheating and the flinging of wineglasses, ended after four years, sending McInerney into the comforting arms of southern belle and jewellery designer Helen Bransford. He once described Bransford, who soon became his third wife, as 'cool, like a guy. The first person I'd been with for any length of time who wasn't wounded emotionally or terribly needy.' Hardly. Insecure about being seven years older than McInerney, she underwent a facelift and wrote a book, *Welcome to Your Facelift* (1997), about the experience.

Bransford claimed she resolved to go under the knife when McInerney interviewed Julia Roberts for *Harper's Bazaar* magazine and returned home smitten. 'I told her about you,' he allegedly remarked to Bransford: 'Well, everything but your age.' McInerney now dismisses the Roberts vignette as 'largely bullshit; but it made a good story for her to tell on talk shows'.

Charmed by Bransford's southern airs, McInerney took little convincing when she suggested they move to a ranch in Tennessee. From these bucolic years came *The Last of the Savages* (1996), a multi-generational saga of the deep south that confounded critics, much as Tennessee did McInerney.

New York's bright lights eventually drew him back: 'It was a sojourn and I'm glad I had it, but I won't be retiring to the south. I was always an outsider, observing, and I could never really belong there.' When Bransford suggested kids, McInerney obliged, though he'd always felt he could postpone fatherhood indefinitely. But she was 43 when they married and, after a series of miscarriages, the couple resorted to a surrogate mother. Bransford arranged for a friend who was a country music singer to donate eggs.

As the gestational carrier chain-smoked throughout the pregnancy, Bransford published an essay addressed to their unborn twins in *Vogue* magazine: 'Please know I'll do better by you when you come out. You won't have to breathe smoke, eat McDonald's or listen to Country Music TV day and night.'

The transition from man-about-town to father wasn't easy for McInerney. 'A part of me was afraid of growing up, afraid of assuming responsibility for anyone else.' For the most part, he managed to abstain from going out until after their children, John Barrett McInerney III and Maisie, were asleep.

He felt, too, that his work needed to mature. In 1998, he'd just published *Model Behaviour*, about a 32-year-old writer of celebrity profiles who is abandoned by his model girlfriend. It received respectable reviews, but McInerney realised it was past time to move on from writing about over-privileged youths behaving badly. When he tried to embark on a new novel, however, he found himself blocked for three years. 'I hadn't figured out how to make the transition to something more mature,' he says.

Gary Fisketjon, a friend from college and his career-long editor, remembers McInerney as deeply troubled during those years: 'He had always got writing done, so it was a horrible shock to find himself in a period when he wasn't producing pages.' As well, McInerney's marriage to Bransford was collapsing, and he became clinically depressed. Two years of therapy and antidepressants followed, and a return to drug abuse.

Bransford won custody of the twins on their divorce in 2000

and moved to the Hamptons, but McInerney remains on friendly terms with her, and visits his children most weekends. The 14-year-olds relish Googling their father's name and assailing him with questions about his playboy past. His daughter, McInerney boasts, is a precociously talented poet.

After the September 11 terrorist attacks, McInerney struggled to justify the ironic voice that had sustained his career. 'There was a strange congruence between my own mood and that cataclysm which affected everybody so deeply,' he recalls. He witnessed the destruction of the World Trade Centre from his apartment: 'I just never felt the same about looking out that window, so I left that building very shortly thereafter.'

When McInerney told Norman Mailer of his plan to centre a novel around the attacks, the late novelist advised him to wait a decade — the time, he insisted, that any writer would need to make sense of it. But, says McInerney: 'I wanted to record the emotional impressions while they were still fresh. It was such a defining moment of New York's history, and my own personal history, that it seemed foolish to ignore.'

So he wrote *The Good Life*, about two Manhattan families rocked by the bombings into re-examining their lives. That novel, which finds the characters of *Brightness Falls* (1992) in midlife, helped McInerney overcome depression. It also marked a turning point in his work. 'I found a way to write about middle age,' he says, 'about marriage, about fatherhood, about mortality.' Fisketjon considers *The Good Life* McInerney's best work, with characters marked by a new complexity.

Since July 2008, McInerney has been working on a novel about a New Yorker forced to reinvent himself after losing his financial and social standing, and it's as though he's writing it in real time. 'I just didn't imagine that current events would seep into the novel quite as much as they have,' he says.

He speculates that his next work will also address the meltdown of the Wall Street money culture. Not, he stresses, because he has ever tried to capture a zeitgeist, but because Manhattan is, and always will be, his subject. 'New York is going to be a very different place in the next year or two,' he says. 'I don't want New York to descend into poverty and chaos, but I think that a bit of sanity, a bit of gravity, is a good thing.'

— *January 2009*

Rick Moody

By his own admission, Rick Moody once seemed among the most unlikely of writers to grow bored with himself. After satirising his Nixon-era WASP childhood in his best-known novel, *The Ice Storm* (1994), his memoir, *The Black Veil* (2002), intercut his history of drug and alcohol abuse with the story of an ancestor who wore a veil in penance for inadvertently killing a friend: 'Get to know my book the way you would get to know me,' Moody wrote, 'in the fullness of time, hesitantly, irritably, impatiently, uncertainly, pityingly, generously.'

But as he sips herbal tea in a Brooklyn café, with no outward signs of his manic prose or unstable past, Moody says he now finds himself a dull subject. *The Black Veil* belongs to a different era; he submitted the final draft on 10 September 2001. 'After 9/11, I really wanted to deal with the culture as a whole instead of just navel-gazing,' he says in his slow drawl.

The three novellas of his newest book, *The Omega Force* (2008), explore post-September 11 paranoia. 'K&K' follows a drudge at an insurance brokerage unravelling the mystery of an anonymous colleague posting menacing notes in the suggestion box. 'The Albertine Notes' is cyberpunk sci-fi set in a bomb-flattened Manhattan; the surviving New Yorkers are afflicted by an epidemic of the drug 'Albertine' that stimulates happy memories from before the blast. In the title story, a retired government official becomes convinced that his island sanctum is being invaded by 'dark-complected' foreigners.

In Moody's view, the protagonists of the three novellas 'have a mania that induces them to interpret wrongly. It's the illness of the Bush administration to be constantly reading into things and imagining conspiracies around every corner.'

With his disaffected characters and hip style, Moody is sometimes grouped alongside Dave Eggers, David Foster Wallace, Jonathan Lethem, and Jeffrey Eugenides as a generation of American postmodernists reacting against their realist forebears. But there's little that's conventionally cool about Moody. A slight man of 46, he wears a beige cardigan over a faded R. L. Burnside T-shirt. Off alcohol and nicotine (and also sugar, caffeine, and meat), he practises yoga and plays in a folk-band.

Moody is an agnostic who goes to church because he loves ritual, and feels 'you have to believe in something'. In 1997, he co-edited *Joyful Noise*, a collection of essays on the New Testament: 'I had a theory that the only way for the Left to have a cultural impact in the way it did of old was to reco-opt the Bible, which I felt had been hijacked by the Right.'

His debut novel, *Garden State* (1992), examined the travails of aimless New Jersey teenagers. Moody checked himself into rehab halfway through writing it, aged 25, after suffering an alcohol- and cocaine-fuelled breakdown, and hallucinating that he'd be punished for his transgressions by being sexually violated by a man. 'You can see that like a big fault line running through the book — the before and the after. I think it's a truly dreadful book, but it's emotionally really accessible and vulnerable, and I admire that.'

Accustomed to writing while intoxicated, it took him six months after sobering up to write again. Returning to the church in which he was raised helped restore his mental health. Lacking moderation, he never again drank. 'There wasn't some halcyon period where I could have one or two drinks and be witty at a party. I'd have six or eight more and try to fuck other people's girlfriends. I was sometimes so drunk that I couldn't read what I was typing.'

Drying out made him a better writer. 'Emotionally you can't really understand other people when you're drinking. There's always this simulated quality to the characters of people with advanced alcoholism.' He doesn't regret his years of substance abuse, since it was 'something I had to go through to be the person I am now. Seeing as it's a problem in my family as a whole, there wasn't a lot of chance that I wasn't going to do it.'

Repeatedly talking about his month in a psychiatric hospital while promoting *The Black Veil* was 'like a full-on trip through hell', which made him sometimes regret publishing the book. Digressive and claustrophobically intense, the memoir polarised critics and led the notorious literary hitman Dale Peck to dub Moody 'the worst writer of his generation'.

Moody only read the first paragraph of Peck's screed, which sparked an international debate about the ethics of book-reviewing. Yet while he's never spoken publicly about Peck, Moody is quick to slap down the charge that writing a memoir at 40 was premature and self-indulgent. 'Where's it said that you have to have a lot of events to describe to write a memoir?' The September 11 attacks didn't stir him to change the closing lines, which he stood by on tour: 'To be an American, to be a citizen of the West, is to be a murderer. Don't kid yourself. Cover your face.'

Moody traces his tangled and experimental style to *Purple America* (1996), about an alcoholic layabout attempting to care for his dying mother. 'When I was writing the short, declarative sentences of *The Ice Storm* or *Garden State*, it was because I thought I had to. I felt people missed the strain of feeling in my work because I come from a culture that doesn't express its emotions directly very often. So I decided with *Purple America* to write a book that would be almost operatic in its ambition to display feeling.'

The Ice Storm traced the moral decay of two Connecticut

families, and became an acclaimed film by Ang Lee. That it remains
his most famous book is 'Hollywood's fault, not mine,' Moody says,
dismissing it as an apprentice work. 'There's not a sentence in it that
I would memorise. It just doesn't sing.' He flirts with the idea of
writing a sequel 'to get right what I got wrong'.

After *The Ice Storm*, some critics anointed Moody heir to John
Cheever and John Updike, both known for chronicling the malaise
of the suburban upper-middle classes. Moody finds the comparisons
lazy: 'It typecasts me as a WASP writer. I don't really bear, beyond
having written one book about the suburbs, even a passing
resemblance to them.'

Moody's family was hurt but understanding about *The Ice Storm*.
'It may not be easy always, but they recognise that writing is how I
try to handle stuff,' he says, adding, 'it's not really very fictionalised
at all.' Moody's mother divorced his father, an investment banker, in
1970, creating a wound that Moody struggled to resolve even as an
adult. 'For some people, it just takes it out of them. My brother and
sister felt less aggrieved by it than I did.'

His paternal grandfather, an automobile salesman, gave him
an ear for trade language. 'He had that kind of hail-fellow-well-
met salesman discourse that I found really winning. I'm a reluctant
social person, a little bit awkward, and I like the ease and confidence
that salespeople can project.'

As an undergraduate at Brown, he was taught by postmodern
novelists Robert Hoover, Angela Carter, and John Hawkes. Lazy
and drug-addled, Moody doubts he made an impression, but all
three teachers meant a lot to him. He recalls Hawkes' 'avuncular,
sweet, generous aspect' and Carter's playfully abrasive manner. 'On
the first day, the class was over-enrolled. She basically got it down to
fourteen people by scaring people out of the room. Some guy raised
his hand and said, "Well, what's your work like anyway?" She said,
in her mild-mannered way, "My work cuts like a steel blade at the

base of a man's penis." '

Moody also took courses in semiotics, and developed an appetite for post-structuralist jargon. 'The density of it was so aggressive. I love Derrida's long, tangled sentences. I liked its rebelliousness and its unwillingness to compromise. I like marginalised, ambitious discourses.' Moody's fondness for italicising words and sentences in unexpected places suggests Derrida's influence, but he attributes it to the Austrian novelist Thomas Bernhard ('a great italiciser').

Moody's windy sentences reflect his attempt to pin down elusive reality. 'My experience of language is that Lacanian experience of constantly wanting to capture something in prose that I can't get to. So there's this excess of words and clauses and paragraphs. "Shambolic" to me is a term of great praise.'

He remains opposed to forms of conventional realism that presume reality can be captured by language. 'Realism, especially insofar as it relies on epiphany and formulaic structure, is politically dubious. If literature is not trying to move to a new way of thinking about how we might describe life then it's just cooperating with what *is*, and what *is* in this country is hard to stomach.'

Yet in the title short story of his collection *Demonology* (2001), Moody abandons all artifice, writing about the death of his elder sister, Meredith, from a seizure aged 38. 'I should fictionalise it more,' the narrator writes. 'I should conceal myself. I should consider the responsibilities of characterisation.' Moody wrote the story in the two months following Meredith's death. '"Demonology" is what it looks like — a perfectly realistic story.' He kept using his sister's photograph of him on his books until he'd aged so much it looked absurd. 'It was hard for me to not have her name on the book jackets any more,' he says.

After becoming heavily involved with Meredith's children, he subsequently decided to marry his partner, environmentalist Amy Osborne, and eventually have children of his own. 'I'd been until then too preoccupied with my own trajectory as a writer to think much about kids. Suddenly the idea of having kids had much more appeal, out of an epiphanic diminishment of selfishness.'

Moody's shift towards gazing outward at the world rather than inward at himself will reach a new stage with his next novel, partly set on Mars. It will be even more dystopian than 'The Albertine Notes', Moody says, but he's cheerful because — not in spite — of his despairing outlook. 'My belief in the exploitative nature of human psychology frees me up to feel good about things. I expect the worst of people and institutions. When they do not perform to type, I'm surprised and delighted.'

— *March 2008*

Toni Morrison

Toni Morrison dedicated *Beloved*, her 1987 masterpiece recently named by *The New York Times* as the best American novel of the last 25 years, to the 'Sixty Million and more' black people said to have perished under America's slave trade. There was no appropriate monument to commemorate American slaves, she lamented at the time: no plaque, tree, or statue. Not even a bench by the side of the road.

In July 2008, an international society of Morrison scholars and admirers gathered to lay a six-foot-long bench on Sullivan's Island, South Carolina, by what was once a port for slave ships. 'I really liked it because it was simple and unpretentious; it was open, anyone could sit there,' Morrison says by phone in her slow, whispery voice. 'It wasn't some traditional memorial.'

The Nobel laureate is more than just a literary figure: to many readers, she's an icon who helped reclaim the African–American experience from white history. Even critics sometimes find her prose abstruse, but Oprah Winfrey has endorsed four of her books, and they sell in the millions. When *Beloved* was passed over for the National Book Award, four-dozen African–American writers issued a statement of protest, and it subsequently won the Pulitzer Prize. Winfrey produced and starred in Jonathan Demme's 1998 film of the novel.

Now 77, and with her ninth novel *A Mercy* (2008) recently published, Morrison is keen to shake off the image of national conscience. At a talk in London, she corrected an audience member who called her a spokesperson for the African–American community: 'I don't speak for you, I speak to you.'

For most of her four decades as a novelist, Morrison embraced being categorised as a 'black woman writer', choosing to see it as liberating rather than limiting. 'That whole labelling business is just so tiresome — you can't escape it, but you can try to own it,' she laughs. 'I don't think I was successful at all.'

Beloved devastatingly shows how slavery deformed the ability of black women to care for their children. The novel was triggered by an old newspaper clipping Morrison read about an escaped slave, Margaret Garner, who killed her own daughter rather than see her returned to bondage. *A Mercy* explores similar territory, following a black slave, Florens, who is separated from her mother and sent to the smallholding of an Anglo–Dutch farmer, Jacob, as payment for a debt.

Yet *A Mercy* is set in the late 1600s, two centuries before *Beloved*, when slavery was not yet linked to skin colour. Morrison wanted to imagine what it felt like to be a slave but not subject to racism: 'That's why I had to go back before the institutionalisation of racism, when it became law.' Various European nations and empires were laying claim to the land in the 17th century, and Morrison 'was interested in who those people who came to the continent were — the ordinary people who were running away from something and hoping to find it in this new world'.

When Jacob dies of smallpox, his charges — among them a Native American servant and two white indentured labourers — struggle to hold up in the harsh terrain. After Jacob's widow also falls sick, Florens sets out to find a blacksmith with curative powers — a free African man, and the object of her sexual obsession. 'I was trying to erase racism from the American narrative,' Morrison says, 'to take it out and see people from different places, different classes, different parts of the world, trying to form a family, a kind of a unit.'

The working title was simply *Mercy* — a typical Morrison one-worder, following her previous three novels *Jazz* (1992), *Paradise* (1999), and *Love* (2003). But she felt that *Mercy*, which refers to an act in the book's last chapter, was too general; so it became *A Mercy*. 'It's just one human gesture, and you don't get anything for it,' Morrison says. 'You don't get to feel good. You just suddenly do what only humans can do, which is offer mercy.'

A Mercy was originally slated for publication in 2009, but Morrison's publishers pushed it forward to time with the American election. The novel's portrayal of racial commingling thereby gained added currency. Barack Obama personally phoned Morrison to ask for her endorsement, and she wrote him a letter describing him as 'the man for this time'.

Obama's victory was seen widely as a landmark for racial progress, but Morrison took an unlikely view. Her decision to back Obama against Hillary Clinton had nothing to do with race, she says. 'I'm not interested in him because of his race at all. It's just overdone. It's like Othello — everybody plays that role like the play is about his being a Moor. They all dress up and blacken their faces and redden their lips and get hysterical. The play's not about that at all!'

Observing the discussion of race in the lead-up to the election, Morrison felt as if a boil was being pierced — a cleansing process that, once complete, will allow people to talk about something else. 'People tried to say it and not say it, then use it and reject it, then try to develop a language that was about race, where you could say alien, foreigner — everything except race.'

Upon awarding Morrison the Nobel Prize in 1993, the Swedish Academy praised her as a writer of 'visionary force and poetic import' who 'delves into language itself, a language she wants to liberate from the fetters of race'. A small but vocal coterie of black writers construed her victory as owing more to political correctness than merit. 'Attacks?' Morrison protests. 'What attacks? Who attacked?' Stanley Crouch, for one, who called *Beloved* a 'blackface holocaust novel'. Morrison softens, refusing to be drawn into sparring: 'Oh, Stanley, that's his living.'

The black novelist Charles Johnson has criticised her for negatively depicting men and whites. Yet Morrison once opposed the attempt by a prominent African–American lobby group to censor Mark Twain's *Huckleberry Finn* because of its use of 'nigger'. She also defended O. J. Simpson and Bill Clinton against the charges of feminists. Writing in *The New Yorker* magazine in 1998, Morrison described Clinton as America's first black president — a remark she must now regret? 'I didn't even say that. [For the record, she did.] I said he was treated like one — that is, with complete disrespect, complete, "You're guilty already." '

Morrison grew up in the poor steel-mill town of Lorain, Ohio, which was divided along lines of class rather than race. Her neighbours and schoolmates came from many cultures. Racism was an abstraction: 'My parents were from the Deep South, so I knew there was another world, but it was their past, not my present.' Her father, George, a welder, didn't let white people into their home. But her mother, Ramah, a homemaker, 'always judged people one person at a time'; a strong believer in political change, she once wrote to President Roosevelt about the weevils in their flour.

As an undergraduate at Howard University, the so-called Black Harvard in Washington DC, Morrison was derided for proposing to write a paper on Shakespeare's black characters. There, the author, born Chloe Wofford, picked up the nickname 'Toni' (an abbreviation of her middle-name, Anthony). She wrote her master's thesis at Cornell on alienation in the novels of William Faulkner and Virginia Woolf. Later she returned to Howard University to teach, before becoming a book editor.

Her first novel, *The Bluest Eye* (1970), was about a black girl who dreams of blue eyes and blonde hair. The novel was hardly autobiographical, but Morrison wrote it because 'I never read about "me" in any of the literature I loved — "me" meaning one of the most vulnerable people in the society: a child, a female, and a black female child.' Morrison worked on it over five years, waking up every morning at 4:30am to write while employed as an editor at Random House. She was also alone in raising her two sons, Harold and Slade, after divorcing their father, Jamaican architect Harold Morrison, in 1964.

Morrison never remarried, and has said that she and the older Harold clashed because he expected her to be subservient. Of her late turn to writing, she remarks: 'I enjoyed having something of my own to think about so much.' There were few black female literary voices in the 1960s, and they didn't offer models for the gritty fiction she aspired to write. 'Most were about how really and truly noble characters were in the black world. I was writing about what the pain really was.'

At Random House, she nurtured the literary careers of African–American writers such as Toni Cade Bambara, Angela Davis, and Alice Walker, and edited a groundbreaking scrapbook of black history, *The Black Book* (1974). Only after publishing *Sula* (1973), *Song of Solomon* (1977), and *Tar Baby* (1981) did she leave to write full-time. Morrison felt economic insecurities, which she traces to her Depression-era childhood.

In her 1992 book, *Playing in the Dark: whiteness and the literary imagination*, Morrison argued that black characters are central to the American literary canon. The white view of Africanness, she wrote, 'deployed as rawness and savagery ... provided the staging ground and arena for the elaboration of the quintessential American identity'.

It heartens her that critics no longer read African–American fiction mostly as sociology. Morrison recalls a review of *Beloved* in

The New Yorker that opened by comparing the family in the novel to that of black television sitcom *The Cosby Show*. Now, she says, 'They talk about it as literature — about the language, the structure, its relationship to other kinds of novels. You can't just get away with saying, "This is a black world novel." '

— *November 2008*

Paul Muldoon

Like any event that becomes legend, it's hard to disentangle fact from fiction in accounts of Paul Muldoon's first meeting with Seamus Heaney. Even Muldoon mistrusts his memory. As he vaguely recalls it, he was 16 when a teacher introduced him to Heaney at a poetry reading in Northern Ireland with the epithet *rara avis* (Latin for 'rare bird'). He subsequently posted Heaney some poems, asking, 'What can I learn from you?' Heaney's response: 'Nothing.'

Already at 21 Muldoon had published his first book, *New Weather* (1973) — after Heaney, then Muldoon's tutor at Queen's University in Belfast, showed his work to Faber and Faber's poetry editor. Now, after ten volumes of poetry (not counting his selected and collected poems) no Irish poet rivals Muldoon for the Nobel laureate's mantle.

But aside from his wayward mop of hair, Muldoon shares little with his former mentor. Muldoon's playful verse — where recondite allusions rub up against colloquial diction, and emotion is undercut by irony — contrasts with Heaney's high seriousness and polish. Next to Muldoon's brazen experiments, Heaney's pastoral lyrics seem old-fashioned.

In person, Muldoon is equally puckish. Boyish in temperament and appearance, despite his 58 years, he has a rotund figure and bouncy walk. He's so soft-spoken and mild-mannered that it's hard to see where the poetic fireworks come from. His lilting Ulster vowels remain, despite two decades in the United States, where he teaches at Princeton University. With his tweed sportscoat and shaggy hair, he's a cross between professor and ageing rock star. In 2004, he co-founded the 'three-car garage band' Rackett with the Princeton poetry scholar Nigel Smith — Muldoon writes lyrics and plays guitar.

He's surprised by his reputation for cryptic verse, insisting he's not trying 'to present riddles or conundrums, but to engage readers'. Even Helen Vendler, perhaps the pre-eminent American poetry critic, has suggested he publish with explanatory notes. 'Certainly, I can imagine a circumstance when a few notes would be useful, absolutely — but we'll leave that for someone else to do,' Muldoon says. 'John Donne and William Shakespeare need annotations, but they weren't doing their own.'

It perplexes him, too, that poetry is often seen as inherently more difficult than film or music. 'We've spent so much of our lives watching movies that we're not conscious of how sophisticated we are at it,' he says, peering through black-rimmed spectacles beneath a brown-and-grey fringe. 'In the silent movies, that famous caption, "Meanwhile, back at the ranch", had to be shot up because there was no understanding that what was happening in one frame was synchronicitous with the next frame, rather than in advanced time.' And, he goes on, 'we've learned a very sophisticated grammar of popular music. Poetry is not something people read, and they say, "I don't understand this."'

Muldoon's poetry has a sonorous quality that makes it inviting even when resisting comprehensibility. His fondness for unlikely rhymes has led some to joke that he could rhyme 'knife' with 'fork'. Although rhyming verse has fallen out of fashion, Muldoon doesn't see it disappearing. 'These little chimes are delightful to us,' he says. 'They make things memorable. In popular culture, rhyme is a very potent force, in everything from rap music through to advertising.' Referring to his love of demotic culture, Muldoon once described himself in a poem as a 'prince of the quotidian'.

For such a worldly poet, Muldoon's origins are surprisingly provincial. The eldest of three siblings, he was born into a Catholic family in county Armagh, Northern Ireland. His parents were opposed to political violence, and Muldoon inherited their legacy, with his poetry maintaining an even-handed view of the sectarian conflict.

His father, Patrick, was a market gardener and mushroom farmer, whom Muldoon describes as a life-battered but jubilant man. In his poem 'The Mixed Marriage', Muldoon recounts how Patrick left school to market himself as a labourer at a hiring fair: 'When he left school at eight or nine/He took up billhook and loy/ To win the ground he would never own.' In fact, his father was 12. Though virtually illiterate, Muldoon Senior once heard his son's poem broadcast on the BBC and commented, 'God, you made me very wee.'

His mother, Brigid, was a tough-minded schoolmistress, whom Muldoon admits to having 'probably demonised more than appropriate'. In 'Oscar', Muldoon relates a visit to his parents' grave, where he imagines that 'though she preceded him/by a good ten years, my mother's skeleton/has managed to worm/its way back on top of the old man's/and she once again has him under her thumb.' Muldoon used her maiden name, Regan — an anagram of 'anger' — for the dedication of *The Annals of Chile* (1994).

'The mother' — as Muldoon refers to Brigid in conversation — educated her children through general-knowledge magazines. Today, Muldoon remains 'less interested in literature with a capital L than just books about interesting aspects of life — history, geography, biology, almost anything'.

He started writing poetry aged 15 at St Patrick's College, where he recalls several great teachers who fostered a love of poetry in their students. 'They made it cool. Lots of people around me were writing poems. One of our past students was the Irish poet John Montague, so there was a sense that one could be a poet without having lived in some previous era.'

It was at St Patrick's that he discovered Donne, the 17th-century English poet known for his mastery of the 'metaphysical conceit' — extended metaphors that yoke together two unlikely ideas. 'A lot of my poems operate in simular ways — the idea of the quite fanciful, far-fetched metaphor,' he says. 'I love John Donne — the range, the control, the craziness. He's so witty, so airy, so grounded. He's a model poet.'

His rich poetry education was, he laments, rare. 'It's usually taught at the pretty banal level of, "Oh, so here we have our poem for today. You'll notice in the first stanza some *alliteration*. And notice what a *hard* sound that word 'hard' has."'

Not all poetic techniques are so obvious. When Muldoon submitted 'Capercaillies' to *The New Yorker* magazine in the 1980s, the editors seemed not to notice that it was an 'acrostic' — a poem in which the first letter of each line spells out a message — reading, 'Is this a New Yorker poem or what?' Despite Muldoon mimicking what he saw as the magazine's preference for revelatory pastoral lyrics, the answer to the acrostic was clearly negative — *The New Yorker* rejected it. The barb didn't stop *The New Yorker* from hiring him as poetry editor last year — a post that he holds on top of his demanding Princeton schedule.

But Muldoon doesn't want more time to write, having only ever written about a dozen poems a year. 'I try not to get involved in writing a poem unless I'm fairly sure that it's going to be demi-semi interesting,' he says, 'when I have an image or phrase or two that I think, in my innocence, are going to be explosive.' For 13 years, before decamping to the US in 1987, he worked as an arts producer for the BBC in Belfast, and 'in those days, as today, everything I wrote, I wrote at lunchtime or at the weekend'.

He's rarely conscious of form when he writes. 'I would never know that something was going to be a sonnet, unless it was part of a sonnet sequence — that's just something that develops. But I'm apt to write a sonnet because the structure is predisposed to us. The basic idea of the sonnet, which in many cases is, "Here we have this, then we have that", corresponds to a very basic way of thinking.'

Poetry doesn't get easier with experience. 'Poetry is made out of the stuff of one's own self, out of one's innards,' he says, grasping his stomach. 'And for that reason it becomes more and more difficult, in the spider sense of weaving from its own innards, to spin out as one gets older. Poets disimprove as they go on. It's just a fact of life.'

However, there are signs that Muldoon is improving, if anything. In 2003, he won the Pulitzer Prize for *Moy Sand and Gravel*. And his 2006 volume, *Horse Latitudes*, was published to high acclaim. Although critics never question Muldoon's verbal dexterity, some, like Vendler, have criticised his work for appealing more to the head than the heart. But reviewing *Horse Latitudes* in *The New Republic*, Vendler wrote that 'age has deepened Muldoon's poetry' and applauded his ability 'to bear aloft both grief and playfulness'.

In 'Incantata', published in *The Annals of Chile*, Muldoon elegises a former girlfriend, the Irish artist Mary Farl Powers, who died of cancer in 1992. He recalls, '[Y]ou detected in me a tendency to put/on too much artificiality, both as man and poet,/which is why you called me "Polyester" or "Polyurethane."' But Muldoon downplays the claims that his work has become more emotionally charged. 'I can see how there might be more evident emotion, but there was always emotion.'

In 'The Mudroom', the poet merges Jewish and Irish imagery to celebrate his marriage to his Jewish wife, US novelist Jean Hanff Korelitz. Muldoon ruminates on his children's mixed heritage in 'At the Sign of the Black Horse, September 1999', where he sees in the face of his newborn son, Asher (now nine), 'a slew of interloper/not from Maghery ... [but] that kale-eating child on whom the peaked

cap, *Verboten* / would shortly pin a star of yellow felt.' In 'The Birth',
he evokes the first moments of their daughter, Dorothy, now 16: 'I
watch through a flood of tears / as they give her a quick rub-a-dub /
and whisk / her off to the nursery, then check their staple-guns for
staples.'

Flights of fancy pervade Muldoon's essays, not just his poetry. In
2006, he published *The End of the Poem*, which consisted of the 15
lectures that he had delivered over his five-year tenure as professor
of poetry at Oxford University. Although applauded for their
inventiveness, his close readings of 15 poems were too idiosyncratic
for some. The Oxford literary scholar Valentine Cunningham
described them as 'Bedlam — an associative madness.'

Names are important to Muldoon. He reads Marianne Moore's
poetry as a struggle against its own tendency for the excessive
ornamentation typical of *Moorish* (or Islamic) art. He suggests that
the Portuguese poet Fernando Pessoa wrote under heteronyms
because of an obsession with personality stemming from his
name 'pessoa' (Portuguese for 'person'). 'Poets do, consciously or
unconsciously, have relationships with their own names,' he says.
'I've seen many times my students unconsciously rendering their
own names in their poems.' Muldoon describes his affinity with his
name as 'profound' (recall 'The Mudroom').

The End of the Poem is not the funeral lament for the form
that its ambiguous title may suggest; it refers instead to Muldoon's
belief that, after taking in the shape of a poem, the reader might
reasonably start at its end. He thinks that the early 21st century is a
particularly vital moment for poetry. 'What I like now is that there
are no figures that have a monopoly on the poetic situation. There
are many voices from all around the world. One can appreciate a
poem by Les Murray, say, without getting involved in some kind of
notion of the Herculean figures. In my day, the ones represented as
such were [Ted] Hughes, [Philip] Larkin and [Thom] Gunn.'

And now there are Heaney, Murray, and Muldoon? He smiles bashfully: 'Well, see, I wouldn't know that.'

— *January 2007*

Harry Mulisch

In Holland, Harry Mulisch is looked to as a national conscience: the leading post-war writer of a society troubled by its history of Nazi occupation. But, for his part, Mulisch does not feel Dutch. 'I was born in Holland, but in a way Holland was never born in me,' he muses, pointing out that his parents were foreigners.

Interviewed in his canal-side Amsterdam apartment, on the cusp of his eightieth birthday, Mulisch looks a decade younger than his years. Wearing a pink-and-white-striped shirt and white loafers, he sports an elegant set of black-and-silver bracelets. And although supremely at ease with his importance, he surprises with flashes of ebullience. 'I have a theory that everybody has an absolute age which he will always have. My absolute age is 17.'

To flag his birthday, Mulisch's Dutch publisher commissioned six novellas from noted Dutch authors, taking Mulisch's novels as their departure points. It was an unlikely homage to a writer whose exuberantly inventive, philosophical works depart from the understated realism of most Dutch literary fiction. 'Dutch writers and painters are naturalists, describing normal life. That tradition is not mine,' he says.

Dutch writing is far less internationally famous than Dutch painting; even Mulisch has seen only one-third of his work translated into English. He is best known for two books: *The Assault* (1982), a compact, intense thriller that probes the decades-long reverberations of a political assassination in Nazi-occupied Holland; and *The Discovery of Heaven* (1992), a 700-page saga of divine intervention, in which Mulisch incorporates characteristically exhaustive displays of his encyclopedic learning, on topics ranging from astronomy, philology, and theology to architecture.

He is sometimes misreported as believing that *The Discovery of Heaven* is his best work. Mulisch likens asking authors to choose between their books to the malicious question in William Styron's *Sophie's Choice* (1979): 'You may not ask a mother which of her children they love most.' But if, he says, an immoral God — 'and if there is a God, he would be immoral' — were to offer him a choice of destroying all his books but not *The Discovery of Heaven*, or destroying all *The Discovery of Heaven*s but not the rest, he would choose the former. 'Not because I love it most, but because it's the book in which all my obsessions and themes come together.'

The Assault tracks 35 years in the life of Anton, an anaesthetist, whose innocent family was shot by the SS as a reprisal for the murder of a collaborationist police officer in 1945. Only the first of five episodes is set in the war. Mulisch says that for 'young people used to novels about the war — *The Diary of Anne Frank*, for instance — the four scenes after the war gave them a contact with the war'.

The novel was made into a film that won the 1987 Oscar in the foreign-language category. Mulisch admires the film, but is relieved that no one has described it as an improvement on the book, which would be 'the worst thing' that could happen to him.

The novel's tension reaches its height when Anton confronts the former underground member who indirectly caused his family's slaughter, killing the thug despite knowing that the Nazis would take revenge on local civilians. 'What interested me was the difference between guilt and responsibility,' says Mulisch.

He is well placed to probe the moral ambiguities imposed by history. His mother was a Jew whose entire family was exterminated, while his father was a Gentile who saved his wife and son by working for the Nazis as a director of the bank where Holland's

Jews were forced to deposit their assets before being deported.

Mulisch's mother was incarcerated in 1943, but his father's access to power meant that she was released three days later. Mulisch's unusual parentage has elsewhere led him to declare: 'I didn't so much "experience" the war; I am the Second World War.'

He recalls how once during the war, at the cinema, the lights came on to reveal Nazis surrounding the auditorium. All men whose identity cards showed them to have three Jewish grandparents were arrested, while those with one Jewish grandparent were sent to work in German munitions factories. But Mulisch, as a half-Jew, was free. 'Two Jewish grandparents meant that you were not Jewish enough to be murdered, but you were too Jewish to be allowed to work in the German factories.'

His formal education ended in 1944 when he decided not to risk attending school any longer. Although originally set on a career in science, he turned to writing at 18, a few months after the war's end. His first effort at a short story was published in a newspaper. His father was serving three years in prison for his service to fascism, and Mulisch continued writing to earn enough money for two meals a day.

At 23, his first novel, *Archibald Strohalm* (1951), won the Rein Geerlings Prize for young writers and high praise. Money was scarce, but he found himself a patron: 'A girlfriend, who had a job, thought that I was a genius — very clever girl! — and I lived on her, more or less. I was very poor, but after the war everybody was poor.'

Over subsequent novels, Mulisch distinguished himself from his contemporaries with his intellectual game-playing and fondness for the mythical and uncanny. He feels more affinity with the lofty aesthetics of Catholicism than with dour Protestantism, which he says explains the Dutch resistance to fantasy and ornamentation: 'Catholicism — that is statues, prayers, the Pope, and holy priests — is all gone in Protestantism.' Some churches in Holland are still bare from when their monuments were destroyed in the Reformation. 'As a writer, I'm not in favour of destroying beautiful statues. I help make them.'

A sculptor of words rather than a reader, Mulisch hasn't read a novel for two decades. He enthuses about his close friend of five decades, fellow Dutch writer Cees Nooteboom, but admits unabashedly that he isn't familiar with his books. 'People ask me often, are you still reading novels? But that's the same as if I ask a reader, are you still writing novels? If I read one page of a book, standing in a bookshop, I know whether it is OK, or nothing. I don't need to read a whole book to see that.'

Mulisch reads only the non-fiction that forms research for his novels. He gestures towards the walls of his capacious, book-lined study — here, books about theology used for *The Discovery of Heaven*; there, others about Nazism that he drew on for his 1962 essay on the trial of Adolf Eichmann, *Criminal Case 4061*.

His report on the trial advanced a theory of Eichmann's ordinariness similar to Hannah Arendt's study of 'the banality of evil' in *Eichmann in Jerusalem* (1963). 'My book was first,' says Mulisch, noting that Arendt cites his work approvingly.

He revisits the question of evil in his most recent novel, *Siegfried* (2001), which centres on Rudolf Herter, an aged and self-important Dutch novelist famous for his 1000-page opus, *The Invention of Love*. During a publicity jaunt, Herter is inspired to tackle Hitler when he tells an interviewer: 'He's been examined from all sides. All those so-called explanations have simply made him more invisible. Perhaps fiction is the net that he can be caught in.'

Mulisch offers his own account of Hitler: 'Nobody said he had this power not although he was nothing, but because he was nothing. He was a kind of black hole.' *Siegfried* imagines that Hitler had a son, and then considers his reaction to discovering that the child is 1/32nd Jewish. Mulisch wondered whether Hitler would murder him. 'He made 55 million people die, but none of them with his own hands, only one — he himself. I thought: "Wasn't there something of love in this man? Was it just all hate and destroying?"'

Mulisch speaks proudly of his nomination for the 2007 Man Booker International Award for an author's body of work, but speculates about the envy of other Dutch writers. 'It's a small country, but this smallness is also in the Dutchmen themselves. If there's suddenly somebody who is a really big man — let's say, Spinoza — he's thrown out.' But as he looks forward to a 1000-strong birthday reception, and the array of media profiles, public literary forums, and book publications welcoming him into his ninth decade, Mulisch surely knows that he is exaggerating.

— *July 2007*

Haruki Murakami

Haruki Murakami would seem the very picture of the Japanese writer-prophet. He gazes out over the rooftops of Tokyo's chichi suburb of Aoyama, speaking in low, urgent tones about Japan's rightward lurch. 'I am worrying about my country,' says the 60-year-old writer, widely considered Japan's Nobel laureate-in-waiting. 'I feel I have a responsibility as a novelist to do something.'

He is particularly concerned about Tokyo's popular governor, the novelist Shintaro Ishihara. 'Ishihara is a very dangerous man. He is an agitator. He hates China.' As Murakami discusses plans to make a public statement opposing Ishihara, and weave an anti-nationalist subtext into a novel, it's hard to recognise the writer often derided by the Tokyo literati as an apathetic pop-artist — a threat to the political engagement of Japanese fiction. Yet Murakami always distanced himself from the Japanese tradition of the writer as social admonisher: 'I thought of myself as just a fiction writer.'

Murakami's resistance to literary cliques has led him to be seen as thumbing his nose at Japan and its literature. He refuses to fulfil the typical public duties of writers — participating in talk shows, judging panels, and literary festivals — and declines all requests for television and telephone interviews. As dreamy and introverted as his disaffected protagonists, Murakami has no literary friends and never attends parties. He has spent large stretches of his adult life in Europe and America. 'I'm not interested in Japanese literature or literary people. I have no models in Japanese literature. I created my own style, my own way. They don't appreciate this,' he says.

As a teenager, Murakami kicked against the reading tastes of his parents — both lecturers in Japanese literature — by consuming pulpy American mystery novels in English. He read 'to get away from Japanese society'. Murakami's idols remain American writers — Fitzgerald, Carver, Chandler, and Vonnegut. His offhand prose, studded with references to American low culture, contrasts with the formal elegance of Japan's literary lodestars — Yukio Mishima, Kenzaburo Oe, and Jun'ichiro Tanizaki.

The heroes of his surrealistic, genre-bending narratives are under-employed drifters, without children or long-term partners, who refuse to genuflect to the Japanese group ethos of the family and the corporation. They are more likely to eat spaghetti, listen to Radiohead, and read Len Deighton than drink saki or quote Oe. 'It seems natural to refer to Radiohead songs because I love music. It's just like a movie soundtrack. But I don't listen to music when I write. I have to concentrate on writing.'

In his short story 'The Rise and Fall of Sharpie Cakes' — collected in his 2006 collection of stories, *Blind Willow, Sleeping Woman* — Murakami allegorically depicts the ructions that he touched off after netting an award for his debut novel, *Hear the Wind Sing*, in 1979. The protagonist is a finalist in a competition for a new recipe of an age-old confection known as a 'Sharpie'. His updated Sharpie cake causes bloody tumult among the wizened crows judging the competition. The young relish his recipe; the old guard does not.

Blind Willow, Sleeping Woman (2006) draws together 26 short stories, penned over twenty-five years. In the chatty introduction, Murakami writes that 'I find writing novels a challenge, writing short stories a joy.' 'A "Poor Aunt" Story' illustrates Murakami's belief that 'with one idea, one word, you can write a short story'. His narrator, who styles himself as 'one of those people who try to write stories', falls in thrall to the random image of a poor aunt, commenting: 'for some reason, things that grabbed me were always things I didn't understand'.

Murakami works on short stories in the intervals between novels. 'You can test your new technique in a short story for your next novel. The first draft is done in two or three days. So it's an experiment — a game.' *Sputnik Sweetheart* (1999) grew out of 'Man-Eating Cats', in which the narrator disappears after being lured by an intoxicating melody to climb a hill in the Greek countryside. Typically for Murakami, loss and suicide sound the keynotes. 'Many of my friends committed suicide, so I have several empty spots in my mind. I think it is my responsibility to look at them. Life is conflict with many obstacles. Sometimes you just want to get away from this world. When you commit suicide, you don't have to worry about anything. You don't get older. You don't feel pain anymore. Sometimes it's very tempting.'

Murakami's most famous novel, *Norwegian Wood* (1987), originated as 'Firefly' — about an introverted college student, Toru, who pines after his mentally unstable girlfriend. Like Toru, Murakami was raised in Kobe, and moved to Tokyo to study drama and film at college. There Murakami witnessed the rupturing of his generation's idealism, with the quashing of the 1968 and 1969 student riots. Although Murakami didn't participate in the demonstrations, his characters often wrestle with feelings of emptiness arising from the defeat. 'Spiritually I was with the protesters, but I couldn't cooperate. I'm a lone wolf.'

Despite his reading, Murakami was an unremarkable, ill-motivated student. 'My heroes don't have anything special. They have something to tell other people, but they don't know how, so they talk to themselves. I thought I was one of those ordinary people.' Although harbouring loose aspirations to become a scriptwriter, Murakami finally realised that 'to make a movie is a collective art. So I gave up wanting to be a scriptwriter.'

At university, Murakami met his lifelong partner, Yoko, and together they managed a jazz bar, Peter Cat, for seven years. 'I wasn't interested in working for a big company like Toyota or Sony. I just wanted to be independent. But that's not easy. In this country, if you don't belong to any group, you're almost nothing.'

Typically, his characters, he says, 'are looking for the right way, but it isn't easy to find. I think that's one of the reasons why young readers like reading my novels. Among the many values in life, I appreciate freedom most. I'd like to keep that freedom in my characters, so the protagonist won't have to commute to the company or office. They are not married, so they are free to do anything, free to go anywhere.'

The itch to write hit him with all the random force of a trigger for a story. Murakami points out the window to the stadium where, one night in 1979, he 'was just watching baseball and drinking beer and thought, "I can write."' He worked on his first novel over the following six months, writing in the small hours after 14-hour days at Peter Cat. He wrote the initial chapters in English, before translating them into Japanese. 'I didn't know how to write fiction, so I tried writing in English because my vocabulary was limited. I knew too many words in Japanese. It was too heavy.'

He writes like a jazz musician extemporises — guided by impulse, without a plan. 'I didn't have a teacher or a colleague as a writer, so the only way I knew was good music — rhythm, improvisation, harmony. I just know how to begin. If I knew how to finish, it wouldn't be fun because I'd know what would happen next. If you read a book, you can't wait to turn the pages. The same thing happens when I write. I can't wait to turn the pages. Writing is like dreaming when you're awake. When you're sleeping, you cannot dream a continuous dream. But when you're a writer, you can continue your dream every day. So it's fun.'

The couple closed Peter Cat in 1980 after Murakami's second

novel, *Pinball, 1973*, became a bestseller. International recognition arrived with his following novels — *A Wild Sheep Chase* (1982) and *Hard-Boiled Wonderland and the End of the World* (1985)— kaleidoscopic dreamscapes, which fused conventions of the hard-bitten detective novel with sci-fi overlays and off-the-wall comedy.

In 1987, Murakami surprised readers by producing a traditional rites-of-passage novel, expanding 'Firefly' into *Norwegian Wood*. 'I had to prove I could write in a realistic style.' But by dipping his toe into realism, Murakami triggered a tsunami. *Norwegian Wood* shifted two million copies. To Murakami, it was too much of a good thing. 'It became a phenomenon. It wasn't a book anymore. I was so uncomfortable with being famous, because being famous didn't give me anything precious or important. I felt betrayed. I lost some of my friends. I don't know why, but they left. I was not happy at all.'

He decamped to Europe with Yoko to escape the heat, shuttling between European countries for five years before taking up a writers' fellowship at Princeton in 1991. From abroad, Murakami witnessed the bursting of Japan's bubble economy. Suddenly, mainstream Japan was made to confront the questions that trouble his characters. 'We had to stop and think — what is truly good for us? What is our value? We lost our confidence, so we had to find something else as the purpose of society. After the war we had been getting richer and richer, and we were confident that we would keep getting richer.'

'We are in chaos at this moment,' continues Murakami, 'and there is nationalism, and we are searching for new value. So some things are dangerous, but basically I think things are getting better. Young people in Japan are not like we were twenty or thirty years ago. In the 1960s, we used to be more idealistic, and people were very confident.'

The gap between Murakami and Japan narrowed further in 1995, when the country was rent by another two convulsions. On

17 January, Kobe was hit by an earthquake, killing 6,500 people. Two months later, Aum cultists released toxic nerve gas into the Tokyo subway system at rush hour. Murakami, who had spent the previous four years at Princeton writing his opus *The Wind-Up Bird Chronicle* (1997), returned from self-exile. 'It wasn't a patriotic thing. I just wanted to do something for my people.'

The sharpening of Murakami's social commitment was heralded by *after the quake* (2000) — a set of six bleakly absurd stories, portraying the aftershocks of the Kobe earthquake. He'd also recently turned to non-fiction with *Underground* (1997), a collection of interviews with the doomsday cultists responsible for the gassings and the subway riders who survived them. Murakami came to empathise with the work-obsessed salarymen and office ladies who he had previously felt were not worth writing about: 'Many people expected that I would be sympathetic to the cult people because they're outsiders. But that was not the case. They're shallow, but the common people have the depth of real life.'

Childless, like his characters, Murakami is free to pursue his daily regime of writing, translating and fitness. After rising at 6.00am, he writes for about six hours, broken by an hour-long jog or swim. 'When I stopped running the jazz club, I started running because I needed a physical outlet.' His evenings are spent listening to jazz and translating American novels into Japanese.

As a translator, Murakami has introduced the Japanese reading public to over 40 works by the likes of Truman Capote, John Irving, Tim O'Brien, and Grace Paley. 'Writing fiction is like making your own puzzle, but translating is just like resolving the puzzle. In other words, when you're writing your own stuff, you're making up your own video game. When you're translating, you're playing that game. So it's fun. Writing fiction, you get egotistical. You have to have confidence. But translating, you have to respect the text, so your ego shrinks to normal size. It's good for your mental health.'

Asked about his decision not to have children, Murakami comments that he fails to share the post-war idealism of his parents: 'I'm not so optimistic.' He also notes that 'books are more important to me'. He pauses, pensive, then half-grins — perhaps implying that these are mere equivocations: 'I didn't want to be a parent because I knew my children would hate me.' He refuses to be drawn on his difficult relationship with his parents, saying only that 'they had their own values and I had my own. I was an only child, and their presence was heavy.'

Despite what Japan's most hidebound pundits argue, Murakami's writing has always been closer to his homeland than the fictional universes of Fitzgerald, Carver, and Chandler. Occidental critics ritually compare Murakami with postmodernists such as Don DeLillo and Thomas Pynchon. But in Japan, as Murakami tells it, 'people do not think my stories are postmodern'.

In Japanese spirituality, the divide between the real and the fantastic is permeable, so his tales of unicorn skulls, six-foot tall frogs, star-patterned sheep, and Colonel Sanders are 'very natural'. 'You know the myth of Orpheus. He goes to the underworld to look for his deceased wife, but it's far away and he has to undergo many trials to get there. There's a big river and a wasteland. My characters go to the other world, the other side. In the Western world, there is a big wall you have to climb up. In this country, once you want to go there, it's easy. It's just beneath your feet.'

— *May 2006*

Ben Okri

Ben Okri is admiring a designer bottle of mineral water. 'Isn't it a beautiful colour?' he says, holding the sapphire-blue glass up to the light. He asks the waiter for another bottle and a bag to carry them home. 'Shhh,' he whispers over the expensive water in London's ritzy Langham Hotel. 'I don't want to be seen carrying these drinks. I don't want them to become too popular. I collect them.'

It's not surprising that a bottle should invite wide-eyed wonder from Okri. In the alternate realities of his novels, everyday objects assume talismanic qualities, auguring fertility and famine, birth and annihilation.

His 1991 Booker Prize-winning novel, *The Famished Road*, followed the spirit-child Azaro, who flits between human and spiritual realms against the backdrop of a West African civil war. He has since written ten more books, fusing a broadly African aesthetic with New Age spirituality and the magic-realist techniques popularised by Latin American writers.

Critics are divided about Okri's oracular style, but he enjoys a devoted following; Bridget Jones vowed to finish *The Famished Road* as part of her self-improvement regime.

Okri's worldview has the intentional naivety of a man who has kept modern-day sophistications at bay, who doesn't drive, own a computer, or use a mobile phone. He makes a dramatic gesture of bewilderment when I present two voice-recorders, questioning my reliance on technology.

I explain that it's because I share his technophobia that I double up, but Okri seems not to have heard. 'I'll show you something', he says, presenting a pen and paper to write silently, and leaving a 30-second interregnum on the recording. 'A computer can't pick that up, can it?' he says, cryptically adding that 'silence is the highest action'.

He sees himself as an artist of silence who is frustrated by having to use words: 'The text of experience is extremely rich and mysterious, but the text of prose is so visible. Another genre is inside me trying to express itself through this medium.' In his latest novel, *Starbook* (2007), he literally gives silence a voice, writing: 'There was a long silence as the silence spoke.'

Starbook is a meandering narrative of fables, aphorisms, and vatic disquisitions on topics such as 'authenticity', 'truth', and 'seeing'. It tracks the efforts of a sickly prince to woo a poor maiden from an invisible tribe of artists, which channel the wisdom of the gods into prophetic sculptures. Their courtship sparks an enigmatic prophecy of a dark time ruled by 'the white spirits', which will be vanquished only by love. The prince's enlightenment incites the ire of his tribe's elders, protective of their monopoly on power.

He tried to draw silence into *Starbook* by dividing it into 150 short chapters, Okri explains. Likening the effect of a chapter division to 'the wind blowing over a vast empty landscape', he brings a chapter to a close when he wants 'to perch the narrative into an expressive silence'.

Okri gesticulates with the slow, controlled rhythms of a martial arts connoisseur. He began practising martial arts as an adolescent to compensate for being less physically developed than his peers. Both his prose and fighting stem from the Taoist philosophy 'that you should have no style, that a style is a limitation; that however the fight is you go with the fight'.

Despite his rhythmic, ornate syntax, Okri insists that he doesn't aim for elegant language. 'I don't want you to look at how pretty my hand movements are when I'm supposed to be knocking you out.' In *Starbook*, the tribe of artists lacks a word for beauty; they excised it from their vocabulary because style is a hindrance to higher consciousness.

Starbook's opening line, 'This is a story my mother began to tell me when I was a child,' was the fountainhead from which the novel flowed. 'If I didn't have that sentence, I would never have had the book. You have no idea how long it took me to get such an obviously simple sentence.' Beginning a novel is a process of finding the right rhythm, because 'the universe is musical and there's a precise beat by which something can be true'.

In *Starbook*, which reads like a kaleidoscopic dreamscape, the gods communicate with people through dreams. Okri says that he 'cannot' — that is to say, will not — comment on the role of dreams in his creative process, but remarks that many of his favourite novels — such as *The Pilgrim's Progress*, *Don Quixote*, *Dr Jekyll and Mr Hyde*, and *Eugene Onegin* — originated as dreams. 'Many of our greatest scientific discoveries came in dreams. Creativity and dreams share the same matrix.'

Okri is as elusive as his characters because, as with his writing, he formulates ideas abstractly, skirting over concrete feelings, motivations, and events. He says that the years of writing *The Famished Road* were the bleakest of his life, but will not be drawn on the reasons. 'It was a long, long, long night that I thought was going to go on forever. If I hadn't come through that, I wouldn't be here right now, alive.'

After finishing *The Famished Road*, he produced eight books in as many years. 'It was like all paths of my life jammed, and this thing came along and freed me.' At five years in the writing, *Starbook* was relatively slow coming. 'What happened was there was a backlog gushing out, and now it's the river again.' As a young writer, he often worked feverishly into the night, but now writes at a more considered pace. He sees ambition as hostile to writing because 'what made this universe is not ambition, but simplicity'.

Starbook's repeated allusion to 'the book of life among the stars' reflects Okri's interest in how our lives participate in an infinite story that is inaccessible to the human mind. 'There are ancient philosophers who believe that all of reality is a dream in the mind of God — a book, a perpetual narrative.' Okri's novels don't so much end as taper out because 'the true purpose of art is to keep you on an endless journey'. With *Starbook*, he sensed the climax 'when it touched that point that touches all other points — the point where it touched the stars'.

Okri's detractors argue that he privileges gaudy magical effects over character and plot. The narrator of *Starbook* puts the criticism succinctly when he states that 'too much myth, an excess of magic, and the road to heaven is undone: what amazes the eye blinds the soul to its true goal'. Critics who see his work as undisciplined fail to look beyond its veneer, according to Okri: 'Sometimes the surface deliberately mirrors the very problem that it's trying to address, like fighting fire with fire.' But surely through mimicking the problem he also risks falling under its spell? 'No, not if you just listen to the building block of that universe, which is a beat,' he replies with typical woolliness. 'If the beat is clear the spirit is clear.'

For Okri, history has an ambivalent relationship to mythology. 'The ancient kingdoms all go through a period of excessive magic. Egyptian kingdoms were at the point of their decline when they believed in too much myth. That has been one of the greatest problems of Africa — the triumph of myth and magic over clarity.'

The settings of his novels are unnamed but often presumed to be Okri's native Nigeria. Yet when he won the Booker Prize in 1991, he resisted media attempts to cast his triumph as a milestone for African writing, preferring to situate himself within a universal storytelling tradition: 'I'm interested in what is universal in the African.'

Born in 1959 in the nut-growing village of Minna, central Nigeria, Okri moved to London when he was 18 months old, after his father won a scholarship to study law there. He remembers himself as a precocious, vagrant six-year-old, reading Shakespeare and *The Times* from cover to cover, while regularly losing himself in the streets and asking for directions back home. Together with his gang, modelled on *The Bash Street Kids* comic-book heroes, he roamed London deflating tyres and trespassing into homes.

The family returned to Nigeria after his father qualified as a barrister. Okri was devastated. Refusing to enter the ship, Okri was tricked into embarking when his mother, after telling him that he could stay alone in London, lured him on board to say goodbye as the ship set sail. Civil war erupted shortly after their return, but Okri refuses to discuss his wartime experiences. 'It's not every day that one is plunged into such a thing in your childhood. The scope for meditation is immense because it's part of what's made you. That's why I don't talk about it.'

His father was so ambitious for his son that he pulled strings to get Okri enrolled in secondary school at the age of nine. 'I was in the same class as bearded people who had big muscles. I never totally got away from that feeling of bewilderment.' He initially wanted to be a scientist — more particularly, an 'inventor' — but that ambition ended when his university application was rejected. Having graduated from secondary school aged 14, the university administrators thought he was a fraud. 'I'm lucky I didn't become a scientist. It would be too boring just to be that which you wanted to be. It's much more interesting to be frustrated.'

The rebuff coincided with his family's fall from prosperity, for reasons Okri will not disclose. He passed the following four years frugally at home, reading English literature and ancient philosophy. 'If we'd still have been rich and successful, I would have been hanging out with my old mates and going to gigs. Those years in which I didn't have anything to do were actually the real formation of me.'

At 19, now bent on becoming a writer, Okri headed to England to study comparative literature at the University of Essex: 'London draws the mind — I mean, Shakespeare, Dickens, *hello!*' He sees his return as a reprise of his father's journey 18 years earlier. 'It's not surprising that later on I'd come back here — to write. We human beings are very echoistic. We're very musical.'

Two years into his degree, Nigeria went into an economic tailspin, and the government withdrew his scholarship. When the house of his uncle that Okri shared was knocked down, he took to the streets for several months, sleeping in the Tube, but continuing to read even while his ribs began to protrude.

Okri regards his down-and-out months as central to his formation as a writer, arguing that contemporary literature often lacks authenticity because writers are alienated from ordinary life. Asked whether his post-Booker Prize celebrity threatened his writing, Okri says that 'it takes much more character to cope with success than with adversity. More people have done themselves in on account of being rich, famous, and successful, than poor.'

Okri's spirit has obviously survived the trials of material success; he insists on footing the steep bill. I tell him that I'm surprised he owns a credit card, given his Luddism. 'I am, too', he says. The machine rejects his card. Okri tries again unsuccessfully, before concluding that the machine is broken. As the waiter leaves to seek counsel about the equipment, I glance at Okri's card. It expired three days earlier.

– September 2007

Per Petterson

When Per Petterson worked in an Oslo bookstore in the 1980s, and aspired to write fiction that reflected his working-class origins, he looked for inspiration to the American 'dirty realist' writers — Raymond Carver, Richard Ford, and Jayne Anne Phillips. Petterson was due to visit Carver with one of his Norwegian translators when the writer died of lung cancer in 1988. Carver's widow suggested that they come anyway; Petterson slept for four nights in Carver's library.

With their spare style and attention to the textures of everyday life, Petterson's novels are well worthy of the epithet 'Carver-esque'. His most recent novel translated into English, *Out Stealing Horses* (2003), sold 200,000 copies in Norway, which has a population of fewer than five million. After taking out the 2006 Independent Foreign Fiction Prize, it beat shortlisted novels by J. M. Coetzee, Julian Barnes, Cormac McCarthy, and Salman Rushdie to the 2007 International IMPAC Dublin Literary Award which, at €100,000, is the world's richest literary laurel.

A coming-of-age story with none of the kitsch or melodrama that often attaches to that genre, *Out Stealing Horses* finds 67-year-old Trond Sander reflecting on the transformative summer of 1948 that he spent with his father in a rural town near the Swedish frontier. A widower since his wife was killed in a road accident, Trond renovates the secluded cottage where he intends to pass his remaining years in solitude while recalling how, when he was 15, his horse-thieving soulmate became the unwitting perpetrator of another tragedy.

Over coffee during the New York leg of an American publicity tour, Petterson is as jaunty and jokey as his books are brooding and dark. In contrast to his meticulous prose, he talks nineteen to the dozen without making a passing glance at his water. 'When I read, it's the other way around,' he says, grinning. 'I have to drink all the time.'

Petterson sees *Out Stealing Horses* partly as a homage to Nobel laureate Knut Hamsun who, before becoming an ardent Nazi sympathiser, wrote novels about alienated outsiders who worm their way into tight-knit communities in Norway's Arctic north.

Hamsun's novels defined what Petterson terms 'the Norwegian kind of Buddhism — the need to go into the forest for the solitude, to be alone in nature doing ritual things'.

Petterson likens the international success of *Out Stealing Horses* to a 'freak accident' but, with a personal history buffeted by tragedy no less than his fiction, that is no light metaphor. In 1990, the Scandinavian Star ferry caught fire, claiming 158 lives, including Petterson's parents, brother and niece. Petterson was supposed to be on board with his family, travelling to their holiday home in Denmark, but was fortuitously delayed at the last moment.

Petterson's autobiographical novel *In the Wake* (2000) opens as Arvid Jansen, a blocked novelist, wakes dishevelled, slumped against the door of the Oslo bookstore where he once worked, unable to remember how he got there. Through flashbacks we learn of how he arrived at this nadir, and of the deaths of his parents and two brothers in a freak ferry accident six years earlier.

Petterson formed a support group with survivors and other family of victims, propelled by adrenalin for two years after the tragedy. 'I was running around talking about what happened. We externalised everything and talked and talked and talked. Everybody had three deaths in the family, or had just survived by one inch. Everybody was crazy, but nobody was aware of it.'

Petterson hadn't spoken about the death of his other brother, who passed away seven years before the ferry disaster, because he felt that it had no significance outside of his family. After the nationwide mourning process that followed the Scandinavian Star incident, he understood how his parents' generation sometimes spoke nostalgically of the wartime years. 'You stood shoulder to shoulder with your allies, your neighbours. Whatever happened to a family, there was a kind of sharing in it.'

Writing didn't assuage his grief: 'Writing is not confessional. You should do therapy with your therapist.' Petterson began *In the Wake* seven years after the tragedy, having psychically resolved all that he possibly could. 'I couldn't have written it if I was in a fragile state.' The novel is less about the ferry tragedy than the fraught family dynamics that it prompts Arvid to ponder. 'I didn't want to be "the Scandinavian Star writer", writing about the ship and all that happened. A maximum of four pages is devoted to what happened on the ship.'

Most of Petterson's work centres upon father-son tensions, and his own ambivalent relationship with his father made his death particularly difficult to come to terms with. His father worked in a shoe factory, and was an outdoorsy type who was suspicious of speech. As a teenager, Petterson rejected his values, only later appreciating the love of physical work and nature that he planted in him and which pervades his fiction. 'I regret that we didn't talk and that I didn't explain to him why I sort of left him when I was young. I thought, "I will some day." And then he died.'

In Petterson's final conversation with his mother, she told him that she hoped his next book would not be 'childish' like his first two novels, which featured Arvid Jansen as a child. She might not have liked his books, but Petterson is sure she was proud of him becoming a writer. She passed her days working in a chocolate factory, but by night devoured great literature, which she read in five languages.

To Siberia (1996) was a fictionalised account of his mother's adolescence in Nazi-occupied Denmark, focusing on her relationship with her idolised older brother, who died of a brain tumour aged 25. 'When she talked about her brother she got this glow in her eyes,' says Petterson, who describes his mother as a tough-minded woman who refused to complain about life's trials. 'When she talked about my father, she didn't have the same glow in her eyes. So I understood from a very early age that her older brother was the man in her life.'

Petterson dropped out of college before training as a librarian, which he aborted after two years. 'I fear academics, because I think they know something that I don't. The bookshop was my university. For twelve years I read books all the time and talked with normal people — readers and customers — about books.'

By 18, he wanted to be a writer, after reading Hemmingway and realising that the language and subjects of fiction could be drawn from ordinary life. 'I always wrote seriously, but I never finished anything because I would see that it was crap.' At 34, Petterson completed his first story after a friend pointed out that he was already halfway through life, and that if he didn't make a name for himself now, he probably never would. 'I was so scared that suddenly I could do it. It was like when I stopped smoking; it really terrified me.'

He moved to the country in 1993 at the urging of his second wife, Pia, a kindergarten teacher. 'I had to move to get the girl. No chance in Oslo — she wanted out.' As he renovated the cottage in Eastern Norway where he continues to live, in much the same way as Trond, he put to use the skills that his father had browbeaten him into acquiring. 'It was like a blast from the past. I thought, "Oh, I should have thanked him, because I see now how what he gave me, by forcing me into the woods, was important."'

Petterson's father never mentioned his books, but Petterson is convinced that he read them. He remains a crucial, if unlikely, influence on his writing, which is spare in dialogue but rich in its description of physical work. 'My father couldn't formulate the things that were important to him — he did them with his body. But when you are younger you don't understand that what he has given you is something other than talk. I'd like to thank him for that, because as a writer now that is extremely important to me. Talk is entirely overvalued, I think.'

— *October 2007*

José Saramago

In *On Late Style* (2006), Edward Said suggested that the approach of death often provokes one of two reactions in writers. Some embody the popular image of the old sage, whose work reflects a new serenity and reconciliation with the world. For others, ailing health manifests as irresolvable contradiction and discord, provoking them to reopen unsettling and intractable questions of meaning and identity.

In José Saramago's *Death at Intervals*, death is not only the central theme but also the principal character. First published in his native Portuguese in 2005, the book was translated into flowing English by Margaret Jull Costa in 2008. Now 86, the novelist seems almost to parody the death-obsession of a writer with his eye on the hourglass. Yet by comically personifying the Grim Reaper as a woman, is Saramago going gently into the night, or mounting a futile rebellion against the injustice of mortality?

Death at Intervals sits between Said's two categories of 'late style' — it offers neither unbridled indignity nor the reassurance of moral closure. Outwardly, it's a fable about the importance of death to civilisation. The population of an unnamed country suddenly stops dying — Saramago grants humankind its age-old wish for eternal life in order to imagine its hellish consequences. But this is also a postmodern novel with a self-conscious authorial voice, drawing attention to its constructed nature and insisting on alternative interpretations.

It is the Portuguese novelist's 16th work of fiction (counting a collection of short stories and a novella) — a significant achievement for any writer, particularly one born into a family of illiterate peasants in southern Portugal. 'We were a poor family with no education, with limited horizons, in a continuous line of illiterates, generation after generation,' says Saramago in an email interview. 'I read everything I could get my hands on — even newspapers I picked up off the floor. From reader to writer was a logical step.'

He published his first novel in 1947, in his mid-twenties, but then abandoned his literary pursuits and worked variously as a mechanic, a translator and, more latterly, as a journalist. 'I didn't think I had anything worthwhile to say,' he says. It was only in his fifties that he came back to fiction. He has written full-time ever since, and won international attention with his 18th-century romance *Baltasar and Blimunda* (1982). Acclaim followed, and in 1998 he was awarded the Nobel Prize for Literature — the first Portuguese ever to win the accolade. The award committee commended his 'parables sustained by imagination, compassion and irony'.

Saramago's work has not been universally applauded, however. In 1992, the centre-right Portuguese government barred his heretical novel *The Gospel According to Jesus Christ* from being nominated for a European literary award — Saramago moved to the Spanish island of Lanzarote in protest. 'It made me indignant,' he says. 'After fifty years of fascist dictatorship, a democratic government decided to ban a book!'

Even the critics remain divided. Harold Bloom has labelled him our greatest living writer, but both Tim Parks and John Banville, for example, construe his technique of introducing fantastical elements into real-world scenarios as frivolous. Banville has criticised Saramago's magic realism by arguing that 'reality itself is magical enough without inventing whimsicalities'.

'How is reality "magical enough?" ' protests Saramago. 'Reality contains nothing magical. Magic is the imagination. To classify my books as 'magic realism' is Banville's responsibility, not mine. I consider myself to be a realist author, who is free to walk along different paths and press different keys.' In Saramago's 2003 novel *The Double*, a history teacher seeks a mandate to teach history in reverse from the present to the past — like this fictional protagonist, Saramago inverts reality in order to illuminate it.

Both Saramago's moralising and his subversive streak are typical of his work more generally, not just his newest book. Stylistically, his punctuation is unorthodox. There's an improvised quality to the writing that makes it read like speech.

His run-on sentences spill into paragraphs that are often several pages long. Eschewing quotation marks, the dialogue of his characters merges with that of the omniscient narrator to create a sometimes disorientating melange of shifting voices: 'Punctuation is a convention. There are languages that don't use it, but the speakers still understand what they read. When we talk, we don't use punctuation.'

'My style,' continues Saramago, 'began in 1979 when I was writing *Risen from the Ground*. The world I described was rural Portugal during the first two-thirds of last century — a world in which the storytelling culture dominated, and was passed on from generation to generation, without using the written word.' Saramago resembles the old provincial porter in *Death at Intervals* who is briefly consulted about an archaic proverb, and laughed at because 'he still spoke as if he were sitting by the fireside telling stories to his grandchildren'.

The first half of *Death at Intervals* has little plot, and considers the social and political consequences of death's departure. The state ponders how future generations will support a burgeoning population on old-age and disability pensions. Insurance companies seek loopholes to relinquish payments to the permanently undying. Republicans agitate for a presidential system with fixed mandates, rather than a monarch subsisting in a vegetative state. People euthanise their living-dead family members by transporting them across the frontier where death remains active. The undertaking industry is reduced to arranging funerals for animals.

This is obviously a satire on human vanity, with its yearning for immortality. But Saramago doesn't have the science-fiction writer's impulse to explain his scenario: why people continue to die outside the country's borders, and death still happens to animals and plants. In fact, he deliberately refuses to dwell on the logic of the situation, writing: 'We confess that we are unable to provide explanations that will satisfy those demanding them.'

The octogenarian author has never reached for the consolations of an afterlife. His old-fashioned atheism is most clear in *Gospel*, which depicted a megalomaniac God who engineered the martyrdom of Jesus to expand his following beyond the Jews. *Death at Intervals* again thumps his message home: despairing of the paradox whereby the cessation of death also spells the death of god, the clergy feverishly spin new myths to keep their straying flock within the fold. Of religion, Saramago declares: 'It is out there and so am I. I can't tolerate it; it can't tolerate me.'

After seven months' leave, death resumes her operations, albeit now delivering violet-coloured letters to her victims to signal their imminent demise. The novel's pointed satire evaporates in its second half with the entrance of the personification of death (spelled with a lower case 'd'). A plot finally emerges as one of death's lethal notices is inexplicably returned to her subterranean lair. Flummoxed that someone has eluded her summons, death takes human form as a beautiful woman to pursue her quarry — a solitary, middle-aged cellist, and prototypical Saramagan everyman.

Saramago's fiction frequently notes class differences and the rapacity of market forces. He joined the Portuguese Communist party in 1969, when it was a vital source of opposition to the dictatorship of António Salazar, and remains committed to the ideology. 'The Christians took refuge in Jesus to persevere in their faith, as I take refuge in the principles and ideals of equality and solidarity,' he says. 'It seems that everyone would like me to move over to capitalism, after the disaster of communism as it was put into practice. I'm sorry to disappoint anyone. Being a communist, in my understanding, is a state of mind. I shall never renounce that.'

He has delivered lectures at international conferences attacking the International Monetary Fund and the European Union, and is most notorious for a visit to Israel in 2002 when he compared Ramallah to Auschwitz. Today, Saramago says: 'In Ramallah I found the spirit of Auschwitz. While there is one Palestinian still alive, the Holocaust continues. Israel will never accept the existence of a sovereign Palestinian state.'

Fortunately, his fiction is less dogmatic. *The Cave* (2001) finds a potter and his family living on the outskirts of an ominous housing complex and mall known as the Centre, which deprives them of their livelihood. In *The Stone Raft* — published in 1986, the year that Portugal and Spain joined the European Community — Saramago's vision of Iberia as a free-floating landmass signified his concerns about Portugal's sovereignty when it aligned with its more economically powerful northern partners.

'I've never used literature to convey my political ideas, but my politics are easy to spot in my writing,' Saramago says. 'I believe that I'm an essayist at heart. I have a strong tendency towards reflection, which in theory would manifest more appropriately in the form of essays. But I don't know how to write essays, so I use the novel as a substitute.'

While most of Saramago's novels resemble fables, they never hinge on simplistic moral truths. His hallmark is to establish an absurd scenario, then trace its ramifications with clinical rigour. In *Blindness* (1995), a city's population is afflicted by an epidemic of blindness; but it's whiteness, not darkness, which replaces sight. *Blindness*, he says, was his most difficult novel to write: 'It is a thankless task to create horror with one's own hands, even in the world of literature. I paid for it with several months of anxiety.' *Death at Intervals* developed in a similar way: 'In *Blindness*, I tried to look at the question: "What if we were all blind?" Here the question was: "What if death no longer killed us?" The idea came out of the blue.'

Blindness remains Saramago's most famous novel, but it's also probably his most overrated. Although he creates a haunting conceit to show how political tyranny blinds people to humanity, his difficult, undisciplined prose impedes the flow of the adventure story.

Saramago's narratives are typically late to develop. It's only midway through *The Double*, where a depressed history teacher discovers a duplicate appearing as a bit actor in various films, that the rivals meet and a thriller launches. This verbosity and delay would be frustrating in a lesser writer.

The real joy of reading Saramago is not his plots but his voice — by turns generous and barbed, earthy and urbane, philosophical and pedantic. His characters, often unnamed, are mostly timid and undistinguished — proofreaders, clerks, bit-part actors. But they refuse to act predictably — they chat to Common Sense in *The Double*, and an entity called 'the spirit hovering over the water of the aquarium' in *Death at Intervals*. A speaking plaster ceiling features in *All the Names* (1997) — a portrayal of a lowly clerk employed by a Central Registry of Births and Deaths.

The epigraph from *Death at Intervals* quotes Wittgenstein's hypothesis that thinking about death requires 'new linguistic fields'. One suspects that Saramago chose these words ironically, to mislead us into thinking that death will be invoked indirectly through figurative language, rather than the absurdly literal death with her petty bouts of irritation that we eventually meet. The female death persona would not seem odd to a Portuguese readership — 'death' is a feminine noun in Romance languages. 'As far as we know, death has no gender,' Saramago says. 'Either that, or it carries the gender attributed to it by the language in which we mention it. I had no doubt that, in my book, death would have to be female.' There's a sense in which, by decapitalising death, Saramago also decapitates her, puncturing her authority.

Saramago forgoes capitals for all proper names, deflating god, marcel proust, socrates, and the catholic apostolic church of rome. As he writes: 'words have their own hierarchy, their own protocol, their own aristocratic titles, their own plebeian stigmas'. His unconventional grammar levels these disparities. But no character is better placed to ponder the slipperiness of human language than death herself. Explaining to her incredulous scythe that there are at least six words for 'coffin', she comments: 'That's what these people are like, they're never quite sure what they mean.'

Saramago's interest in how reality is shaped by the contingencies of language is most visible in *The History of the Siege of Lisbon* (1989), where a proofreader alters the historical record by inserting the single word 'not' into a scholarly account of the city's 1147 siege. Despite playing with language, however, Saramago lacks the nihilism of postmodern writers who regard truth as unattainable.

In *The Year of the Death of Ricardo Reis* (1984), Saramago's titular hero is one of the four main heteronyms employed by the Portuguese poet Fernando Pessoa. As with the doppelganger in *The Double*, Saramago creates a character who cannot logically exist; not to cynically suggest that the self is an illusion, but rather to question what it means to be an authentic being.

Saramago's works play with traditional stories. In *The Cave*, he reworks Plato's allegory to show how truth has been replaced by the virtual reality of consumer capitalism. *Death at Intervals* subverts the late-medieval allegory of the dance of death. In the Middle Ages the dance of death was a popular trope demonstrating how death draws everyone into its dance regardless of social rank — its appeal to Saramago's political sympathies is unsurprising. In the novel, rather than death being the musician leading people to their demise, it's now the human cellist who seduces death.

The denouement of *Death at Intervals* hints at a possible return to its beginning, creating a circular structure which echoes the cycle of life. It implies that, even if death continues to reign and human existence remains finite, the storytelling impulse is unending. The novel ultimately lacks the imaginative reach of Saramago's rendition of Inquisition-era Portugal in *Baltasar and Blimunda*. And there's little here of the metaphysical richness of *The Double* or *All the Names*. But the author's eccentric voice is as engaging as ever.

Umberto Eco suggests in *Turning Back the Clock* (2007) that the best way for an aged intellectual to face mortality is to recognise the stupidity of the world that they will leave behind. Perhaps this is why with *Death at Intervals* Saramago's satirical impulse is unrestrained.

His narrator comments: 'We human beings can't do much more than stick out our tongue at the executioner about to chop off our head.' Saramago gives death an impish tongue-poke — but he also resigns himself to its inevitability. *Death at Intervals*, according to Saramago, 'brings to light the one absolute certainty we have on this subject — we cannot stop death. By accepting this, I think, we show our wisdom.'

— *December 2008*

Graham Swift

In Cool Britannia, where authors gain media notice through spouting headline-grabbing opinions and flaunting their eccentric lifestyles, Graham Swift is an unusual figure. His media persona is unpretentious and his opinions demure. An A-list writer with a low-key celebrity profile, his personal history is as seemingly unremarkable as the characters in his work.

Across an oeuvre of eight novels — most notably his 1983 saga, *Waterland*, set in the low-lying, marshy terrain of the British fens, and his 1996 Booker Prize-winning novel, *Last Orders* — Swift has emerged as Britain's chief practitioner of artful banality. His work is free of the flamboyant plots or linguistic pyrotechnics of contemporaries Martin Amis, Salman Rushdie, and Julian Barnes. He sculpts compelling drama from unassuming scenarios, creating lyrical visions out of quotidian language.

Swift's most recent novel, 2007's *Tomorrow*, stemmed from the desire to write about happiness. It's a simple idea, but a challenge that few novelists take on. As Leo Tolstoy famously opened *Anna Karenina*: 'All happy families are alike; each unhappy family is unhappy in its own way.' Because drama hinges on conflict, domestic bliss is inherently undramatic. 'There's no real story in happiness,' says Swift, 60, by phone from London.

So he wrote about a close-knit family whose serenity is jeopardised. 'The way to write about happiness and make it nonetheless dramatic is to write about it at a point where it is vulnerable.' *Tomorrow* opens at 1.00am as Paula, a successful art dealer and mother of 16-year-old twins, lies awake, anxiously anticipating the later morning. After sunrise, Paula and her husband, Mike, the prosperous CEO of a science-publishing company, will tell their children the truth about their origins.

The novel ends several hours after it begins, at the dawn before the announcement, and the reader can only guess the aftermath. 'One possibility is that this family will go on being happy, but nonetheless the happiness is threatened. The possibility of losing happiness gives the happiness a sense of urgency.'

Writing about happiness doesn't make the creative process unusually pleasurable. 'It doesn't matter whether you're writing about grief or joy; you get the buzz when it's working.'

Swift's prose appears effortless, at times even flippant, but it's the work of a master craftsman. In *Tomorrow*, seemingly throwaway phrases are repeated at meticulously timed moments so that clichés such as 'sometimes mothers can just tell things' and 'mothers only want the best for their children' attain a poetry and resonance that one might never have thought possible. 'It's not as though I earmark a certain word or phrase as something which will be repeated. That's very much intuition.'

But writing isn't primarily about words for Swift. 'One of the great challenges of writing is to attempt to put into words something which most people most of the time would find very hard to put into words. It's not the words themselves that count, but the feelings they're trying to express.'

The authenticity of Swift's novels owes much to their first-person narrators. 'We all exist in the first person, so if you write in the first person you're automatically so much closer to life as it's really lived. With a first-person narrator, you know why the story is being told. The story in the third person has to come out of the blue from some mysterious point the author has decided on. I always have a slight sense of the third person as the author taking a superior stance.'

Last Orders was the watershed book that freed him to employ a demotic style. 'I relied on narrators who were not particularly educated. I discovered that seemingly limited language was capable of being very expressive.' As with *Last Orders*, *Tomorrow* is narrated on a single day. 'I'm attracted to the intensity and the atmosphere that you get when everything is being related during a short period.'

Yet *Tomorrow* also stretches back fifty years, as Paula imaginatively reconstructs the events surrounding her husband's birth during World War II, while his father was away fighting. The war forms a historical legacy for many of Swift's characters.

Born in 1946 to a father who served as a naval pilot, Swift developed an early interest in combat. In his adolescence, he began to question the glamourised view of war that he grew up with. 'I was dealing with both the real effects of history and the way that history can be mythologised and comparing the two — not a bad formative process for a future novelist. It taught me that ordinary little lives could get swept away by very big things.'

After gaining an English degree at Cambridge, Swift studied for his PhD in English literature at the University of York, but spent more time working on short stories than on his doctorate. 'Its chief value was that it gave me time to work on my writing.' With no interest in an academic career, he supported himself over the following decade working as an English teacher, a security guard, and a farmhand.

His first novel, *The Sweet Shop Owner*, was published in 1980. 'There was a very long chunk of my life when I was effectively just by myself and out in the cold, an unpublished writer. When I looked around at my contemporaries in very comfortable jobs, I might have a moment's pause for thought and even envy. But then I'd come back to the fact that I was lucky to have discovered the thing that really was going to drive me.'

Fame arrived in 1983 with his third novel, *Waterland*, an ornate historical chronicle. 'It's not typical of my usual style, which is much quieter, more intimate, and more internal, as in *Tomorrow*.'

The sea forms an atmospheric backdrop in several of Swift's novels. In *Tomorrow*, the beach is the site of both a decades-long love affair and a near-drowning. 'Any waterline, any coastline, is on the edge, where one element meets another. It has that inherent drama. It can have a latent danger as well as being something that people enjoy.'

Tomorrow is about the importance of offspring to human identity. Swift thumbnails its central theme as 'biological continuity and how much that matters for sustaining our sense of continuity'. So why do Swift and his lifelong partner, Candice, not have children? 'It's simply a matter of choice. We're pretty happy without. The novel is very much not a reflection of my personal experiences.'

His diffident public image has not made him immune to controversy. Shortly after *Last Orders* won the Booker Prize, *The Australian* carried a letter from Melbourne University academic John Frow, charging Swift with improperly borrowing from William Faulkner's *As I Lay Dying* (1930). Debate raged in the British media, with Booker judge A. N. Wilson writing in *The Independent* that if the jury had been aware of the parallels with Faulkner's novel, Swift wouldn't have won.

Having acknowledged his debt to Faulkner's novel, Swift was stunned by the plagiarism allegation. 'The story of what people do with the remains of the dead is a story we've been dealing with for as long as we've been around. Faulkner had no monopoly on it. If I hadn't won the Booker Prize, I don't think that story would have been a story at all. Unfortunately, when your profile is high you're a target for all kinds of mischievous activity in the press.'

— *April 2007*

Tobias Wolff

As his co-workers at *The Washington Post* investigated Watergate in 1972, Tobias Wolff was a negligent obituary writer. A colleague, aware the cub reporter wasn't following protocol, phoned in a fake death notice. Another journalist saved Wolff from exposure by warning him about the ruse. But the emerging short-story writer often wondered what would have happened if he'd mistakenly published the death notice of a living man.

From his undistinguished stint as a journalist came the story 'Mortals', about a man craving recognition who calls in an obit for himself and furthers the deception by complaining when it's printed. This bleakly comic tale is included in *Our Story Begins* (2008), an omnibus volume of Wolff's stories, which combines selections from his three previous collections with ten new pieces.

Mainstream success arrived for Wolff with the memoir of his troubled youth, *This Boy's Life* (1989), furthered by the 1993 film adaptation in which he was played by Leonardo DiCaprio. Until then, he was best known for his role in the American renaissance of the short story. Along with Richard Ford and Raymond Carver, he was tagged as a pioneer of 'dirty realism', denoting the new orthodoxy of sombre and minimalist fiction about blue-collar life. (Wolff tetchily dismisses the term as 'utterly meaningless'.)

His stories often explore the lies people tell to reinvent themselves and colour their underwhelming lives. Wolff himself owes a lot to bluffing. As a delinquent 14-year-old in the backwater town of Chinook, Washington, he won a scholarship to study at an elite East Coast preparatory academy, the Hill School, by forging straight-A grades on blank report cards and fabricating testimonials on school letterhead. 'I felt full of things that had to be said, full of stifled truth,' he wrote in *This Boy's Life*. 'I believed that in some way that was not factually verifiable … I was an Eagle Scout and a powerful swimmer, and a boy of integrity.'

The boy's talent for dissembling seemed destined to land him in prison, where his father, an alcoholic and conman, did time for passing bad cheques. Instead, Wolff made a career out of telling truth through fiction. His stories build towards old-fashioned epiphanies in spare and unsentimental prose. As the title *Our Story Begins*, suggests, they respect traditional form, with clear beginnings, middles, and ends. Wolff contrasts his work with the stories of John Barth and Donald Barthelme — 'adventurous but not very narratively based fiction: fiction about the conventions of fiction, and experiments in time'.

Yet he feels indebted to the numerous postmodern stories he wrote, though never published, in the 1970s. 'It taught me a great deal about the construction of stories — to look upon the story form as a malleable, constructed thing rather than taking it as a received and sacred charge,' Wolff, 64, reflects by phone from California, where he teaches writing at Stanford. 'I bury my experiments in my work because that's not what I want the reader's attention to be on.'

Another important literary influence was his brother, Geoffrey, also a writer, and older by seven years. Their parents divorced when Tobias was five: he moved with his mother to the west coast, while Geoffrey lived with their father on the east. Before the brothers were reunited, when Tobias was 15, they lost touch for six years. But the siblings independently became aspiring writers. 'I discovered my brother — who I looked up to, especially in that way that you look up to someone who you hardly ever see — to be completely besotted with literature.'

They have remained close ever since and their relationship — at least as the more famous sibling tells it — has always been remarkably free of rivalry. It helped, he suggests, that Geoffrey never wrote short fiction, and the age gap meant that his elder brother assumed the role of mentor rather than competitor.

The brothers' shared literary leanings may have owed less to uncanny coincidence than heredity; their father, Arthur, was an inveterate teller of fictions — a scam artist as charismatic as he was duplicitous. Not until he was 19 did Wolff, now a practising Catholic, learn that his father was of Jewish extraction rather than the Episcopalian he claimed to be.

Geoffrey recounted his life with their father in *The Duke of Deception* (1980). A decade later, Tobias wrote about his upbringing with their hard-up but endlessly optimistic mother, Rosemary, in *This Boy's Life*. Her second husband was no improvement on Arthur; Dwight, a mechanic, relished humiliating his stepson and terrifying him on drunken car rides. 'She was feckless in her decisions about men,' Wolff admits. Initially uncomfortable with her son writing about her, 'She warmed right up when all the reviews came out and kept talking about my beautiful, plucky mother.'

Before heading to the Hill School, Wolff visited his father and brother. Arthur, who suggested the family reunion, had a nervous breakdown two weeks after Tobias' arrival and spent most of the summer in a sanatorium. Still, Wolff warmed to him. 'There was something very dear and vulnerable about my father. I think it was that very vulnerability, that made him so fearful of derision or prejudice, that drove him to disguise himself.' Wolff felt less forgiving after the first of his three children was born. 'When I realised what it was to have a child, it became unimaginable to me that someone could just walk away from them.'

'The Hill', as it was known, confirmed his desire to be a writer. 'It was an atmosphere in which literature was honoured above all things. The English masters were the aristocrats of the place.' The school hosted a reading series in honour of its former pupil, the critic Edmund Wilson, and William Golding and Robert Frost visited during Wolff's time there. He recalls 'the tremendous competition to get into the honours English class, which in the final year was taught by the headmaster himself'. But Wolff failed to rise to the academy's standards. After flunking a crucial mathematics exam, his scholarship was withdrawn, forcing him to leave.

His 2003 novel, *Old School*, depicts the intrigue and rivalries at an exclusive boys' boarding school in the 1960s. The narrator, a closet Jew, plagarises a story in an effort to win a literary competition where the prize is a private audience with Ernest Hemingway. In writing the novel, Wolff drew upon 'the crisis of identity that was triggered in me by my transformation from a rural school in Washington State to this very expensive, socially conscious and literarily conscious school'.

Old School was not, contrary to its publishers' reports, Wolff's first novel; but his 1975 debut, *Ugly Rumours*, is long out of print and omitted from his list of published works. Pressed as to why, he replies firmly: 'I don't acknowledge it. I don't like it. So maybe we could move to the next question.'

After leaving The Hill, he spent four years in the army, including a year's stint in Vietnam. 'It seemed almost inevitable for me to join up,' he says. 'All the men I knew when I was growing up had served. Vietnam wasn't on when I joined up, so there wasn't the counter-cultural questioning of the obligations of military service.'

It felt significant that several of his literary idols — including Norman Mailer, Ernest Hemingway, Erich Maria Remarque, and James Jones — had served in the military. 'I thought that as a writer it was something that I should know about.' The lessons of combat proved less glamorous, though: 'I discovered within myself the temptations to abuse authority and power.'

After Vietnam, he spent six months preparing for the entrance exams at Oxford, where the former school drop-out went on to graduate with a First in English. Bill Clinton was also a student there and, though they weren't friends, Wolff jokes that he may have passed Clinton the joint he didn't inhale.

England attracted him as a chance to escape the constant talk about Vietnam in the United States. 'That stuff about Vietnam veterans being terribly treated by people when they got back is mostly bullshit, but people really just wanted to pump me about it all the time.' It was two decades before he began work on the memoir of his Vietnam days, *In Pharaoh's Army* (1994), which was the time necessary 'to find a form for those memories and see myself in them from a distance'.

If he writes a third memoir, he says, it will be a recollection of the literary life in America. It's an intriguing remark given how rarely he's written about writing in the past. In *This Boy's Life*, Wolff tells of how he renamed himself 'Jack', after Jack London, at age ten. But the book contained few other literary references. 'I wanted to avoid the usual underlining in literary memoirs, where every little thing that points to the future writer has to wear a hat over it.'

Asked what remains in him of the scamp from *This Boy's Life*, Wolff mentions 'the longing for home, for family, and that tendency towards mythologising'. But, he adds: 'I don't self-mythologise anymore: I'm just too tired, too old.' It's safe to say that the fibber who improvised his own reference letters will not be writing his own obituary.

— July 2008

A. B. Yehoshua

When A. B. Yehoshua began *The Liberated Bride* in 1998, the Middle East peace process had reached its high-water mark. A hopeful resolution to the Israel–Palestine quagmire seemed finally to be in sight. By 2001, as he was writing the book's final chapters, Israel was once again haemorrhaging out of control. 'We had been already touching peace,' says Yehoshua, his voice thickening with a mix of frustration and grief. 'We touched peace, and now we are back to all this killing.'

Many scenes from the novel, such as those depicting the formerly permeable borders between Israel and the occupied territories, now seem utopian. Yehoshua's protagonist, Rivlin, a Jewish Orientalist, darts casually between the Israeli checkpoints, attending the concert of a singing nun in Jenin and a festival of romantic poetry in Ramallah. 'I was going without weapons, without anyone in my car, to all these places,' Yehoshua says. 'They were so peaceful. It was amazing how much they had invested in the infrastructure for tourism.'

The novel is set in 1998, three years before the outbreak of the Second Intifada. It follows Rivlin's pursuit of his twin preoccupations over the course of the single year — his academic quest to comprehend the historical roots of the Algerian terror of the 1990s and his personal mission to disentangle the mystery surrounding his son's divorce.

But with the onslaught of the suicide attacks, Yehoshua allowed some faint drops of blood to percolate a narrative otherwise marked by optimism and light farce. Yehoshua seeded the novel with subtle portents of the coming uprising. He modelled the convener of the Ramallah poetry competition on the Palestinian rebel Marwan Barghouti ('a very brave man'), now serving a prison sentence for his role in the resurgence of terrorism.

A fifth-generation Jerusalemite, Yehoshua was born in 1936, two streets away from his fellow novelist and contemporary Amos Oz. Having retired several years ago from his long-standing position as professor of comparative literature at Haifa University, Yehoshua lives in the port city with his wife of 48 years, a psychoanalyst who is not above turning the tricks of her profession on her husband. 'I'm under analysis all the time,' he says. 'I am afraid to tell her my dreams.' Yehoshua likens his role as a writer in Israel to that of a communal psychoanalyst: his aim is 'to get out the unconscious of the people and point out hidden truths'.

When *The Liberated Bride* was published in Hebrew in 2001, it was made the subject of a brutal vivisection in the prominent Israeli broadsheet *Haaretz* by Yitzhak Laor, a radical anti-establishment Tel Aviv poet and literary critic. Laor's 3000-word attack slated the novel as the literary equivalent of ethnic cleansing in its 'ferocious, racist hatred of Arabs'. Laor is briefly lampooned in the novel as a formidable but ruthless intellectual who exploits the Israel–Palestine conflict to settle scores with his adversaries.

Yehoshua dismisses Laor's efforts to impale him as wholly personal. 'He was thinking that I was the man who blocked his way to Haifa University,' Yehoshua says. 'So many Arabs were admiring this book.' But the vendetta, one suspects, is as political as it is personal.

Despite his standing as a stalwart of the Israeli Left and as a long-term campaigner for the creation of a Palestinian state, Yehoshua was also one of the country's most vociferous advocates of former prime minister Ariel Sharon's security wall through the West Bank.

It is a policy Laor equates in his review to 'the ghettoisation of the Palestinians'.

The Liberated Bride is an allegory about the need for borders. The novel explores the violation of boundaries existing between fathers and sons, husbands and wives, and teachers and students, as well as the muddying of cultural barriers between Israel's Arab minority and its Jewish population. Each comes to stand for Yehoshua's belief in the imperative of a wall separating the two peoples. His characters are never extricable from their political context. Their relationships function as metaphors for the challenges of the Jewish state.

Yehoshua's militant Zionism at times finds him at loggerheads with younger Israeli writers, such as Etgar Keret, who fail to share the traditional Israeli conception of the writer as prophet. Where Yehoshua composes epic tomes that stridently draw attention to their political significance, Keret's micro-stories flaunt their irreverence in hip rebellion against the ideological zeal of the generation that came of age with the state.

Yehoshua recalls when he was brought together with Keret on a panel at a conference in Greece, and a wrangle ensued over the Jews of the Diaspora. Keret stressed the affinities binding the Jewish people, while Yehoshua maintained his controversial belief that exile is the 'disease' of Judaism for which Zionism is the sole 'cure'. His books might distil the alienation and despair of contemporary Israel, its idealism dried up and replaced by cynicism, but Yehoshua's Zionist fervour has lost none of its heat.

It is the borderlessness of the Jewish people and the resulting vagueness in their identity that Yehoshua holds to be the root cause of their historic persecution: 'Because there is something unclear in their identity, the anti-Semite can easily project his problems, his fantasies, on the Jew. The Jew is like a text with a lot of gaps. As a Zionist, I know our purpose is to be among ourselves and not to wander again in the world. The Diaspora Jews have to know that the structure of their identity invites anti-Semitism. They need to decide themselves if the price is too high.'

His persistent call for the Israeli government to dismantle the settlements in the occupied territories derives from this principle. 'Because we wanted to grab a bit of territory from the Palestinians, Israel betrayed the most sacred rule of Zionism — we broke our borders.' Only by living within the clear boundaries of Israel does he believe the pathological impulses of anti-Semitism can be stemmed: 'The Palestinians are hating us, but they don't have these anti-Semite fantasies.'

For Keret, Yehoshua's position on the Diaspora Jew is ostensibly 'a case of asking the victim to take responsibility for what happened to him'.

'It's not much different than the "she shouldn't have worn that dress" reaction to rape victims,' Keret says. 'Claiming that the Israeli is the complete Jew seems very strange and wrong to me. The archetypal Israeli is more an anti-Diaspora Jew than a complete one. If the Diaspora leaders were intellectuals, the typical Israeli political leader is a general or a farmer, preferably both. The Jewish cosmopolitan and self-reflexive critical thought is also hard to find in the archetypical Israeli who is more ... simple, pragmatic, and straight to the point, which doesn't at all seem to me a continuation or improvement of Jewish thought.'

Laor sees what he terms Yehoshua's 'deformed nationalism' as a reflection of the novelist's fragile sense of belonging as a Jew of Middle Eastern ancestry. 'Since (Yehoshua) is a Sephardic Jew, who never had a 'real belonging' to the Western fantasy that Zionist Israel lives, he keeps denying the simple fact that our people, like every people in the world, is a collective of many different human beings, colours, faiths, desires, fears, choices. For him, every Jew that remains outside the domain of Israel threatens his own definition of himself as member of a national majority. This is exactly his weakness as a writer: he is unable to think about people outside their national identity.'

Yehoshua admits that as a developing writer he avoided writing about his Sephardic origins, but says that the accusations that he was effacing his ethnicity are misguided. As an emerging voice in the Israeli intelligentsia, Yehoshua sought to be defined by his national rather than ethnic identity. Only after establishing his Israeli selfhood did he return to his Sephardic background as grist for his work. 'When the majority of the newcomers were coming from countries, it was easy for them because all their background was left in the Diaspora,' he explains. 'My marks of identity were here, so there was a certain effort to detach myself from the ethnic side.'

The milieu of Israeli Orientalists has been familiar to Yehoshua since his childhood. His father was an Arabist who spoke the language fluently and fostered in his son a belief that the Arabs were 'part of the family'.

'They were really excellent people who tried not just to understand the politics of the Arabs, but the deep layers of their conscience. They thought that because we are coming back to this country and we want to live with them forever, we have to understand our neighbours.' But unlike his son, Yehoshua's father was not a dove in his political convictions. 'Because he'd read their stuff, he was saying to me, "Never will there be peace with them." Sometimes I think he was right.'

This background gave Yehoshua the confidence to feel he could dissect the Arab mind just as effortlessly as he would analyse the Jewish psyche. The death of his father in 1982 coincided with Israel's invasion of Lebanon. These twin events precipitated the crafting of his ambitious 1990 city portrait *Mr Mani* ('my great novel'), drawing from his father's 12 published studies on Jerusalem. The novel consisted of five one-sided 'conversations', each narrated by a member of the same family marooned within an epochal moment of Jewish history. 'For the first time, I felt I cannot understand my fellow people,' he says. 'It was as if I discovered a member of my family had gone crazy. This was a kind of psychoanalytic process to go to the past to understand the present.'

Some day he'd like to live in Australia, jokes Yehoshua, but only if he could bring all the Jews of the world along with him. 'I would love to have a small Australia to collect all the Jewish people of the world. Then you will see there will be no anti-Semitism. To live among ourselves in our territories, clear within our borders, this is our dream. But you will not offer Australia to us.' He laughs. 'If you could cut a part and surround it by sea, it perhaps could work. But inside Australia we will be immediately in Melbourne and Sydney.'

— April 2004

Part II
Non-fiction

Ian Buruma

On a weeknight at *The New Yorker* Festival, a fashionable young crowd has gathered to think about monsters. Or, rather, to watch Martin Amis, ageing prince of literary chic, discuss with Ian Buruma the origins of evil. Amis slouches low inside his black leather jacket, growling provocations about the Koran in his nicotine-cured voice.

Buruma sits straight-backed in suit and tie, speaking in BBC English about the alienation that led Mohammed Bouyeri, a second-generation Moroccan Dutchman, to slay journalist-provocateur Theo van Gogh in 2004. 'But Ian', Amis breaks in, 'don't you think that it *is* important that it's Islam.'

'No,' Buruma replies calmly. 'I think it's incidental.' Islamic fundamentalists, he argues, could just as well have chosen a secular ideology to justify bloodshed.

Buruma has none of Amis' celebrity aura — his rumpled cool, irreverent wit or flamboyant speech. However, he matches Amis' stage presence. He provokes without polemicising, convincing with erudition rather than style. In a further paradox, Buruma is standing in for Ayaan Hirsi Ali, the Somali-born anti-Islam crusader who collaborated with Van Gogh on the propaganda film *Submission* (2004). Buruma, who is Anglo–Dutch by birth, criticised her dogmatic view in his 2006 book *Murder in Amsterdam*, a meticulously sober account of the decline of multiculturalism in his native Holland.

Buruma's refusal to take extreme positions has earned him wide respect, if not exactly fame. Included in the 2008 *Foreign Policy / Prospect* list of the world's top 100 public intellectuals, he is a prolific author of history, reportage, and cultural commentary on both Asia and Europe. *The China Lover* (2008) is his second novel. But nuance doesn't sell, and Buruma has never offered glib sound-bites about the clash of civilisations or the return of history.

Buruma identifies as a liberal who prizes freedom above equality while believing in modest wealth distribution. Of all democracies, in his opinion, the United States best balances liberty and equality. According to writer David Rieff, a friend: 'It's remarkable that he seems quite untouched by either the fanaticism of the Left or the Right in this time of duelling fanaticisms. He was able, on the one hand, not to fall victim to political correctness, but also not to be tempted by panic about Islam or neo-conservative fantasies.'

Buruma lives in a kitschy new apartment complex in Harlem, New York, supposedly influenced by the architecture of the Kalahari Desert. He's impeccably courteous and agreeable, if not quite friendly or inviting smalltalk. Japanese and modern styles mix in the airy penthouse.

He has spent his life writing about different cultures. When he won the coveted Erasmus Prize in 2008 for his 'contribution to culture in Europe', the Dutch jury praised him as a 'new cosmopolitan'. The annual laurel felt like a vindication to Buruma, after being attacked in the Dutch press for *Murder in Amsterdam*.

'There was this rather provincial sense of envy of the person who left and comes back,' he says. 'A feeling of, "He might think he's a big shot in New York, but who is he to come here and tell us what Holland is like?"' The book revealed how Holland's post-war consensus on multiculturalism, liberal immigration policies, and generous welfare services bred a culture of complacency and denial that made it powerless to engage with its new Muslim minority.

In 2007, Buruma wrote a cordial profile of Tariq Ramadan, a moderate Muslim philosopher and proponent of European Islam, for *The New York Times* magazine. Neo-conservative journalist

Paul Berman responded with a 28,000-word rebuttal in *The New Republic*. He charged Buruma with glossing over Ramadan's history of supporting abuses against women and promoting anti-Semitism, while turning his back on Hirsi Ali, a former Muslim fighting for Enlightenment freedoms.

On being called an apologist for radical Islam, Buruma responds with typical equanimity: 'The people who say that see this debate in terms of friends and enemies and do not wish to challenge Hirsi Ali at all. If Tariq Ramadan is an enemy, then anybody who has anything good to say about him is a traitor to Enlightenment values. I was trying to explain why the Muslim women who Hirsi Ali is speaking up for didn't support her, and why her support is mostly from white, intellectual middle-class Dutch people. She's a little zealous in the way that converts always are.'

Buruma's politics are decidedly closer to Hirsi Ali's. 'I'm not a religious person and I don't share Tariq Ramadan's rather old-fashioned, Third Worldist leftism. But if you're looking for somebody who can have a positive influence on educated Muslim believers in Europe, in the sense of integrating them into democratic society, then there's more hope with Tariq Ramadan, simply because he is a believer and she is an atheist.'

Born in The Hague in 1951, Buruma grew up in a bilingual household where the British were seen as saviours. Buruma's mother, born in England to assimilated German–Jewish immigrants, lost relatives in the Holocaust. His father, a lawyer and the son of a Dutch Mennonite minister, was forced to work in a German factory during the war.

Buruma spent summer holidays with his maternal grandparents in England, which seemed like an idyll. In his 1999 book, *Voltaire's Coconuts, or Anglomania in Europe*, Buruma reminisces about how 'a visit to Holland by my grandparents felt like the arrival of messengers from a wider, more glamorous world'.

Buruma's mother dressed him like an English schoolboy in knee-length socks and long flannel shorts, making him stand out from his classmates. The boy would imitate her elegant handwriting, associating it with English refinement.

The headmaster once reprimanded Buruma for drawing swastikas. 'Every member of the older generation, it appeared, had been in the resistance,' Buruma writes in *The Wages of Guilt* (1994), which compares German and Japanese memories of their military pasts. The book argues that Germans faced up to their wartime atrocities, but that the Japanese remain in denial.

The Shoah didn't properly enter public consciousness until the late 1960s, Buruma says: he read about it for the first time in Harry Mulisch's 1963 report on the trial of Adolf Eichmann. So, although he and his friends knew that one history teacher had been on the wrong side in the war, 'that didn't really bother us very much because he was popular and rather a nice guy'.

Speaking two languages at home set Buruma apart from his peers in culturally homogenous The Hague, which he recalls as a buttoned-up, snooty place that he 'couldn't wait to get out of'. The 1968 protests in Amsterdam felt remote but, in any case, Buruma 'was never terribly interested in going to demonstrations or being an activist'.

When Buruma was 20, his mother died of cancer. He had recently left The Netherlands for London, and says: 'The excitement of living a life on my own in some ways helped me over it rather easily, possibly too easily.' His father, who was taking care of Buruma's two younger sisters, was more deeply affected: 'He didn't find anybody like that again.'

As a student of Chinese at Leiden University in The Netherlands, Buruma was neither a Maoist nor an aspiring Sinologist like his fellow students. He had little interest in going on a state-organised tour of Mao's China, or scrutinising party texts and photographs for hints of subversions of state power. As he writes in *Bad Elements,* his 2001 book on Chinese dissident communities: 'I was never a China watcher.'

Yet he became enamoured of Japanese film and theatre. With aspirations to direct movies, he went to Tokyo on a scholarship to study film in 1975. There he met Donald Richie, a renowned Japanophile, who became an important mentor. Says Richie, now 85: 'In a way, he's an innocent, always ready to entertain both sides of stories. He still retains his freshness, which is unusual among New York intellectuals. He's absolutely open to new ideas.' Richie found him work reviewing films for the English-language daily *The Japan Times*, and used Buruma's photographs to accompany the text of their 1980 book, *The Japanese Tattoo*.

Buruma's film ambitions were encouraged by his maternal uncle, filmmaker John Schlesinger, best known for *Midnight Cowboy* (1969). They were especially close because Schlesinger, who was gay, had no children. But there was some tension in their relationship: 'He always talked about how his work was instinctual: it didn't come from ideas. He was very self-conscious and uncomfortable with people he called intellectual. He always saw me as an intellectual who was rationalising, conceptualising. I suppose I've always in a way wanted to be more like him.'

Though Buruma made a few documentary films, he eventually realised he lacked the patience for film, and journalism took over. His first book, *Behind the Mask*, was published in 1983 and explored the Japanese underworld of transvestites, massage parlours, and *yakuza* gangsters. After four years based in Hong Kong as culture editor of *The Far Eastern Economic Review*, he returned to London in 1990 to become foreign editor of *The Spectator*.

Buruma admired the magazine's satirical take on left-wing idealism, but found its quaint lunches and respect for moneyed privilege and old-school ties nauseating. When a suicide bomber killed former Indian prime minister Rajiv Ghandi in 1991 and the deputy editor suggested that Enoch Powell would write about it better than the Indian journalists Buruma suggested, he knew he needed to leave.

His centrist politics made for similar strains when, in 2002, he wrote a weekly column for *The Guardian*, with a readership often viscerally opposed to Israel and the US. Buruma confidently describes Israel as a democracy, and calls his friend Tony Judt's proposal for a one-state solution mad. But as a critic of Israel's policies, he has been denounced by novelist Cynthia Ozick as a 'low moral coward … trailing uplifting slogans [about] "seeing the other side".'

In *Occidentalism* (2004), co-authored with Israeli philosopher Avishai Margalit, Buruma attempts to show the flip side of Edward Said's argument in *Orientalism* (1978). To Buruma's mind: 'If there is a Western view of the East that is dehumanising, there is an equally dehumanising Eastern view of the West. Said had one insight and then tried to fit everything else to prove his case. It's had a very bad effect both on academe and on intellectual life in the Arab world.'

His most recent book, *The China Lover*, is based on the life of Japanese screen icon, Ri Koran, and spans East and West. She launched her career in the late 1930s playing Chinese damsels in Japanese propaganda flicks aimed at generating sympathy for Japan's occupation of Manchuria. During the US occupation of Japan she acted in pro-Yankee films under the name Yoshiko Yamaguchi, before reinventing herself as a Hollywood actor, Shirley Yamaguchi.

Yamaguchi kept transforming herself. For 18 years, she was a centre-right Japanese politician. As a television journalist, she embraced the likes of Idi Amin, Kim Il-Sung, and Yasser Arafat. 'She felt she'd been on the wrong side during the war, so that after the war she had to be on the side of the underdog, and that meant having sympathy for Third World leaders,' Buruma says.

Given the extraordinary facts, why write her life as fiction? Buruma considered writing a non-fiction book until concluding that it wasn't simply Yamaguchi's story he wanted to tell: 'What interested me more was how people fantasised about her and how that blended with all kinds of political and historical fantasies.' Thus, he created the novel's three-part structure, each with a male narrator observing the actor from within a different historical setting: Japanese-occupied Manchuria, post-war Tokyo, and 1970s' Beirut.

Buruma first met Yamaguchi in 1987 for *Interview* magazine, but her predictably polished answers made little impression. They have met twice since, but he 'could have written the same book without ever having met her'. When they last spoke by phone in 2001, two days after the New York terrorist attacks, Yamaguchi said: 'Yes, it's a funny old world.'

Buruma left London for New York three years ago, hoping to transform himself. His marriage to Sumie — the Japanese mother of their 23-year-old daughter, Isabel — had collapsed, and the move also made sense because of his part-time teaching position at Bard College, in upstate New York, where he holds the catch-all title professor of democracy, human rights and journalism.

In 2007, he married another Japanese woman, Eri Hotta, twenty years his junior. They met after he gave a talk at Oxford, where Eri was a doctoral student in international relations. The couple have a two-year-old daughter, Josephine, and speak mostly Japanese at home.

In his 1996 collection of essays, *The Missionary and the Libertine*, Buruma explores the stereotype of liberated sexuality for which Westerners have traditionally looked to the Orient. He writes of how, aged 21, he first fell in love with a Japanese girl, the heroine of François Truffaut's 1970 film *Bed and Board*, played by Hiroko Berghauer.

Asked what attracts him to Japanese women, Buruma smiles reticently and says he has always sought out what is different: 'It's not so much anything specific to Japanese women.' Does anything about Eri remain enigmatic? 'No, but I didn't find Japan all that mysterious even when I first went there. I was fascinated, it was different, but not inscrutable.'

Living in New York also seemed natural given his relationship with *The New York Review of Books*, to which he's contributed regularly for more than two decades. Its legendary co-founder, Robert Silvers, 80, has edited the *Review* for 45 years, but word has it that he may name Buruma as his replacement. Would Buruma accept the post?

'It hasn't been offered to me so I can't answer that question,' he answers flatly. 'It's not something I've ever discussed with Bob.'

Silvers enthuses about Buruma's prospects as an editor: 'If I have to slump away from this job, I think Ian would be a marvellous editor — if he wanted to be an editor, but I can't quite believe he would. He's such a great writer. Why would he want to spend his life editing the work of other people? But he's an immensely sympathetic and attractive guy who many writers would work with with pleasure.'

In the breadth of his interests, Buruma has few peers, Silvers continues: 'He commands so many different cultures with extraordinary confidence. Just when you think he's an expert on Japan, he's writing a novel on India, or writing about modern English history, or Islam in Europe. Ian is at home anywhere, but he's also, more than anyone else I know, equally at home in Asia.'

In *God's Dust: a modern Asian journey* (1988), Buruma writes about his fascination with the concept of national belonging: 'I have always wanted to know what it feels like to be entirely and unselfconsciously at home in one country.' But in a 2001 lecture at Leiden, he criticised diaspora writers who romanticise themselves as exiles. It's not a fashion he fell victim to. 'Sometimes I feel a little bit dislocated, but not profoundly,' Buruma says, his gaze fixed sideways. 'I keep going back to Holland and England. I still speak Dutch. So I've never burned my boats. I'm not one of these expatriates who rejected the world I came from.'

— *November 2008*

Noam Chomsky

Noam Chomsky stares back at the black-and-white portrait of Bertrand Russell on his office wall, and feels like he's being judged. 'It's those eyes,' Chomsky says. 'It's as if I've done something wrong.' Asked why Russell's ghost might reprimand him, Chomsky demurs: 'I'm sure he could think of something.' The 80-year-old linguist and left-wing activist has never been one to admit to being wrong.

Chomsky is, according to the Arts and Humanities Citation Index, among the ten most cited thinkers of all time. Ranking higher than Hegel but trailing Freud, he is the only living member of that pantheon. *Prospect* and *Foreign Policy* magazines have named him as the word's top public intellectual.

Plus he belongs to the illustrious group — which includes Pope John Paul II, Gabriel García Márquez, and Mark Twain — of celebrities prematurely declared dead. Venezuelan President Hugo Chávez commended Chomsky's 2003 book *Hegemony or Survival: America's quest for global dominance* during his 2006 address to the United Nations General Assembly, and expressed regret that he never met his hero while he was still alive. (Perhaps Chávez had in mind the now-deceased chimpanzee Nim Chimpsky, used in a study of animal communication.) *Hegemony or Survival* subsequently rose to the top of the Amazon.com bestseller list.

Chomsky, who identifies as a 'libertarian socialist', is an improbable standard-bearer for university campus activists. There's no Che Guevara glamour to the serene, slightly stooped professor seated before me in sneakers, a baggy grey pullover, and outsized glasses. His quiet, froggy voice barely carries across the round table where we sit in his spartan headquarters at the Massachusetts Institute of Technology (MIT). Outside his office are boxes of old red-ragger journals accompanied by a hand-scrawled note: 'Help yourself.'

It's not rousing rhetoric that draws his disciples to pack the auditoriums whenever Chomsky lectures. 'I'm not an actor,' he reflects. 'If I had the talent, I wouldn't use it.' His style, if it can be called that, is to deliver a barrage of historical statistics and examples, making the case — calmly, rationally, and relentlessly — against American hegemony. For all his humility, he must get a charge out of addressing crowds of admirers? 'There are more important things,' Chomsky answers patiently, 'than how you look in the eyes of other people.'

No critic of US foreign policy has a more avid global following, but Chomsky is virtually ignored by the American media. 'Here I'm regarded as more of a threat,' he speculates. Chomsky pulls out a framed 2005 cover from the liberal *American Prospect* magazine, depicting him and Dick Cheney as leering figures looming over a quavering huddle of liberals. 'It's an interesting indication of their self-image as terrified little cowards,' he says.

Some linguists say he is as vital to their field as Albert Einstein is to physics. The era before the Chomskyan revolution is sometimes referred to as BC, or Before Chomsky. In 1957, when not yet 30, he published his first book, *Syntactic Structures*, arguing that our ability to produce sentences is biological and not simply learned behaviour, as the 'structuralist' orthodoxy had it. Chomsky posited a 'universal grammar' that all people share; the task for linguists, then, is to describe these inborn principles, rather than just the grammars of different languages.

Growing up in Philadelphia during the Depression, Chomsky thought deeply about language and politics. His father, William, an emigrant from Ukraine, was a respected Hebrew scholar and an expert on medieval grammar. Elsie, his mother, emigrated from Belarus as an infant and taught Hebrew school. Many in his extended family were unemployed, but Chomsky has happy memories of the pre-war years: 'People were suffering. You could see it everywhere. But it was an intellectually and politically very lively time.'

On weekends, he commuted to New York City to help his disabled Trotskyite uncle run his newsstand business, and Chomsky absorbed the heated debates that took place there. He hung out in anarchist bookstores, read political pamphlets, and chatted with European refugees. When Barcelona fell in 1939, the ten-year-old wrote an editorial for the school newspaper about the ascent of European fascism.

Aged 21, he married Carol Schatz, an old family friend, and the couple spent several months on an Israeli kibbutz, even considering a permanent move. The promise of an anarchist utopia was alluring, but he found the ideological fervour stifling and he was demoralised by the racism towards the Arabs and Mizrahi Jews.

By the mid-1960s his academic celebrity was long established. But as the US started bombing North Vietnam, he felt he had more urgent priorities than pondering syntax. Activism consumed him. Chomsky shared a cell with Norman Mailer after participating in the March on the Pentagon in 1967. In *The Armies of the Night* (1968), Mailer recalled his cellmate as 'a slim, sharp-featured man with an ascetic expression, and an air of gentle but absolute moral integrity'. Carol returned to university to write a PhD on linguistics so she could support the family if Chomsky was jailed or lost his job — no small possibility, with the majority of MIT's budget then coming from the Pentagon.

Their eldest daughter, Aviva, is now a Latin American scholar and a committed activist; son Harry is a violinist and computer programmer. Younger daughter Diane has lived in Nicaragua since her mid-twenties, when she shacked up with a Sandinista activist. She lives in poverty, deliberately eschewing bourgeois comforts. So, does Chomsky feels guilty about his comfortable lifestyle? 'Our lives are remarkably privileged by world standards, but we don't help anyone if we give them up,' he says. I suggest that sounds like an indictment of Diane's lifestyle. He grimaces: 'I'd be happier if she had running water in her house instead of a cold trickle a couple of hours a night, but that's her choice.'

His first political book, *American Power and the New Mandarins*, was published in 1969 and collected his writings on Vietnam. Its arguments would form the cornerstone of his critique of subsequent American military interventions: the government's humanitarian rhetoric is merely a cover for its imperial ambitions, and liberal intellectuals provide the legitimising figleaf for its atrocities.

After Cambodia fell to the Khmer Rouge in 1975, his hatred of American foreign policy led him to write sympathetically about Pol Pot. In 1978, Chomsky and Edward Herman published *After the Cataclysm*, in which they rationalised the Cambodian communists' lethal social engineering as an understandable remedy to the economic devastation caused by US attacks.

Nowadays, Chomsky is more tactful. His writings on the Khmer regime had a specific context, he insists — contrasting the Western media's treatment of crimes committed by the West and its proxies, and those perpetrated by enemy states. 'We compared the Khmer Rouge atrocities and Indonesian atrocities in East Timor. In the case of Cambodia, the atrocities were by an official enemy where we could do nothing about it. There was a huge outcry, great passion, and outrageous lying that would have impressed Stalin.'

In 1975, Indonesian president Suharto, a US ally, invaded East Timor and, by some accounts, killed more than 100,000 civilians. To Chomsky, 'It was our crime, we could do a lot about it, and there was silence and denial. By now, the facts are all there. If you choose to deny them it's a definite choice. It's like Holocaust denial.' By this logic, David Irving would not be out of place among America's liberal commentariat. 'There's a literary genre now — Samantha Power is the leading figure — in which we denounce ourselves for our failure to respond to the crimes of others. But we either totally ignore or else flatly deny our own crimes.'

In her 2003 book, *A Problem From Hell: America and the age of genocide*, Power castigated the United States for looking away from Suharto's massacres. 'We didn't look away, we looked right there,' says Chomsky, who calls Power 'part of a liberal educated intellectual community, which is very clearly subject to Orwell's dictum about the indifference to reality of the nationalists'. But to Chomsky's detractors, few pundits have a shakier grasp on reality than him.

His call for Israel to become a bi-national state makes him a hate figure for many Jews, who argue that a system in which the Jewish people became a minority in an Arab-dominated country would be suicidal. 'I think the hostility would decline,' Chomsky says simply. There are moves towards federal arrangements in many parts of the world, he muses, and Israel should follow suit: 'Life's a complicated and diverse affair. We all gain by having these cultural and linguistic systems enriched.'

Most Jewish critics of the Israeli government bridle at being labelled 'self-haters', but Chomsky wears the tag proudly. 'The first usage of the term is by King Ahab, who is the epitome of evil in the Bible. He condemned the prophet Elijah as a hater of Israel. Why? Because Elijah criticised the acts of the evil king. I'm certainly not insulted by being compared to the prophet Elijah.'

Even those who tolerate Chomsky's extreme views on Israel are usually troubled by his association with neo-Nazis. In 1979, he signed a petition defending the right to free expression of French literature professor Robert Faurisson, who had been suspended from teaching for his Holocaust denial. The petition referred to the 'findings' of the 'respected' academic.

Chomsky wrote Faurisson's publishers an essay describing Faurisson as 'a relatively apolitical sort of liberal', and told them to make the best use of it for the campaign. 'I went through the evidence,' Chomsky tells me, 'and I said, "Well, if this is the strongest evidence that his harshest critics can bring, then he's probably a relatively apolitical liberal."'

When he learned that Faurisson was using the essay to preface his 1980 book *Mémoire en Défense* (*Testimony in Defence*), Chomsky got cold feet, but it had already gone to print. 'I tried to retract it and *that* I feel was a mistake,' he says. 'I knew that in France where there is total irrational hysteria among the educated classes, and also absolute hatred of freedom of speech, it would be grossly misinterpreted.'

For Chomsky, the media is an elaborate mechanism for state thought-control: 'The Western intellectual community is dedicated to lying in support of state power.' So media consumers and journalists are mere dupes with no faculty for independent thought? 'These are tendencies,' he parries. 'There are some very decent people and fine journalists, in fact.'

In an era of obsessive public-opinion polling, it could be argued that politicians are excessively attentive to the whims of popular opinion, not too little. But Chomsky downplays the influence of polls on politicians, adding 'one of the ways of protecting the leadership from the public is simply by not publishing the results of opinion studies. That's the norm.'

Were the revisions to 2007's US$700 billion bailout plan, following nationwide protests, not the work of popular democracy? 'That's only on the surface. The political system has so dissolved that all the public can do is shout, "No." If we had a full, functioning democracy, the public would do more than just scream, "No." They would have proposals and they would insist that their representatives act on those proposals.' Instead, to Chomsky's mind, the US is a four-year dictatorship: 'The way our system works is once every four years you have a choice between two candidates — both whose positions you oppose — and after that, "Shut-up." '

Not everyone opposes Barack Obama, of course, but Chomsky has his own views. 'He is dangerous,' he says flatly. 'He's a centre-right Democrat who insists that the United States is an outlaw state which must violate international law and resort to violence when it chooses.' What hope does his relentlessly cynical vision offer? Much, boasts Chomsky; in fact, he thinks the world is improving. 'If you look at history, you see very definite and significant progress towards a more civilised world. It's true of the last 40 years.' He finds cause for optimism in public opinion — if only we could overcome the deliberate failure of our democratic institutions.

After September 11, Chomsky gained renewed popularity on the hard Left. He was virtually alone among commentators in protesting against the American military action in Afghanistan, which he termed 'silent genocide'. His pamphlet-size book of interviews, *September 11* (2001), sold hundreds of thousands of copies. Yet columnist Christopher Hitchens, formerly a champion of Chomsky, charged him with 'losing the qualities that made him a great moral and political tutor in the years of the Indochina war'. Hitchens, like many, was disturbed by Chomsky's suggestion that president Bill Clinton's 1998 bombing of the Al-Shifa pharmaceutical plant in Sudan was comparable to the September 11 attacks.

Al-Qaeda was mistakenly believed to be using the factory to manufacture chemical weapons. One security guard was directly killed in Clinton's strike, but it's likely that tens of thousands of Sudanese died as a result of not having access to the factory's medicines. I ask how Clinton's bombing, terrible though it was, can be likened to Al-Qaeda's deliberate attempt to kill thousands of people by driving planes into the World Trade Center? Chomsky corrects me: Clinton's strike was morally worse. He starts talking about ants — when we go strolling, we know we'll crush ants; but we don't mean to kill them, as they're not worthy of moral thought. Ditto with Sudan: 'We know we're going to kill lots of people, but we don't intend to kill them because they aren't even considered as individuals deserving of moral judgement. Okay, which is the lower level of morality?'

Carol Chomsky passed away in December 2008, aged 78, shortly after our interview. Speaking of her advanced lung cancer, Chomsky's voice dropped an octave, if that's possible: 'So most of our lives have been together and now she's terminally ill.' Chomsky survived a cancer operation a few years ago, but he's now in rude health. He's not afraid of his own mortality. 'As a child, I thought it was an indescribable horror. That's passed over the years. I feel that I'm already a decade beyond what life is supposed to be according to the holy texts.'

The interview time, however, is up. His assistant throws open his door, truncating our appointment; Chomsky is very busy today — he needs to be photographed for his old primary school. The octogenarian-to-be puts on the school's cap and flashes his gap-toothed smile for the camera. And, for a moment, the professor with no ego or charisma looks rather pleased with himself.

— November 2008

Umberto Eco

Umberto Eco has grown wiser with age, and it shows no better than when he discusses stupidity. Rolling forward in his low couch in the dim-lit lounge-bar of his New York hotel, the oval-shaped Eco advises that the best way to face mortality is to realise how little there is to miss. At 77, the recently retired semiotics professor from Bologna harbours no false expectations of his fellow mortals. When another writer's work displeases him, he just sighs philosophically: 'If he were intelligent he would be the professor of semiotics at the University of Bologna.'

With 34 honorary doctorates (and almost as many declined), Eco's erudition is a rare commodity. His agile intellect, as adept at descanting on Superman as Shakespeare, once prompted Anthony Burgess to declare enviously: 'No man should know so much.' Eco pioneered the academic study of popular culture in the 1960s before it fell into vogue, at a time when 'many academics read detective stories and comic strips at night but didn't talk about it because it was considered like masturbation'.

He then defied the conventional wisdom of publishing that abstruse ideas cannot turn a profit when his 1980 debut novel, *The Name of the Rose*, shifted 50 million copies. Superficially a sleuth story set in a 14th-century abbey, the novel brimmed with such arcana as passages of untranslated Latin and a love scene stitched from the words of religious mystics. 'Readers are not as stupid as publishers believe,' Eco says animatedly, his earlier wisdom deserting him.

'Eco' carries similar clout in publishing to 'Armani' in Italian fashion. His new book, *On Ugliness* (2007), tours the history of unsightliness in Western art — an assemblage of images with a running commentary too thin for any art connoisseur but emblazoned with a name to guarantee the book a place on coffee tables worldwide. A selection of Eco's occasional pieces was recently published as *Turning Back the Clock* (2007); but the book could just as easily have been titled *On Stupidity*, as it charts the decline of public life in the age of media populism.

Eco himself is owlish rather than ugly. Besuited and bearded, with a paunch he likens to the late Pavarotti's, he has the congenial manner of someone who delights in holding court. He is no longer a smoker, but his gravelly voice wears the strain of his former 60-a-day habit, and he sucks on an unlit *cigarillo* throughout the interview.

His name — Italian for 'echo' — is fitting for an exponent of that European academic fixation of 'semiotics', concerned with the limits of language. 'Semiotics is a confederation of competing approaches to the problem of communication, of signification,' the professor explains. 'Confidentially, there is only one approach which is good, which is mine.'

Whereas his fellow semioticians Roland Barthes, Julia Kristeva, and Jacques Lacan were wilfully elitist and obscure, Eco gave his field an approachable face with raffish newspaper think-pieces and jargon-free monographs on topics ranging from medieval aesthetics to the mass media.

He accepts the label 'postmodern' to describe his novels, whose plots often hinge on the ambiguities of language, and pay homage to writers, philosophers, and theologians from throughout the ages. 'Postmodernism is a form of narrativity that takes for granted that everything has already been said before. If I love a girl I cannot say, "I love you desperately", because I know that Barbara Cartland has already said it. But I can say, "As Barbara Cartland would say, 'I love you desperately.'"'

His 1997 philosophical study, *Kant and the Platypus*, described the platypus as a postmodern animal, after considering the debates of 18th-century scientists over whether to classify the duck-beaked, beaver-tailed creature as a mammal, a bird, or a reptile. 'Postmodern texts quote other texts; the platypus quotes other animals,' Eco says. 'Borges said that the platypus is an animal made up of the pieces of other animals; but since the platypus appeared very early in evolution, there are probably other animals made with pieces of platypus.'

As unclassifiable as a platypus, Eco made his fiction debut at age 48, when a publisher commissioned him to contribute to an anthology of detective tales written by academics. Instead, he turned in a 500-page tome: *The Name of the Rose*. Italian literature lacks a tradition of detective fiction, which Eco attributes to Renaissance Italy's abandonment of Aristotle's *Poetics*. 'The *Poetics* is the theory of pure narrativity. The Italian tradition was more interested in language than plot.'

Asked about his late impulse to write a novel, Eco waves away the question: 'It's like you feel the need to piss, so you go and you piss.' Pressed, Eco says that he turned to fiction to compensate for his two children growing up: 'I didn't have anybody to tell stories to any more, so I started writing.'

After *The Name of the Rose* was made into a garden-variety adventure flick starring Sean Connery in 1986, Eco refused all approaches to render his books in celluloid. He illustrates his decision by way of an anecdote — perhaps apocryphal — about a girl who walked into a bookstore and remarked of *The Name of the Rose*, 'Oh, they've already adapted the film into a book.' But, after Stanley Kubrick died, he regretted rebuffing the director's interest in filming his second novel *Foucault's Pendulum* (1988).

Foucault's Pendulum depicts three jaded editors at a Milan publishing firm connecting all the major conspiracy theories in history into an overarching 'Plan', only to find the hoax unravelling from their control. Eco amassed 1500 occult books, gathered from ten cities, to research the novel, which anticipated the *Da Vinci Code* juggernaut with remarkable prescience. 'I invented Dan Brown. He's one of the grotesque characters in my novel who take a lot of trash occult material seriously. He used a lot of material that I myself quoted.'

Brickbats flew with *Foucault's Pendulum*, where critics found Eco's delectation for scholarly exotica difficult to absorb in the absence of its predecessor's thriller plot. With the *fatwa* recently proclaimed on his head, Salman Rushdie found sufficient peace of mind to read *Foucault's Pendulum* and slate it in *The Observer* as 'humourless, devoid of character, entirely free of anything resembling a credible spoken word, and mind-numbingly full of gobbledygook of all sorts. Reader: I hated it.'

Emotion rarely surfaces in Eco's novels, which anti-populist critics sometimes try to dismiss as cerebral game-playing masquerading as fiction. Eco subscribes to T. S. Eliot's notion of literature as an escape from emotion. 'You can only write a real love poem when you're not in love any more and you can look at your previous emotion without being a victim of your passions,' Eco says.

His 2004 novel, *The Mysterious Flame of Queen Loana*, was uncharacteristically sentimental. Containing barely disguised autobiographical traces of Eco's boyhood in Piedmontese Italy, it followed an amnesiac book-dealer whose memory gradually returns upon a visit to his childhood home. His identity re-emerges as he re-encounters the old record covers, books, magazines, and stamps from Mussolini's Italy, which are reproduced as illustrations — for 'illiterate people', Eco jokes — throughout the text. But Eco has no plans to write the memoirs of his adult life, fearing that 'many ladies could be compromised'.

Eco was raised in Alessandria — the company town of Borsalino hats — in a lower-middle-class family. His parents were apathetic about the fascist regime, but Eco launched his literary career, aged ten, by winning an essay-writing competition for 'young Italian fascists' on the topic: 'Should we die for the glory of Mussolini and the immortal destiny of Italy?'

Eco consolidated his interest in medieval symbols by writing a doctoral dissertation on the aesthetics of Thomas Aquinas, published in his early twenties, before spending several years producing cultural programs for Italy's nascent national television network. He also co-founded the 'Gruppo 63' — modelled on Günter Grass' 'Gruppe 47' in Germany — calling for an overhaul of traditional literary techniques. But scholarship remained his life-blood.

After *The Name of the Rose*, Eco could have retired to — even purchased — a private island, but he continued to teach, considering writing secondary to academia. Even post-retirement, he regularly arranges seminars in Bologna, where he likes to live because he doesn't suffer from his public recognisability: 'They know me, so I can go through the streets and nobody cares. I'm a part of the landscape.'

In Anglophone countries, academics engaged in public affairs are often viewed askance by their colleagues, which Eco chalks up to the campus environments of most American and British universities. 'Oxford and Cambridge, Harvard and Yale, are outside of the city, so it separates the university from the political world. In Italy, Germany, France, and Spain the university is geographically at the centre of the city.'

Turning Back the Clock traces the disintegration of Italian democracy under centre-right Prime Minister Silvio Berlusconi, who has exploited his monopoly on media holdings to maintain popular support. 'The Italians who voted for him thought that he would not steal the public money, without considering that in order to become rich he stole money from somewhere,' Eco says.

'Secondly, they thought, "Because he's rich, he will help us become rich", which is absolutely false. It's only because you are poor that I am rich.'

Whereas his 1964 monograph, *Apocalypse Postponed,* inveighed against the demonisation of the mass media by Marxist theorists such as Theodor Adorno, Eco now holds a pessimistic — if not exactly apocalyptic — view of the media. He explains that in the 1950s, when many Italians only spoke local dialects, television played an important role in unifying the Italian language.

There was just one television channel, which broadcast in the evenings, so the programming was very selective, he says. 'Now in Italy we have the possibility of looking at one hundred channels all day, so the quality is low.' Italian newspapers are now almost twice the length that they were, which means 'you invent news, or repeat the same story ten times, or imagine plots and false explanations'.

Eco describes himself as a pacifist, and thinks that war should be made a universal taboo. This wouldn't stop him from defending his family against attack, but means that military invasion wasn't the answer to the Iraq question. He deadpans: 'If Bush were intelligent he would be the professor of semiotics at the University of Bologna.'

— *November 2007*

Robert Fisk

Soon after 11 September 2001, Robert Fisk was bashed by a crowd of Afghan refugees near the Pakistani border. Only the 11th-hour intervention of a Muslim cleric, who called an end, saved the veteran foreign correspondent from death. But Fisk, who has lived in Beirut for 34 years — reporting first for *The Times* and then, since 1988, for *The Independent* — felt no rage towards his assailants: only at himself for fighting back.

'What had I done?' he wrote after recovering. 'I had been punching and attacking Afghan refugees ... the very dispossessed, mutilated people whom my own country — among others — was killing.' He referred to one attacker as 'truly innocent of any crime except that of being the victim of the world', and saw the mob's brutality as 'entirely the product of others, of us'. If he were an Afghan refugee, Fisk wrote, he would have responded to the presence of a Westerner with equal bloodlust.

In an age of carefully impartial media coverage of the Middle East, Fisk's empathy with the Muslim world and moral indignation have won him an avid global following. But some see his treatment of Arabs as patronising — even while trying to kill him, they can do no wrong. His critics charge him with promoting a Manichean vision in which the West is the Great Satan and the Arabs are mere victims of its imperial designs. But even they often grudgingly admire his courage and experience.

Named British international journalist of the year seven times, Fisk has provided dispatches from 11 major Middle Eastern wars, and innumerable insurgencies and massacres. While many fellow commentators unleash opinions from London or New York, being spoon-fed by Washington think-tanks, and recycling news-agency reports, Fisk testifies from the ground and gives a voice to the people affected by Western foreign policy. He avoids working with other Western journalists to stay immune from what he sees as their pack mentality. 'A lot of journalists want to be close to power — governments, politicians,' says the 63-year-old reporter, adding, 'I don't.'

Even so, he has interviewed most of the region's major power brokers — including, on three occasions, Osama bin Laden. In *The Great War for Civilisation: the conquest of the Middle East* (2005) — a 1300-page memoir of three decades as a Middle Eastern correspondent — Fisk recounts how Bin Laden, who has praised his 'neutral' reporting, tried to recruit him. The Al-Qaeda leader told Fisk that a 'brother' had a dream in which 'you came to us one day on a horse, that you had a beard and were a spiritual person. You wore a robe like us. That means you are a true Muslim'. Terrified, Fisk replied: 'Sheikh Osama, I am not a Muslim, and the job of a journalist is to tell the truth.' To which the satisfied jihadist remarked: 'If you tell the truth, that means you are a good Muslim.'

Fisk makes no apologies for favouring the downtrodden, asserting that 'we should be unbiased on the side of injustice'. He explains, 'It's not a football match, where you give 50 per cent to each side. At the liberation of a Nazi extermination camp, you wouldn't give equal time to the SS.' His outrage at the duplicity of Western politicians — and the media's complicity with their lies — burns throughout his latest book, *The Age of the Warrior: selected writings* (2008), a collection of columns from five years.

To Fisk, the 'balance'-fixated objectivity of the press masks its collaboration with oppression, as competing views of well-documented facts are weighed with weasel clauses like 'opinions differ among Middle East experts'. 'I find *The New York Times*' coverage of the Middle East incomprehensible,' he opines, 'because it's so careful to make sure that everybody is able to criticise everybody else. People reading newspapers want to know what the bloody reporter is thinking or knows.' On average, Fisk receives about 250 readers' letters every week, and he notes 'how much more eloquent the language of readers is than the language of journalists'.

Nowhere does Fisk identify more skewed semantics than in press treatment of Israel–Palestine. Israeli-occupied territories are recast as 'disputed territories', Jewish settlements become 'Jewish neighbourhoods', assassinations of Palestinian militants are termed 'targeted killings', and the separation wall is described as a 'security barrier'. His prognosis for Israel–Palestine? 'Eternal war, unless we go back to UN Security Council Resolution 242 — withdrawal of security forces from territories occupied in the '67 war.' But, he hastens to point out: 'I see no eagerness for it. If you keep on building settlements for Jews and Jews only on land that belongs to Arabs and they're illegal, that's a terrible cause of war.'

The actor John Malkovich, aggrieved by Fisk's stance on Israel, remarked to the Cambridge Union in 2002 that he wanted to shoot him. Soon images of the journalist covered in blood were posted online by bloggers threatening to beat Malkovich to the job. The verb 'to fisk' has entered the language of the blogosphere; 'fisking' involves copying an article onto a webpage and debunking it point by point — a practise favoured by his detractors. Little wonder, then, that Fisk doesn't use email or the Internet, which he derides as 'trash' and a 'web of hate'.

'There's no sense of responsibility,' he says. 'It's not something you can sue over. It's caused huge numbers of inaccuracies in stories.'

Fisk rejects the allegation that his work reflects a pro-Arab bias, noting: 'I've been excoriating in my views of Arab dictators.' A controversial figure in Turkey, he was once expelled for reporting that its troops looted supplies intended to relieve Kurdish refugees.

His Istanbul publishers insisted on releasing the Turkish-language edition *The Great War for Civilisation* quietly, without publicity, fearing legal action over the chapter, 'The First Holocaust', in which Fisk documents the killing of 1.5 million Armenians by Ottoman Turks in 1915. Yet his fan-base in the Arab world is such that in 2000, when it was rumoured falsely that *The Independent* might sack him under pressure from the 'Zionist lobby', the newspaper received 3000 emails from Muslims in five days protesting. Recently, he learned of a counterfeit biography of Saddam Hussein, titled *From Birth to Martyrdom*, doing a brisk trade in Cairo. The author: 'Robert Fisk'.

Though fluent in Arabic, he hasn't lost his Englishness or 'gone native' like some foreign correspondents: 'I eat Lebanese food, of course, but I also eat pizzas and French food.' Lebanon is the most well-educated and cosmopolitan Middle Eastern society, he claims, and is also a convenient base for his work: 'Beirut is a bit like Vienna after World War II — everybody is here. Iranian agents and — I'm sure — the CIA are here. If you want to meet someone from Somalia or Sudan, they're here.' Divorced from the svelte *Irish Times* foreign correspondent Lara Marlowe, Fisk has admitted to knowing 'quite a few young ladies'. But he now stonewalls personal questions.

He was born in Kent, southeast England, the only child of Bill Fisk, who served as a lieutenant in World War I. It's not lost on Fisk that he's devoted his life to chronicling the failures of the states created artificially by his father's generation, when Britain carved up the Middle East after 1918 — 'the reason why this place is so screwed up and why I'm here now'. Bill was an authoritarian father who called blacks 'niggers' and hated the Irish. By the time he died in 1992, aged 93, his racism had become intolerable to his son, who refused to visit him in his final days. In *The Great War for Civilisation*, Fisk devotes a chapter to his father's wartime experiences, partly as an attempt 'to apologise to him for not going to see him'.

Despite their differences, Bill supported his son's choice of career. When the Israeli government warned journalists to leave Lebanon during its siege of Beirut in 1982, Fisk's mother, Peggy, called to say she and Bill came to the same conclusion as he had — that he should stay put, since it was merely an attempt by the Israeli government to stop reporting of civilian casualties. The only Western male journalist who stayed in Beirut throughout the 1980s, Fisk survived two kidnap attempts. 'I'd end up spending 90 per cent of my time trying to avoid being kidnapped, and 10 per cent working for the paper. We Westerners love routine, and kidnappers know that. You have to completely break up your Western thinking, and think like them.' So he drove to the airport through Hezbollah areas, where the terrorists would never suspect he might travel.

Fisk was 29 when *The Times* 'offered' him the Middle East, after a few years covering the conflict in Northern Ireland. In his memoir, he recalls anticipating what his foreign editor promised would be 'a great adventure with lots of sunshine': 'I wondered how King Feisal felt when he was "offered" Iraq or how his brother Abdullah reacted to Winston Churchill's "offer" of Transjordan.' The romance soon vanished, however. 'Once I was with the Iraqi army in the front line and the Iranians in the trenches, and watching people get killed around me, the Hollywood excitement wore off. It's not been a happy time.'

Nevertheless, he displays the excitement at danger that once led William Dalrymple to christen him a 'war junkie'. 'If I rush to southern Lebanon and manage to get back safely and file my story, I can go out to dinner at a French restaurant and say, "I made it, I made it!"' Fisk exclaims. Preferring the term 'foreign correspondent' to 'war reporter', he suggests that 'people who call themselves "war correspondents" are promoting themselves as romantic figureheads'.

Seeing Alfred Hitchcock's film *Foreign Correspondent* (1940) at the age of 12 sparked Fisk's desire to become a journalist, and Fisk muses about the possibility of retiring to write feature films about the Middle East. Now collaborating on his first screenplay, he says: 'I'm keener to write screenplays for movies than anything else at the moment. I think that cinema — I don't mean DVDs or TV — is probably the most persuasive medium that exists.'

His next book — titled *Night of Power*, in reference to the evening of Mohammed's ascent to heaven — will centre on the Bosnian war of the early 1990s. The indifference of Western powers to Serbian ethnic cleansing of Bosnian Muslims galvanised the Arab world's resentment towards the West, he says: 'Looking back, I should have been much more alert at the Middle Eastern end of the Bosnian story than I was.'

The Middle East has never looked so bleak to Fisk: 'Every morning I wake in bed here and ask myself, "Where is the explosion going to be today?"' From his apartment in Beirut's fabled Corniche, he heard the blast that killed the former Lebanese prime minister Rafik Hariri in 2005. Fisk didn't recognise the burning body of his friend, who had been the second person to phone after his mobbing in Afghanistan. 'I thought it was a man who sold bread,' he says.

Next to his front door is a postcard reproduction of a photograph showing the Austro-Hungarian Archduke Franz Ferdinand and his wife leaving a town hall in Sarajevo, five minutes before they were assassinated. It's there to remind him that 'you never know what will happen when you leave the front door'. Fisk, though, stresses that he has lasted for over three decades in the Middle East because of fear, not the lack of it: 'If you're not afraid of danger, you'll die. I want to live to at least 93, my father's age.'

— July 2008

Thomas Friedman

Not long into my chat with Thomas Friedman, it becomes clear that we have different agendas. Friedman wants to talk exclusively about his latest book, *Hot, Flat, and Crowded* — a clarion call for a US-led global green revolution. I also want to discuss the Iraq war, which he cheered on with breathless enthusiasm in his twice-weekly *New York Times* column. 'Iraq is a whole other interview,' the three-time Pulitzer winner objects.

The book is an urgent primer on the need for a clean-energy system, engagingly written in his usual folksy and anecdotal style. But as Iraq teeters on civil war and America faces unprecedented hostility from the Arab world, it's hard not to feel that Friedman — perhaps the most prominent liberal columnist to have boosted the invasion — is trying to turn over a verdant new leaf.

He was never persuaded by George W. Bush's argument that Saddam Hussein threatened America's security with weapons of mass destruction. Nor did Friedman swallow the idea of links between Saddam's regime and Al-Qaeda. The security risk, as he saw it, was not WMDs but PMDs (people of mass destruction) — the culture of hate, nurtured by repressive Islamic states, which spawned Osama bin Laden.

So why attack secular Iraq rather than an Islamic country such as Saudi Arabia or Iran? Because, as Friedman argued bluntly, America could. He construed the attack as an opportunity to export American-style democracy to the Arab world, imagining that the toppling of Saddam's Iraq would unleash democratic movements throughout the region.

Pressed, Friedman answers all my questions. After all, the Minneapolis-born pundit is, in his own words, 'Minnesota nice': he never hits back at his critics. By phone, he has the relaxed bonhomie of a country-club regular (allusions to golf, his favourite pastime, pepper his writing), and the upbeat temperament of an adman.

His writing is studded with company and brand names. With their glib metaphors and catchphrases, his columns can read like advertising copy. 'To name something is to own it,' he remarks. The jingle 'hot, flat and crowded', for example, describes the convergence of climate change, globalisation, and overpopulation that defines our 'Energy-Climate Era' (or E.C.E).

In his 1989 book, *From Beirut to Jerusalem* — the product of a decade reporting from Lebanon and Israel — Friedman coined the term 'Hama Rules', referring to the Syrian army's massacre of more than 10,000 Sunni Muslims in the town of Hama in 1982. The phrase became popular shorthand for the arbitrary brutality of despotic Arab regimes.

In *The Lexus and the Olive Tree* (1999), his first book-length paean to globalisation, Friedman argued that countries invest in peaceful futures by accepting the 'golden straightjacket' of market liberalisation. Enmities arising from tribal, national, and historical loyalties (symbolised by 'the olive tree') disappear, he contended, when societies open up to the international marketplace and become in thrall to consumerism ('the Lexus').

Lexus posited the Golden Arches Theory of Conflict Prevention, which has it that countries with McDonald's outlets don't fight each other. Shortly after the book was published, America bombed Yugoslavia, thereby torpedoing the theory. But Friedman protests that he 'was not laying down physics, but a principle of a broad trend'.

The hypothesis became the Dell Theory of Conflict Prevention in *The World is Flat* (2005), with the computer company replacing McDonald's. 'No two countries that are both part of a major global supply chain, like Dell's, will ever fight a war against each other,' he pontificated.

Give Palestinians economic security and material distractions, the argument runs, and its extremists will no longer care enough about holy sites to blow themselves up. Yet the Palestinians have long perpetuated a conflict that impoverishes them. Atavistic sentiments run deeper than Friedman allows.

Flat reconceived the globalised world in terms of 'flatness'. The dotcom revolution and the interdependence of markets, technologies, and populations levelled the economic playing field, Friedman argued, giving people unprecedented access to the world market.

In practice, though, globalisation often means trade within regional blocs rather than an integrated world economy. America and Europe continue to protect their industries rather than compete fairly with less affluent countries, and the international trade regime is dominated by power politics.

Friedman bats away the argument of Nobel economist Joseph Stiglitz that globalisation has made the world less flat by furthering inequalities in the developing world. 'Socialism was a great system for making people equally poor, and what markets do is make people unequally rich. The countries that are least globalised — North Korea, Cuba, Sudan pre-oil — are also the poorest.'

As an internationally syndicated foreign policy guru, he benefits from the flat world. 'This is the golden age of being a columnist. Your opinion can go more places and reach more people. It is the most fun legally you can have that I know of.' Pushed for how he imagines illegal fun, the self-described do-gooder states firmly: 'I'm not going to go there.'

In the Middle East, his photo byline is so well-known that he's constantly approached in the streets. Gail Collins, a former opinion editor of *The Times*, has likened travelling there with Friedman to walking through a mall with Britney Spears. It was Friedman whom King Abdullah of Saudi Arabia (then crown prince) used to float his Arab–Israeli peace initiative in 2002, proposing that Arab states give full recognition to Israel if it withdraws to pre-1967 borders.

It's not surprising that political and business eminences take to Friedman. His pro-globalisation writings sometimes resemble puff pieces for corporate CEOs. He reports the spin of political grandees with unqualified praise. A different picture would emerge if he gave similar airplay to those in the developing world impoverished by free-market economics.

Friedman's intimate voice, Panglossian forecasts, and gimmicky phrases make him a winning middlebrow commentator. But his subjects often call for more sceptical treatment. Indeed, as the Iraq war went pear-shaped, he refused to pronounce it a disaster, emphasising the importance of 'the next six months' — even as 2003 became 2006.

The costs of the war, he now admits, have been staggering. 'I wrote what I wrote at the time because I believed it. I'm just hoping that the phase that it's in right now will produce a decent outcome. Iraq may be coming out of this tailspin. Maybe a year from now things will look different.'

His experience reporting on the sectarian conflict in Lebanon might have given him a hard-bitten view of the Bush team's plan to build democracy in factionalised Iraq. Friedman says that in the build-up to the invasion he experienced 'a struggle between hope and experience — the experience of Lebanon, but also the hope, particularly post-9/11, that the Middle East could give birth to a different kind of politics'.

Hope won out, leading him to embrace the Iraq war. But he's

not inclined to wring his hands or navel-gaze: 'My eyes tend to be focused straight forward and not behind. It's the only way you can really survive if you're sitting where I sit and having the number of people commenting on what you do.'

Outside America, *Hot, Flat, and Crowded* is subtitled *why the world needs a green revolution — and how we can renew our global future*. His diagnosis? 'We're addicted to a dirty fuel system based on fossil fuels or coal or natural gas. In a world that's getting hot, flat, and crowded, that addiction is increasingly toxic. It is driving five problems way beyond their tipping point — and they are climate change, petrodictatorship, energy and natural resource supply and demand, biodiversity laws, and energy poverty.'

According to Friedman, the last two decades have seen the rise of 'dumb as we wanna be' politics in America: the reluctance of political leaders to address big, multigenerational problems. 'We've lost our way as a country, and green for me is how we get our groove back — focusing on a green agenda the way we once did on a red anti-communist agenda.' The working title of the book was *Green is the New Red, White, and Blue* but he changed it after concluding: 'We didn't deserve that title.'

Going green is also a security imperative, in Friedman's analysis. American companies bolster the oil wealth of Middle Eastern states, which sponsor Islamic fundamentalism. Developing renewable-energy technologies would make oil cheaper, he says, forcing Arab countries to build their economies through technological innovation, entrepreneurship, and educating their people.

Friedman became interested in the Middle East after travelling to Israel with his parents in 1968, aged 15, to visit his elder sister, then on student exchange. After studying Arabic language and literature at Brandeis University, he earned a master's degree in Middle Eastern studies at Oxford. While in the UK, he met his wife, Ann Bucksbaum, heiress to a multi-billion-dollar shopping-centre fortune; a board member of Conservation International, she also edits his columns.

Fluent in Hebrew and Arabic, Friedman became *The Times*' Beirut bureau chief in 1982 and was transferred to Jerusalem two years later. He openly identified as Jewish in his dispatches from the Middle East, which most of his Jewish–American colleagues avoided for fear of seeming biased. 'I wasn't a self-hating Jew,' he says.

Even still, Friedman was a controversial figure among Jews. He exposed Israeli culpability for the Sabra and Shatila massacre of 1982, and argued that terrorism played a necessary role in bringing the Palestinian cause to world attention. He was labelled an anti-Zionist by the same right-wing Jewish circles that, since September 11, 2001, have adored him for his excoriating writings on Arab dictatorships.

The editor of *Haaretz* once joked to Friedman that the Israeli newspaper ran his column because he was the only optimist it had. His upbeat outlook is a product of his upbringing, Friedman says. 'I had a kind of *Leave it to Beaver* childhood. I always brought that Minnesota optimism to the world.'

But life did not always resemble a sitcom. When Friedman was 19, his father, Harold, a ball-bearing salesman and keen golfer, died of a coronary. Harold had attained local celebrity for trailing his teenage son during his high school golf matches. Still his father's son, Friedman contributes regularly to *Golf Digest*, and toys with the idea of writing a golf book.

Upon turning 55 last year, Friedman qualified for the seniors' championship at his local club. As the first competitive golf match he had played since high school, it unleashed his sentimental side. 'A huge limb broke off a tree adjacent to the tee and just came crashing to the ground,' he recalls. 'I suddenly had this realisation that that was my Dad, that he was watching. It made me start to cry. I think the old guy was very proud of me.'

His mother, Margaret, died last year, aged 89. In an obituary column, he called her 'the most uncynical person in the world'. A champion bridge player, Margaret served in the navy during World War II, qualifying her for the GI Bill loan with which the Friedmans bought their home. Thomas Friedman has never lost faith in the old chestnut of America as a land of opportunity: 'I thank God every day that I was born in a country that has given me these opportunities.'

For Friedman, America remains more a force for good than ill. The US spends more on AIDS relief in Africa than any other country, he points out, adding that it was the Bush administration which pushed for UN sanctions on Zimbabwe (blocked by China and Russia) in July. 'I don't think the Iraq war is the be-all and end-all definer of the United States today,' he states. Which is perhaps another way of saying that it shouldn't be the sole definer of Thomas Friedman.

— *September 2008*

John Gray

What does it take to be billed as 'the most important living philosopher' by ageing *enfant terrible* writer Will Self? Or lauded by the late dystopian novelist J. G. Ballard for challenging 'all our assumptions about what it is to be human'? Surely, a fine line in pessimism, a flamboyant style, and a bulldozer approach to conventional pieties. Not, that is, a tendency for leisurely, academic mind-games.

Reading John Gray is a disturbing, brain-reconfiguring experience, like touring the history of thought through the dark and hallucinatory lens of a Self or Ballard narrator. Stated crudely, Gray thinks we're doomed. His 2007 book, *Black Mass: apocalyptic religion and the death of Utopia*, argues that creeds which presume humankind can remake society are holdovers of Christian apocalyptic thinking — the illusion that a harmonious world will follow from an event of mass destruction that eliminates conflict.

With the Enlightenment, the yearning to see human history as progressing towards a goal became secular rather than religious; Gray professes that secular ideologies — from Marxism and Nazism to extreme forms of liberalism and conservatism — contain this repressed religious inheritance. By believing that paradise on earth can be created by force, the utopian mind justifies mass bloodshed.

An emeritus professor at the London School of Economics, Gray speaks as a reformed ideologue. He won a mainstream audience with *False Dawn: the delusions of global capitalism* (1998), in which he denounced the neo-liberal ideology he once promoted as an early

champion of Thatcherism. British commentator Francis Wheen
has criticised him for his ideological flip-flops. In *Hayek on Liberty*
(1984), Gray surveyed the work of Thatcher's hero Friedrich Hayek,
and won accolades from Hayek, whom Gray later dismissed as a
'neo-liberal ideologue'. In *Beyond the New Right* (1993), Gray wrote:
'It is by returning to the homely truths of traditional conservatism
that we are best protected from the illusions of ideology'; but with
Endgames (1997), Gray declared: 'Tory politics has reached a dead
end.'

Still, Gray, 60, doesn't see himself as having thrown ideological
curve-balls. 'My anti-utopian stance has been completely consistent,'
he says by phone, sounding — oddly — not the least bit lugubrious.
'But, in the meantime, there have been huge geopolitical changes.'

Gray opines that when communism collapsed, utopianism
migrated to the right. Francis Fukuyama announced the 'end of
history' and the birth of an era of worldwide 'democratic capitalism'.
Gray retorted that history would resume as ethno-nationalist,
religious, and resource-based wars. He advised a pragmatic and
non-ideological approach to post-Cold War conflicts.

Instead, the right followed Fukuyama by imagining global
market-capitalism as an unstoppable force of nature and a panacea.
'The characteristics which had been features of communist
thinking,' he says, 'came about on the right — the militant
progressivism, indifference to the casualties of progress, and the
belief that the whole world was moving towards some single model
and that it should be accelerated by force.'

After breaking with the Tories, he became a supporter of New
Labour under Tony Blair. But when Blair continued Thatcher's
economic project and later became an ardent neo-con, Gray declared
a plague on both houses.

History, however, doesn't bear out Gray's belief that utopianism
is inevitably destructive. Gray argues that campaigns are not utopian

if they potentially can be realised. But many historical strides, such as abolishing slavery, would at one time have seemed as implausible as democratising Iraq. The attempt to bring democracy to Iraq was utopian, Gray believes, because even with better planning it would still have failed: 'The Kurds would still have broken away. There would still have been a conflict between the Sunni, who had been ruling the country, and the Shia — and a fairly strong Islamist force emerging through the Shia.'

In his 2003 book, *Al Qaeda and What it Means to be Modern*, Gray challenges the cliché that the September 11 attacks were an assault on modernity by medieval throwbacks. The idea of using mass terror to refashion the world was absent in the medieval period, Gray says, and only emerged with the French Revolution. He reads Al-Qaeda as an inheritor of the same post-Enlightenment revolutionary tradition as communism, Nazism, and neo-conservatism.

Not all critics were persuaded by Gray's view of radical Islam as modern, however. Sure, Al-Qaeda is headed by a multi-millionaire capitalist, and organises its international network through global technology. But contrary to Stalin and Hitler, Osama bin Laden totally rejects Enlightenment values, and seeks to recreate the seventh-century Islamic caliphate.

Gray thinks that war should only be a last resort for self-defence. 'The Second World War was justified,' he says. 'But war shouldn't be used as an instrument for improving the human condition. That's where I differ from the theories of pre-emptive war and revolution from the neo-conservative right, which to me exhibits the same kind of thinking as communism did.'

He conjectures that the invasion of Iraq sounded the death knell for secular utopianism: 'Iraq practically precludes another large-scale experiment along those lines. No one now, except a few post-Trotskyite neo-conservatives in bunkers, talks about overturning all the regimes in the Middle East and replacing them with democracy.'

The failure of free-market capitalism to establish democracy in post-communist Russia has also eroded the utopian mentality, says Gray. 'After the Soviet collapse, a series of ill-judged economic policies produced poverty and economic collapse, and criminalised capitalism. Russia is back now as an authoritarian state. It's certainly not a Western, liberal market-economy, which in my view it never could have been.'

Gray says his harshest detractors are 'evangelical humanists', hostile to his beliefs that secular movements renew Christian patterns of thought and that 20th-century tyrannies were by-products of Enlightenment ideology. 'They've said things like, "Well, the Enlightenment can't have any role in these episodes because the Enlightenment is pluralistic and tolerant", which reminds me of those gormless Christians who say, "Christianity couldn't have any role in the Inquisition because it's a religion of love."'

The role of atheism in Maoist and Stalinist totalitarianism is rarely acknowledged, says Gray: 'Religion was relentlessly persecuted. Mao launched his attack on Tibet with the slogan, "Religion is poison."'

Though not a believer, Gray excoriates the recent fad for books attacking religion by the likes of Christopher Hitchens, Michel Onfray, and Richard Dawkins. 'The difference between religious believers and secular rationalists is that religious believers are used to questioning their myths, whereas secular rationalists think their myths are literally true. I advocate an attitude of scepticism and critical distance from all these powerful belief-systems.'

Asked if he's a nihilist, Gray laughs, seeming to enjoy the role of heroic dissenter. 'Conventional, respectable thinkers always think that anyone who steps outside their mythology is nihilistic. The belief in progress in the West, as a cumulative advance in ethics and politics, is only two or three centuries old. Was Augustine a nihilist? Was the Buddha? Was Maimonides? Were the great Hindu philosophers? Were the Ancient Greeks?'

Gray doesn't think philosophy should generate ambitious programs for society. He sees its role as being to infuse political debate with 'a degree of historical understanding and scepticism, especially about policies which involve large-scale violence. Big ideas, big utopian positions, need big numbers of casualties. So I don't want to produce a new big idea.'

Mixing philosophy, political science, history, and theology, Gray's work reflects an eclectic approach he inherited from his mentor, the liberal philosopher Isaiah Berlin. 'He linked up questions in political and moral philosophy with more far-reaching cultural and historical understanding. I'm opposed to the type of philosophy which is not closely linked to the history of thought in general.'

In their final conversation, Berlin told his protégé that his foremost influence was not another philosopher but rather the Russian memoirist, novelist, and essayist Alexander Herzen. Gray also believes that the most penetrating books about society have come from writers rather than political theorists, calling Berlin 'an exception'. Gray met Berlin at Oxford, where he won a scholarship to study politics, philosophy and economics in 1968.

What drew a working-class student to become a proselytiser of Thatcherism? One can only speculate, since Gray refuses to discuss his childhood or personal life. The few publicly available facts indicate that he grew up poor in South Shields, coastal Northern England, where his father was a shipyard joiner. Gray says he was attracted to Thatcher's anti-communism, and still believes that she introduced important reforms in dismantling the UK's post-war welfare state.

Though now an opponent of the Right, Gray is no easy bedfellow of the Left. The Marxist theorist Terry Eagleton slammed Gray's *Straw Dogs: thoughts on humans and other animals* (2002) as a 'dangerous, despairing book' that, 'like all the ugly rightwing ecology for which humanity is just an excrescence, is shot through with a kind of intellectual equivalent of genocide'. According to Gray, philosophers who hold that humans are distinct from other animals, and masters of their own destiny, are prisoners of the Christian fallacy of human uniqueness.

He dismisses the Kyoto Treaty as 'irrelevant', and sees Greens (or 'earth-lovers') as motivated by the same folly of world-transformation as neo-cons, free-marketeers, and radical Islamists. 'The idea that we can resolve issues of climate change by switching over to an economy based on windmills and solar power, when you have nine or ten billion human beings who want the comfort and security that the richer parts of the world have, is a complete and utter fantasy.'

Gray argues that ecological degradation is caused by overpopulation rather than industrialisation or global capitalism. Instead of looking to reform human institutions, he sees environmental destruction as inevitable. It's a view perhaps as deterministic as the neo-liberal notion of inexorable global 'market democracy' that he rails against. Societies vary in how they interact with the environment; a minority of nations disproportionately pollutes the world and consumes its resources.

Gray is no postmodern relativist. He acknowledges progress in knowledge, but doesn't see it coinciding with human betterment. 'The modern myth of progress is that what is gained in one part of history can be retained in subsequent periods. But whereas knowledge grows, humans don't change much.'

So what's the value of knowledge? Gray returns to climate change. 'Without technical fixes, without the knowledge that underlies them, we're not going to be able to respond intelligently. The only way to get through the next generations without disaster will be by making maximum use of science and technology.' But he makes no great claims for science. 'You can't repair damaged biological systems by technological fixes. There's no way of arresting climate change now.'

Straw Dogs closes by calling for an attitude of philosophical resignation in place of utopian thinking: 'Can we not think of the aim of life as being simply to see?' But why keep writing polemics if humanity is beyond improvement? Gray's work is a powerful rebuke to any belief-system that refuses self-questioning. Taken literally, however, it justifies political passivity.

Gray is not apathetic; he keeps thumping his message home, in book after book, in a virtuosic style designed to make himself heard. Often he's no less evangelical than his bugbears. His achievement as a controversialist is also the undoing of his misanthropic vision. For it's hard to escape the thought that, in spite of himself, John Gray wants to change the world.

— *March 2008*

Hendrik Hertzberg

Something's not right. I'm sitting in *The New Yorker* headquarters opposite Hendrik Hertzberg, the finest political commentator in the Condé Nast skyscraper, and my mind loops back to high school political studies. Our interview hasn't properly begun — just preliminary small-talk about his imminent New Zealand jaunt — and already he's riding his wonkish hobbyhorse of electoral systems.

He'll be promoting *Politics: observations & arguments*, his 2004 compendium of journalism spanning nearly four decades, but the trip there has an altogether holier grail. Hendrik Hertzberg (or 'Rick' in conversation) is interested in New Zealand as a laboratory for mixed-member proportional voting — the system, adopted there in 1996, that he posits as a template for US electoral reform.

During his four years in the White House, as a member of Jimmy Carter's speechwriting team, Hertzberg became convinced that many of America's ailments stemmed from its single-member electoral districts, which prevent popular majorities being reflected in policy. 'Probably only 10 per cent or 15 per cent of congressional seats are competitive,' says the relaxed 65-year-old, a bejeaned leg slung over his chair arm. 'But with a proportional system, you can have nationwide political mobilisation.'

Worthy talk, for sure. But as his disquisition on world voting-structures clocks ten minutes, it has grown as intricate and winding as a Californian gerrymander, and shows no sign of letting up. Hertzberg, though, is so amicable, so obviously enjoying himself, that it feels churlish to interrupt. I take in his waggish face — all impish eyes, mop-top hair, and lopsided grin — and gird myself to remove the baby's bottle.

Is he often censored, I interrupt, commenting that he rarely pours forth about the gears and levers of democracy on the page? 'There's an unspoken quota of how much I can flog this type of analysis,' he admits, 'but I do it two or three times a year.' His colleagues sometimes jokingly play 'Where's Waldo?' (American-speak for 'Where's Wally?') by scouring his work for covert references to electoral reform.

As *The New Yorker*'s main writer of the weekly 'Comment' essay, Hertzberg has a voice that stands out for its warmth and common sense. Philip Roth has praised its 'uncommon journalistic modesty', at odds with the shrill bellicosity typical of the commentariat.

He's a bleeding-heart liberal, but also a master of takedowns, drawing blood from the cruel hard-Right. After Hertzberg charged former House speaker Newt Gingrich with homophobic bigotry, Fox News host Bill O'Reilly dispatched reporters to ambush Hertzberg on his way to work, and then on his nightly news program aired the full exchange with the bemused and pre-caffeinated writer.

Yet Hertzberg is more an *observer* than an *arguer* — the sequence of words in the subtitle to *Politics* is deliberate. Though he acknowledges writing predominately for those who already agree with him — as most of *The New Yorker*'s 1 million-plus subscribers surely do — he tries to avoid inflammatory language that could alienate others. To those within the left-liberal church, he's known for his unflappable charm, and seems to have no enemies.

Above all, Hertzberg is a brilliant wordsmith. His friend, journalist Michael Kinsley, likens him to a jeweller. Although his analysis is usually unimpeachable, it's his prose that most distinguishes him. According to the *Atlantic Monthly*'s James Fallows, a colleague from his White House years: 'Rick himself would admit that he is not developing truly avenues of thinking for the liberal side, but more expressing them with purity, humour, and grace.'

If his tone is uncommonly modest, that possibly reflects how he sees his profession. In his thinking, journalism is no art but a means to an end. 'It's like a trade,' he says, before qualifying himself: 'Well, it might be in the category of interior design or clothes design — maybe architecture, at best. Philosophy, religion, literature, music, and science are ends in themselves; those are the really important things.'

Not that Hertzberg aspired to anything but journalism. As an adolescent, he tried to become friends with people from other states by demonstrating his familiarity with their local newspapers. At his high school, he sold subscriptions for *The New York Times*, and was so successful that the daily called him in to deliver a talk about his selling technique.

Political convictions often originate in Oedipal rebellion, but Hertzberg was 'basically a dutiful son, politically'. His mother, Hazel Whitman, was a schoolteacher by trade and Quaker by religion. A distant cousin of the poet Walt, she met Sidney Hertzberg, a Jewish journalist, editor, and activist, through the anti-war movement in 1939. Their political temperaments rubbed off on Rick, who, by the age of nine, was distributing campaign buttons for Democratic presidential hopeful Adlai Stevenson.

In his early twenties, he identified as a pacifist and radical, joining the Young People's Socialist League, and contributing to the War Resisters League magazine, *Win*. He's since moved towards the centre, but says that's more 'a matter of style and maturing than really an important shift'.

The emerging newshound's main training ground was the *Harvard Crimson*, the student daily at Harvard University, where he was managing editor. After landing himself on academic probation, he was forbidden to participate in extra-curricular activities, but kept contributing articles under a pseudonym. With customary humility, he credits much of his success to the Harvard old-boy network, as many college peers quickly became salted throughout the higher reaches of American journalism.

William Shawn, then the editor of *The New Yorker*, had a son in Hertzberg's cohort, and noticed his work in the *Crimson*. When Shawn called and said in his soft voice, 'Hello, this is William Shawn', Hertzberg replied, 'Yes, and this is Marie of Romania', before hanging up. Only when Shawn phoned again did Hertzberg believe the caller was actually the legendary editor, inviting Hertzberg to join his staff, rather than a student prankster.

Hertzberg didn't take up the offer — not immediately — feeling too green for *The New Yorker* and 'worried that I would stagnate there because of too much freedom'. The possibility of being drafted to Vietnam also concerned him, so he opted for a one-year draft-deferred post as editorial director of the US National Students Association (NSA), where he edited a magazine aimed at inculcating students throughout the world with American values.

Not until the following year, while working in *Newsweek*'s San Francisco bureau, did he learn that the NSA was funded by the CIA. 'The selling point abroad had always been that our Soviet counterparts were obviously KGB operations,' recalls Hertzberg, 'so it was a crushing blow to discover that we and the Soviets were two peas of a pod.'

In 1966, he enlisted in the navy, which took him not to Vietnam but an army desk job in New York City. Upon being ordered to Vietnam two years later, he wrote a 25,000-word application for conscientious objector status. His file was rejected, but he was mustered out due to a mild medical complication, ending his fantasies of heading to jail as an anti-war hero. So Hertzberg phoned 'Mr Shawn', as he was generally known, and took an office at *The New Yorker*.

The Shawn-era *New Yorker* was an outsized cash cow, which bankrolled a large and mostly unproductive staff. 'You really had to motivate yourself,' says Hertzberg, recalling the three-day weekends and long holidays. 'It wasn't like you were sent out on a story, or given an assignment — it was all up to you.' But the freedom made him feel isolated and angst-ridden about his writing abilities, and he started seeing a shrink. 'I thought real writers were fiction writers,' he says.

So, for a change of pace, he worked as a speechwriter for New York governor Hugh Carey. Within months, he was tapped by James Fallows (a Harvard alumnus, naturally) as a speechwriter for president-elect Carter, becoming chief speechwriter after Fallows departed. 'There was a real exhilaration to the feeling of taking sides and being in the political arena, rather than just peeking over and looking at the fight,' says Hertzberg.

The White House years gave him a new perspective on writing, leading him to 'discover that I was happier having an end — namely, to help change the country in directions that accorded with my values — than worrying about the means, namely writing'.

The history books haven't treated the Carter years well, but Hertzberg remains stubbornly loyal to his former boss, calling him a 'saint'. He's quietly confident that 'Carter will be viewed as a minor president, but in an essentially favourable light, eventually, as a prophetic figure who had a lot of bad luck'.

'When Carter left the White House,' Hertzberg continues, 'the United States was importing less oil than when he came in. There's no other president of whom that can be said. And his emphasis on human rights played, I think, as much of a role in the unravelling of the Soviet Empire as did the military build-up that was accelerated under Reagan.'

Carter was often terse with his speechwriters, convinced that in a just world he'd have time to do all the writing by himself. But

Carter and Hertzberg remain pals, and the admiration is mutual. After losing office to Ronald Reagan, Carter presented Hertzberg with a mock speech, thanking him for his labours, on which he'd scribbled out the fulsome praise. 'He was satirising his own curtness,' Hertzberg says. 'It's a subtle apology.'

Another old-school tie opportunity arose when Martin ('Marty') Peretz, formerly his politics tutor, and by then the owner of *The New Republic*, invited Hertzberg to edit his magazine. Peretz remains to this day a committed foreign-policy hawk, but he wanted a more dovish editor to preserve the magazine's liberal tradition.

The two were at constant loggerheads — over affirmative action, over the nuclear-freeze movement, over the Nicaraguan Contras. Hertzberg once became so enraged that he picked up his desk-chair to hurl through the window. (Finding it too heavy, he had to put it back down.)

Peretz fired Hertzberg in 1984 and replaced him with Michael Kinsley, only to reinstall Hertzberg in the editor's seat five years later: 'It took another three or four years for me and Marty to sufficiently get on each other's nerves to part ways again.'

Kinsley, who is also to Peretz's left, reflects that Hertzberg was deeply troubled by the compromises he was forced to make with his boss. 'I'd be happy to put in a piece I didn't want, so long as I got to put in the pieces I *did* want, but that really pained Rick,' says Kinsley, 'which comes back to the idea of him as a jeweller; he saw every issue as a work of art.'

Meanwhile, at *The New Yorker*, advertising revenues were falling, and there was an increasing feeling that the magazine, which had hardly changed since it was founded in 1925, sorely needed to reinvent itself. So, in 1992, British journalist Tina Brown, famous for her circulation-boosting editorships of *Tatler* and *Vanity Fair* magazines, became the new editor.

Brown coaxed Hertzberg back onto *The New Yorker* staff, after nearly 15 years in Washington, DC; Virginia Cannon, Hertzberg's current wife and main editor, followed Brown from *Vanity Fair*. An office romance sprouted, leading to marriage in 1998. Their ten-year-old son, Wolf, shares little of his parents' interest in politics and journalism — much, Hertzberg says, to their relief.

Brown made *The New Yorker* splashier, more celebrity-oriented, and — say her critics — indistinguishable from other glossies. By Hertzberg's lights, however, she saved the magazine. 'She updated it and made it interested in giving its take on the national and global conversation of the moment,' he says. 'We very rarely, even now, have a long profile of a person that no one has heard of.'

When current editor David Remnick replaced Brown in 1998, he scaled back some of her PR buzz and sharpened the magazine's political focus, appointing Hertzberg to his perch as chief editorialist.

It's different, Hertzberg comments, covering politics from outside DC to 'inside the Beltway, where you feel the throbbing of the conventional wisdom. And that's both good and bad, depending on whether you're conscious of it, or whether it's just making you throb along'.

Remnick supported the Iraq war reluctantly, and Hertzberg dissented with reservations. The gulf between their positions was surprisingly narrow, but 'David was much angrier than I was when it turned out that the administration had misled us about WMDs'.

Last October, they collaborated on a full-throated 4000-word endorsement of Obama. The editorial was a suitable olive branch for the Obama campaign, after *The New Yorker* ran a much-maligned cover depicting Barack and Michelle Obama as Islamic fundamentalists giving each other a terrorist hand-jab in the Oval Office.

Hertzberg wasn't involved in the decision to publish the Barry Blitt illustration that sparked the 'Cover-Gate' scandal, but he concedes that the parody misfired: 'It was just the depiction of

various perfervid right-wing fantasies about the Obamas, without
any context, and without the object of the satire being pictured. It
should have had a little Fox News logo to make its satiric purpose
clear.'

The New Yorker explicitly endorsed a presidential candidate,
Democrat John Kerry, for the first time in 2004, after Hertzberg and
Remnick decided they needed to do everything possible to prevent
the re-election of Bush II.

The magazine's tone has changed unmistakably since the
departure of Bush, as Obamamania has replaced Bush-baiting.
How long does Hertzberg see the media's good will towards Obama
lasting? 'As soon as his approval rating goes below 50 per cent they'll
start jumping all over him. The media is just utterly craven.'

But Hertzberg's romance with Obama will last longer, no
question. 'I've never been more enthusiastic about a candidate for
president than I was for Obama,' he says. 'I can't believe I've lived to
see somebody of that quality elected president.'

'When it comes to writing about the meaning of America,'
Hertzberg goes on, 'no one except Lincoln has done better than
Obama. He gets the vast, vast complexity of it — the strange
mixtures and interflows of identity. It was because of *Dreams from
My Father* (1995) that I really became an Obama devotee.'

I suggest it's risky for a magazine to so unreservedly prostrate
itself before a president who has barely had a chance to prove
himself. Hertzberg tries to say he's not entirely uncritical of Obama,
who he fears may be 'a little too non-ideological … My only real
worry about his presidency is that the policies he's proposing may
not be equal to the situation — that the stimulus package is too
small, that he's not ambitious enough in the proposals. But I think
he has a pretty firm idea of where he wants to go.' Hertzberg pauses:
'You can see I'm a pretty tough critic of Obama, you know, and I'm
going to hold him accountable!'

But does Hertzberg feel less relevant now that the *zeitgeist* has caught up with him? 'When Bush was in power, there was one big thing that had to happen, which was that he and his legacy had to be defeated at the polls. So writing opinions had an obvious end-point. Now that Obama's president, it's basically about adjusting the tiles.'

For the first time, Hertzberg is less than garrulous, as his voice thins and he checks his watch. What I take for fatigue, though, turns out to be anxiety — it's Tuesday afternoon, and he's still without a topic for his Friday deadline. Dorothy Wickenden, *The New Yorker*'s executive editor, describes Hertzberg as 'the most agreeable, funny, and relaxed guy I know — until he starts writing, which casts him inexplicably into near despair'.

Still, before seeing me out, he insists upon showing me around the premises — a kind of museum exhibit of the workspaces of America's greatest journalists, which are incongruously small and mostly vacated. But it's only when he takes an errant turn into the women's bathroom that it fully strikes me why he's so likeable.

He has genuine charm — not that of the typical, marble-smooth American talking head, but someone just daggy enough to be endearing. There's a small but noticeable stain on his pullover, which he's either ignored, or not cared enough to see in the first place. His office is so cluttered with unruly piles of books and papers that it feels like an undergraduate's study.

I leave him to procrastinate. Says Michael Kinsley: 'He's a great agoniser. The idea that he could now produce an article nearly every week is extraordinary to people who used to know him.'

James Fallows concurs: 'While almost everybody who writes for a living has trouble finishing things on time, the spectacle was at its peak with Rick. It was always a down-to-the-wire and overnight process. The last night or two was always a crusade, a campaign, an overnight siege.'

For his part, Hertzberg says he usually spends 24 hours coming up with the lead — tinkering with one sentence, then reclining on the inflatable mattress in his office, where he usually camps out the night before a piece is due. His writing then flows in the final few hours before deadline.

When I call Hertzberg the following Saturday, his breeziness has returned. I ask what he ended up writing about. 'Something a bit unusual for me,' he answers, sounding faintly apologetic. 'Instead of just commenting on the passing scene, I recommended a particular policy — the eliminating of pay-roll tax.'

Clearly, he was in a crusading mood that week? Rick Hertzberg laughs, and admits that he hasn't yet used up his allowance of wonkishness. So I throw him another question before he tries to persevere.

— April 2009

Tony Judt

It must take nerve for Tony Judt, professor of European history at New York University, to check his email. He receives hundreds of vitriolic messages — sometimes threats against his life or, worse, his family. People do not, needless to say, want his head for his scholarly tomes on the history of the French Left. Or for his magisterial 900-page book *Postwar: a history of Europe since 1945*, published in 2005, which was a Pulitzer Prize finalist and helped secure his place in the world's top 100 public intellectuals named in the *Foreign Policy/Prospect* survey in May.

What makes the celebrated British-born academic a target for hate are his essays on Israel and American foreign policy in the Middle East — most famously, 'Israel: the alternative', published in *The New York Review of Books* in October 2003. Describing Israel as an 'anachronism', he wrote that 'the time has come to think the unthinkable': the dismantling of Israel as an exclusively Jewish state and its replacement by a secular and bi-national state of Jews and Palestinians. Since Judt is the son of Yiddish-speaking Jewish refugees, his detractors struggle to label him an anti-Semite.

He has always taken unorthodox positions. A long-term anti-communist, he is a firm believer in state intervention. He is politically progressive, but rejects postmodern theory and finds academic political correctness 'just as annoying as the reactionary politics of Washington'. A historian of French ideas, he is no Francophile. In *Past Imperfect* (1992) and *The Burden of Responsibility* (1998), he attacked French intellectuals for closing their eyes to totalitarianism.

Since 1987, when he moved to America to teach at NYU, after jobs at Cambridge, Oxford, and Berkeley, Judt has been educating Americans about the Continent.

The British historian Timothy Garton Ash says that Judt's commitment to public discourse makes him unique in the English-speaking world: 'He is much more like what we in Britain would think of as a Continental thinker rather than an Anglo-Saxon academic — someone who thinks that ideas matter and that the job of an intellectual is to be engaged in public-policy debates.' Academic and journalist Ian Buruma, Judt's friend and a fellow contributor to *TNYRB*, suggests that Judt's worldliness sets him apart from other historians. 'He doesn't just write history from archives and books. He is more like a journalist, in that he spends time in countries, and reports as much as he writes actual history.'

Judt's varied interests are examined in his newest book, *Reappraisals: reflections on the forgotten twentieth century* (2008), a collection of 25 essays written over 12 years. They range from pieces on Jewish intellectuals, such as Arthur Koestler, Primo Levi, Manès Sperber, and Hannah Arendt, to quirky portraits of countries such as Romania and Belgium, to essays on American foreign policy during the Cold War, and on the decline of social democracy.

His polemic style is on display. He likens French neo-Marxist theorist Louis Althusser, to 'some minor medieval scholastic, desperately scrabbling around in categories of his own imagining'. He charges Eric Hobsbawm, a leading living historian and an unrepentant communist, with having 'slept through the terror and shame of the age'. Fellow liberals, such as David Remnick, Michael Ignatieff, and Thomas Friedman, are excoriated for supporting the Iraq war. 'In today's America,' Judt writes, 'neoconservatives generate brutish policies for which liberals provide the ethical fig leaf.'

He explores how international opinion turned against Israel after its victory in the 1967 Arab–Israeli War. In 'The Country That

Wouldn't Grow Up', he equates Israel with a narcissistic adolescent that believes itself to be unique and universally misunderstood.

Some of the essays first appeared in *The New Republic*, which listed Judt as a contributing editor until 2003. After 'Israel: the alternative' was published, *TNR*'s literary editor Leon Wieseltier removed his name from the masthead. 'He does not wish to be held accountable for things that he has not himself done or to be regarded as a representative of anyone but himself,' Wieseltier wrote about his formerly close friend. 'Why must Israel pay for his uneasiness with its life?'

The troublesome essay is conspicuously absent from this collection. 'I really didn't want reviewers and readers to immediately turn to that and then read the book as though it was a footnote to that essay,' he says.

By 2003, Judt had become convinced that the creation of separate Jewish and Palestinian states was no longer possible. 'Israel controls the water, the economy, and the power to the state militarily,' he says. 'It owns the land, and has chopped it up in a way that will make a coherent Palestinian state impossible. One should recognise that, rather than talking as if, at some point in the near future, the Israeli settlers will miraculously go away, Israel will walk away from the land, and there'll be a Palestinian state.'

Fears, even among left-wing Jews, that the one-state solution would mean Jews becoming a minority in Greater Palestine, are exaggerated, he says. 'A substantial segment of the Palestinian population, which is still the best educated and most secular of all the Arab populations, will be very happy to live with and work with the majority of the Jewish population. We're not talking about Israel getting into bed with Saudi Arabia. Although Israel has done its best to turn the Palestinians into angry Islamicists, they are not yet.'

When Judt published an op-ed about the Jewish lobby in *The New York Times*, an editor called to ask that he insert somewhere that he is Jewish. Would Judt have entered the fray if he were not Jewish? 'I might be, like many of my non-Jewish friends here, inhibited for fear of being accused of being insensitive to Jewish suffering or the Holocaust or anti-Semitism,' he says. 'One has to live in the United States to realise how oppressive the silence about American policy in the Middle East is, especially compared with similar conversations pretty much anywhere in the world, including Israel.'

In October 2003, Judt was scheduled to deliver a speech at the Polish consulate in New York about the 'Jewish Lobby'. An hour before Judt was expected to arrive, the Poles cancelled the talk, after receiving calls from the Anti-Defamation League and the American Jewish Congress. ADL director Abraham Foxman dismissed allegations that the Jewish organisations silenced Judt as 'conspiratorial nonsense', but the consul-general clearly felt under intense pressure. In *TNYRB*, 114 intellectuals signed an open letter to the ADL denouncing its antics.

Writing in *Slate*, Christopher Hitchens ridiculed Judt's outrage by arguing that no one has a democratic right to speak at a private institution. A controversial critic of Israel himself, Hitchens mocked: 'What a chance I missed to call attention to myself.' 'I don't respond to Christopher in public,' counters Judt, 'on the general principle that you should never mud-wrestle with a pig because you both get filthy, and the pig likes it.' *Slate* later launched a humorous quiz entitled: 'Are you a liberal anti-Semite?' Second prize was a dinner with Tony Judt. 'I hate dinners, so I'd be a lousy dinner companion,' Judt says. 'It would be a real punishment.'

Judt was 15 when his mother, a hairdresser, and father, a bookseller, concerned about his lack of social life, sent him to a Zionist summer camp in Israel. He says he was 'sucked into the whole youthful enthusiasm — dancing in a circle, singing songs, being both left-wing and nationalistic'.

At 19, at the end of his first year at Cambridge, he organised a group of volunteers to replace the soldiers called up for the Six-Day War in the fields. Later that year, he drove trucks and translated Hebrew and French for Israeli officers. His romance with Zionism unravelled, however. 'I started to see a side of Israel that I didn't know very well,' he recalls. 'I listened to Israeli soldiers talking about how, "We now have all this land and we will never give it back", and, "The only good Arab is a dead Arab." You didn't have to be a political genius to see that this was a catastrophe in the making.'

Another fantasy dissolved during two years in Paris, where Judt researched his Cambridge doctorate at the École Normale Supérieure. 'I became less besotted by France,' he says, 'and less disposed to be a Francophile in the superficial sense of loving French food and wanting to be seen smoking Gauloises and wearing black berets.'

When he first taught at the Institute of French Studies at NYU two decades ago, France-bashing had not yet become an American sport. 'France and things French are now seen as a marginal elite preference, where once they were thought simply to be what the cultivated person cared about, spoke, and read,' he says.

In 1995, Judt founded the Remarque Institute at NYU to facilitate dialogue with Europe; but, even in the post-Bush era, he holds out little hope for the future of US–European relations. 'The substantive content of the relationship probably won't change hugely, because the American way of looking at the world is very different from Europe's,' he says. 'Europeans look at Turkey or the Middle East as frontier issues, whereas Americans see them as long-distance menaces.'

In *Postwar*, Judt describes Europe 'as a paragon of the international virtues' and 'an exemplar for all to emulate', before concluding that 'the twenty-first century might yet belong to Europe'. For a generally hard-nosed historian, it's a remarkably sentimental vision. 'The European model of how to live a Western pluralistic democratic life in the globalised world,' he says, 'is probably the only available model to us — that is to say, which combines the reality of nation-states with the necessity of transnational institutions, legislation, and cooperation.'

Garton Ash calls *Postwar* a landmark achievement: the first history of post-war Europe to integrate the histories of Western and Eastern Europe. He also feels that Judt exaggerates the divergence between Europe and America: 'I think both sides of the Atlantic are likely to come back to what I call a Euro–Atlanticist agenda, to a kind of a strategic partnership. Tony [was] deeply marked by his experience of the last eight years in the United States under the Bush administration,' he says.

Buruma suggests that Judt 'sometimes overstates to further the discussion'. He sees Judt's idealisation of Europe as a way of expressing his disillusionment with the US: 'He's a passionate man, and I think sometimes takes up very passionate positions and then feels disillusioned. The disillusionment is sharper because of the passionate enthusiasm he had at first. It's true of Israel, and it's true of the United States.'

— *June 2008*

Robert Kagan

There's a view of neo-conservatives as a cabal of shadowy figures — cloistered in Washington think-tanks, vastly influential but accountable to no-one — who connived to hoodwink a dim-witted president into invading Iraq.

Robert Kagan, the movement's most eloquent spokesman, has a different conspiracy theory, in which the ideologues are victims. They were scapegoated, he alleges, by a public ashamed of having cheered on the invasion. 'A war which had overwhelming American support, and was voted 77–23 in the US Senate, suddenly became a plot by six or seven people,' says Kagan.

Not that the neo-cons — whose pin-ups include Richard 'Prince of Darkness' Perle and *The Weekly Standard* editor, William Kristol — have had it too rough. After the American defeat in Vietnam, the war planners were shunned by their colleagues, savaged by the commentariat, and booed at public debates. But the architects of Operation Iraqi Freedom generally escaped such opprobrium.

Indeed, Kagan, at 51, is a man in his prime. A monthly columnist for *The Washington Post* and senior associate at the Carnegie Endowment think-tank, he was one of the chief foreign-policy advisers to Republican presidential hopeful John McCain. He was named as one of the world's top 100 public intellectuals in *Foreign Policy / Prospect*'s 2008 survey.

He is, in many ways, a typical neo-conservative — in his moral clarity and conviction that America should be prepared to unilaterally declare war to uphold its values. But the label is meaningless to Kagan, who argues that there is nothing 'neo', or new, about his philosophy. Instead, he places himself within a long tradition of foreign policymakers — encompassing the likes of Dean Acheson, John F. Kennedy, and Ronald Reagan — who stress the importance of US global leadership.

In his 2006 book, *Dangerous Nation* — the first of a projected two-volume history of American foreign relations — Kagan attempted 'to disprove the idea that America is traditionally an isolationist nation that only occasionally heads off into the world'. Some reviewers charged him with revising history to legitimate the neo-con vision of an imperialist America.

For all his bellicose rhetoric, he's surprisingly congenial. Physically large but baby-faced, with a wry, slightly unnerving smile, he wears an open-necked shirt and introduces himself as 'Bob'. The bookshelves of his office in Washington, DC are empty — he's just returned from three years in Brussels, where his wife, Victoria Nuland, a former adviser to Dick Cheney, served as US ambassador to the North Atlantic Treaty Organisation.

Gore Vidal once said of Kagan that he is 'in the grip of a most unseemly megalomania, speaking for no-one but political hustlers within the Washington beltway'. But his muscular prose and deft analysis of geopolitical trends regularly draw plaudits from his political adversaries. Henry Kissinger, whose realist outlook is often opposed to the values-based vision of neo-cons, has called Kagan's 2003 book, *Paradise and Power*, a 'seminal … discussion of European–American relations'.

As the world's lone superpower, the US naturally favours an international order where might prevails, Kagan argued. By contrast, European countries — militarily weaker, more geographically exposed to the risk of war, and shadowed by the memory of World War II — push for diplomatic solutions over military action, seeking regulation through international cooperation rather than the anarchy of nations.

'Americans are from Mars and Europeans are from Venus,' Kagan wrote, offering a ready-made sound-bite at a time when the transatlantic relationship was imploding over Iraq. *Paradise and Power* became an international bestseller, and was distributed by European Union foreign policy chief Javier Solana to every EU ambassador. Though just 100 pages, it drew comparisons to such epoch-defining texts as Francis Fukuyama's *The End of History and the Last Man* (1992) and Samuel P. Huntington's *The Clash of Civilizations and the Remaking of World Order* (1996).

Kagan ignited fresh debate with his most recent book, *The Return of History and the End of Dreams* (2008), in which he outlines his proposal for a global league of democracies — a cornerstone of McCain's foreign-policy platform. For Kagan, the resurgence of China and Russia as great-power autocracies calls for a forum where the world's 100-odd democracies can meet to advance their shared values.

The title alludes to Fukuyama's hypothesis that history in the form of ideological struggle ended with the fall of the Iron Curtain and was replaced by inexorable market-capitalist democracy. 'When we started the post-Cold War period, we thought that there wasn't a challenge to democracy — that it was just an issue of fostering economic development,' Kagan says. 'But we have in the world two powerful autocracies that seem pretty well entrenched, not undergoing this anticipated evolution based on economic growth. Democracies need to begin acting together in a more concerted fashion, whether it's dealing with problems like Zimbabwe and Burma, or showing solidarity against the resurgent ambitions of Russia.'

For a man of fighting rhetoric, Kagan can be surprisingly sensitive, as Kurt Campbell, the current assistant secretary of state for East Asia and the Pacific, discovered at a dinner last May when he made the mistake of cracking jokes about neo-cons in Kagan's presence. It has been said, Campbell mused, that neo-cons are vampires — except whereas a silver bullet can kill vampires, neo-cons are immortal. Nor, Campbell continued, are neo-cons werewolves: whereas werewolves are sane during the day, neo-cons are crazy around the clock. Kagan was unimpressed, and refused to share a podium with Campbell at a conference the next day.

Few would agree with Kagan that he belongs 'very much in a bipartisan mainstream'. Nonetheless, it's true that neo-cons cannot be neatly identified along party lines. In the 2000 presidential election, Kagan voted for Al Gore against George W. Bush's pledge to scale back the US's international commitments. 'I spent much of the Nineties fighting against the Republican Party, which was opposed to intervention. It's only later that people have revised this history and created this fiction of a neo-conservative movement distinct from liberal interventionism, which has been the mainstream policy since the Cold War.'

After September 11, 2001, Bush reversed his foreign policy, and Kagan, who had long pressured the Clinton White House to force regime-change in Iraq, was suddenly in white-hot demand. As were Kagan's father, Yale historian Donald Kagan, and brother, Frederick, who in 2000 co-authored *While America Sleeps*, calling on Washington to increase its defence budget.

Kagan was a teenager during the Jimmy Carter years — 'such a down period for America,' he says. 'We heard all about the limits of American power and how the United States was in decline and fading.' When Reagan came to office in 1980, Kagan admired the new president's 'refusal to accept that the Soviet Union was in a state of inevitable ascension and that there was no hope for the democratic world'.

After a degree from Yale, he worked in the State Department for much of the 1980s, while watching the fall of Augusto Pinochet and Ferdinand Marcos, and seeing cracks appear in the Soviet edifice. 'That was the period when we shifted from a policy of pretty blindly supporting dictatorships to supporting more moderate and centrist democratic forces in both Latin America and Asia, with really some quite astonishing successes. It's one of the reasons I don't share the general scepticism that there's anything we can do to support democracies in countries where there isn't democracy at this moment.'

He remains optimistic about the possibility of a democratic future for Iraq following the 2007 troop surge. 'When they finally changed strategy after four years, we saw the results. What was assumed to be an inevitable civil war between Shia and Sunni was, in fact, the product of our failure to provide security.'

It must concern him that McCain's running mate, Alaska governor Sarah Palin, seems to have little knowledge of the world beyond her state? 'She has at least as much foreign-policy experience as some of McCain's other potential vice-presidential choices,' Kagan retorts. 'But because they were men, no one was raising any questions.'

So ignorance about foreign policy is the norm among McCain's inner circle? Kagan flashes his sardonic smile. 'This whole idea that only a certain elite foreign-policy community can be trusted with American foreign policy is false. I trust the average American to make better decisions about many of these issues.' That's the McCain votary speaking, not the foreign-policy mandarin — the latter is quick to tar Barack Obama as a foreign-policy naïf.

'McCain has been engaged in national security issues for decades,' he says, 'whereas Obama has only been in the Senate for a few years, and he did not make foreign policy the number one topic of his public persona. There have been times when he's said, "We should talk to Iran", then he's said, "We shouldn't talk to Iran without preconditions." He's talked about bombing Pakistan, and then about how the United States shouldn't behave that way any more. You can hear anything you want to hear in Obama's foreign policy.'

On the challenges that McCain would face in reviving US legitimacy on the world stage, Kagan says: 'Most nations act according to their interests, and their interests are not necessarily affected by who's president of the United States. The behaviour of governments in the international system is not fundamentally anti-American.'

Asian countries increasingly look to the US for protection against rising China, he says, adding that America enjoys much closer relations with Europe than two years ago. The attempt by France and Germany to counterbalance American power by embracing Russia failed, Kagan contends, under pressure from the new eastern and central European EU member states — countries whose anxieties about the Kremlin have increased since its military action in Georgia.

So what of his idea that Martian Americans and Venusian Europeans have irreconcilable worldviews? 'I don't think that the things that make Americans and Europeans different have changed,' he says. 'But international circumstances are driving Europeans and Americans closer together again, as we see the rise of two great autocratic powers.'

According to Kagan, there are already two democratic clubs in existence — NATO and the EU — but they fail to reflect the new global reality of democracies dispersed throughout the world, whereas his proposed democratic concert would incorporate countries in Latin America, Africa, and Asia.

The UN Security Council may be 'hopelessly paralysed', as Kagan puts it; but, for my money, it's surely safer to have major world powers united under a single organisation, where democracies are forced to negotiate with illiberal regimes, than split into two competing camps.

The world, it could be said, is not polarised as neatly into democracies and autocracies as Kagan suggests, but an exclusive democratic club would risk creating such a divide. If Kagan were less influential, his proposal could be dismissed as mere nostalgia for the bipolar world of his State Department years. But it's an idea we'll be hearing much more of if US voters elect McCain.

— *September 2008*

Paul Krugman

By the time Paul Krugman was awarded the Nobel Prize in Economics, in October 2008, he didn't seem like a maverick. A CNN poll earlier that year had found George W. Bush to be the least popular American president in modern history, and the United States was about to elect a Democrat president who opposed the Iraq War. But in the run-up to the Iraq invasion, Krugman was one of the few pundits in the mainstream press to unflinchingly attack Bush.

Since beginning his twice-weekly *New York Times* column in January 2000, Krugman relentlessly accused Bush of lying — about the motives behind cutting taxes for the rich and trying to roll back Social Security, for example, and about 'weapons of mass destruction' in Iraq.

After the 11 September 2001 attacks, newspapers and magazines of the liberal centre ricocheted to the right. As *The Times*, *The Washington Post*, *The New Yorker*, and *The New Republic* fell obediently in line with the Bush administration, Krugman's heretical columns made him a cynosure for the anti-war Left, and a hate figure to neo-cons.

'I was largely alone on the major op-ed pages,' says the mild-mannered 56-year-old Princeton economics professor. 'We look back now at 2002 and say, "Nothing really bad happened to people. We did not have a new era of McCarthyism." But that was very far from clear at the time. It was pretty frightening.'

Of celebrity-economists, such as Joseph Stiglitz, Jeffrey Sachs, and Amartya Sen, Krugman enjoys the highest public profile. In 1991, he won the John Bates Clark Medal for an American economist under 40, and with his influential work on economic geography and international trade — explored across 15 books and hundreds of journal articles — Krugman was long regarded as a shoo-in for the Nobel.

In the fevered climate of post-9/11 America, his outspokenness attracted death threats. But Krugman, a self-described pussycat, accustomed to the sedate groves of Ivy League academe, never set out to fight political battles. 'It has been a much less easy life than I expected to be leading at this point. I should be sitting around in well-stuffed armchairs reflecting upon my life's research work.'

When Krugman was approached by *The Times* to write a column in 1999, he wrongly presumed it wouldn't be too time-consuming. The main burden would be financial — the newspaper's conflict-of-interest rules prohibited him from giving corporate talks, for which he commanded up to US$50,000.

With the American political scene calm and the economy booming, Krugman expected to write about business deals, the internet, and developing world financial crises. But the 2000 presidential election politicised him. 'A funny thing was happening. The candidate of one major party was being blatantly dishonest in what he said — at that point about economics — and no one was calling him on it.'

Krugman argues that the media gives a soft ride to mendacious politicians because journalists are trained to consider two sides of any issue. 'If Bush said that the world was flat, the headline on the news analysis would read "Shape of Earth: Views differ",' he quipped in 2000. In *The Great Unraveling: losing our way in the new century* (2003), Krugman explains why many people failed to grasp the radicalism of the Bush agenda: 'People who have been accustomed to stability can't bring themselves to believe what is happening when faced with a revolutionary power, and are therefore ineffective in opposing it.'

He understands why journalists feared speaking up. 'There really has been, for the most part, no reward for having gotten in front of the story and reporting what was going on,' he says. 'On the contrary, people who got it right have been fired, and there's no cost to having gotten it wrong. Most news outlets are owned by large corporations. The journalists may be mostly highly educated people from the north-east, who tend to be liberal, but the ultimate decisions on the coverage are made by people who are, on the whole, Republicans.'

Whereas most *Times* columnists are career reporters, Krugman's academic background means he was never socialised to follow the dominant media line. Other political journalists chase contacts at Washington dinner parties, but Krugman maintains his independence by leading the relatively secluded life of a university professor in New Jersey.

Though sometimes criticised for not doing much original research, Krugman doesn't see any reason to interview executives or government officials. 'I'm not trying to do the beat-reporter style. That's not my brief. Overwhelmingly, what I'm writing about is policy issues, and some carefully neutral words are not going to help me sort it out.'

Even Krugman's admirers sometimes flinch at his savagery. 'He steps over the top,' says Stiglitz, a Nobel Prize-winning economist and close acquaintance of Krugman. 'He doesn't titrate his tone to the magnitude of the outrage.'

Krugman's father was a politically liberal insurance-company executive. As a teenager on Long Island, Paul Krugman fantasised about becoming a 'psychohistorian' — one of the prophetic mathematicians of Isaac Asimov's *Foundation Trilogy* (1951–53). He decided at college that economics was the next best thing to Asimov's fictional science.

After gaining an undergraduate degree at Yale, Krugman went to Massachusetts Institute of Technology (MIT) for his PhD, where he consolidated a refreshingly non-ideological approach to economics. Satisfying neither hardline free-marketeers nor dogmatic interventionists, Krugman styles himself as a 'free-market Keynesian'. 'In practice, it is a common position. You believe in government intervention, but also have a strong appreciation for the power of markets and where you can rely on the market.'

In 1979, he formulated the first model to explain currency crises. But Krugman remains best known among academic economists as a founder of so-called New Trade Theory. In the classical model of 'comparative advantage', a country's relative share of natural resources was alone seen to dictate the success of its industries on the world market. Krugman showed that specialisation and technological sophistication are sometimes enough to account for market domination.

This influential research led to a stint as a member of Ronald Reagan's Council of Economic Advisers in 1982. Krugman says his year as a Washington insider gave him a revelatory insight into the policy-making process. 'Key decisions were being made on the basis of rather obscure "I talked to a businessman who told me" sort of reasoning.' Krugman discovered the reluctance of government officials to amend policies. 'Most things stay the way they are unless there's very strong pressure to change.'

He happily returned to scholarship the following year. 'As a subordinate I was okay, but in terms of being a government official at a more senior level, my fundamental lack of tact would become a really serious problem.'

By 1984, though a full professor at MIT, he was dissatisfied. 'I had a good job and a good income, and from the point of view of what the vast majority of the world has, I was doing fine. But I wasn't at the top of the heap in terms of the academic pecking order. My reference group were the people who were really the star economists.'

His star rose during Bill Clinton's 1992 campaign, when his work on income inequality was used by Clinton's advisers to help demolish Republican claims that the widening wage-gap was a myth. Many speculated that Clinton would appoint Krugman as chairman of his Council of Economic Advisers.

When he was passed over in favour of Berkeley economist Laura Tyson, Krugman was bitter. He dismissed Tyson as 'a third-rate interpreter of other people's work' and denounced two of Clinton's other appointees as 'pop internationalists' who 'repeat silly clichés but imagine themselves to be sophisticated'.

Krugman now downplays his ambitions to be part of Clinton's team. 'I'd have liked the analytical parts of the job, but I'm a terrible manager and I'm not tactful, so I don't think I belong in that kind of position.' He speculates that he alienated Clinton during their first — and last — meeting in 1992. 'I was dismissive of concerns about industrialisation, which were a favourite theme of his. If that was an audition, I failed.' Stiglitz admits that Krugman's 'firebrand [temperament] which serves him well, in some ways, in journalism, may not be that great in the political context'.

Stiglitz feels that Krugman underplayed the achievement of the East Asian economies before the 1997 financial meltdown. 'He suggested that there was no miracle — that they had just saved a lot,' Stiglitz says. 'My response was that it was a miracle that they had saved that much. No other countries had succeeded in saving at that rate and investing that level of savings well.'

As Krugman predicted, the Asian boom economies collapsed, and Bush's rationales for invading Iraq are now widely recognised as canards. Yet rather than relaxing with the satisfaction of a vindicated dissenter, Krugman is hard at work on his academic career. He is revising an introductory economics textbook co-authored by his wife, Robin Wells, and preparing the reading list for 'Economics 553'. 'It's very pleasant to be thinking about which of the latest trends in research I should be devoting a full week to.' It's a lifestyle to which he says he could imagine fully returning.

But Krugman's reference group is now not just star economists, but also political columnists. Some see him as the most influential political commentator in the US. He will want to keep it that way. Abandoning the spotlight for the ivory tower seems unlikely.

— *May 2008*

Bernard-Henri Lévy

Waiting with diminishing patience for Bernard-Henri Lévy in the Washington, DC hotel lobby, I can't help but wonder if his deriders are right — right to dismiss France's most famous public intellectual as a self-regarding dandy, a 'limousine leftist' chauffeur-driven in a tinted-glass Daimler. I imagine the bouffant-haired philosopher, filmmaker, journalist, and socialite preening himself in his suite, or on the phone to his actress-chanteuse wife, Arielle Dombasle, in their 18th-century Moroccan palace.

His opulent lifestyle, self-conscious glamour, and shameless name-dropping make him a sitting duck for satire. Frequently parodied on nightly television puppet show *Les Guignols de l'Info*, he has also been struck several times by anarchist cream-pie thrower Nöel Godin. With French philosophers notorious for their arcane theory and dogmatic politics, I was tempted to indulge one who reports on the ground from forgotten African conflicts and challenges knee-jerk hostility towards the United States and Israel. Yet now my watch suggests that BHL (as he's known in France) is not just late, but has probably stood me up.

A call from his publicist: 'Are you still coming?' I've been directed to the wrong hotel, but there's no drama, as Lévy is resting. When we finally meet, his hair suggests a recent nap. It's a mess — or, rather, studiously 'wind-blown'. I remind myself that the indefatigable author of some 30 books needs just four hours sleep and, moreover, does not have bad-hair days.

Lévy's latest book, *Ennemis Publics* (*Public Enemies*), a

collaboration with bad-boy novelist Michel Houellebecq due out in English translation in 2010, hasn't helped his reputation for narcissism. It collects six months of correspondence between the two self-described whipping boys of the French intelligentsia. 'I can give every possible and imaginable explanation of my work,' Lévy writes to his pen pal. 'All I do is worsen my reputation as a bourgeois swine who has no grasp of social realities and only pretends to be concerned about the world's oppressed so as to make headlines.'

The most enraged attacks on Lévy often come, not surprisingly, from fellow leftists. The occasion of his American tour is the English-language publication of *Left in Dark Times* (2008), a book of ruminations in search of an 'anti-fascist Left'. Activists Arundhati Roy, Noam Chomsky, Robert Fisk, and Slavoj Žižek are lambasted, along with most gurus of French postmodernism. Today's typical leftist, as Lévy sees it, blames America for Islamic radicalism while ignoring anti-Semitism and Muslim violations of human rights. How, Lévy asks in the book, did the Left forget the liberal values for which the activists of May '68 went to the barricades?

Despite Lévy's firm opposition to the Iraq war, his general enthusiasm for the United States sets him at variance to most French intellectuals. 'Anti-Americanism is a terrible tool of blindness, of stupidity,' Lévy proclaims with a typical rhetorical flourish and sweep of his arm. 'The few of us in France who understand that are not popular.'

Left in Dark Times opens with Lévy receiving a phonecall from France's centre-right President Nicolas Sarkozy during his 2007 election campaign. 'When are you going to write me a nice little article?' asked Sarkozy (an old friend, of course). Lévy replied that the Left is his family and that 'you can't change families the way you change shirts'. Not known for changing his shirts, either, Lévy never deviates from his signature black suit and white shirt unbuttoned to his lower chest. But Sarko had a point when he spluttered: 'Your family? These people who've spent 30 years telling you to go fuck yourself?'

The Left, Lévy agreed, parted ways with him by failing to take action to halt the bloodshed in Chechnya and Darfur. But still, Lévy endorsed Sarkozy's Socialist Party rival, Ségolène Royal, whom he considered 'the lesser evil'. Sarkozy's presidency has turned out much as Lévy predicted: 'He promised that he would be a president of human rights, but he supported Putin, and backed down on his threat to boycott the Beijing Olympic Games.'

The book's subtitle, *a stand against the new barbarism*, alludes to his 1977 polemic, *Barbarism with a Human Face*, which sold millions of copies and won Lévy cover-profile treatment by American *Time* magazine. It launched Lévy, aged 28, as the leader of the so-called New Philosophy movement. Along with André Glucksmann and Alain Finkielkraut, Lévy broke with Marxism by calling it a tool for brainwashing rather than freedom. 'In the past, anti-Marxists had said that Marxism was guilty of spreading revolution,' Lévy explains. 'I said Marxism prevented people from revolting. It was a cement of the brain to make people obey dictatorships.'

Lévy's political temperament dates to childhood conversations with his father, Andre, who left his native Algeria to fight in the Spanish Civil War and then with the French Resistance against Hitler. Andre Lévy taught his son that 'no compromise of any sort should be made with fascism'. These days, Lévy uses 'Islamo-fascism' unhesitatingly to invoke the threat presented by radical Islam.

Bernard-Henri was born in 1948 in the north-west Algerian town of Béni Saf. The family moved to Paris when he was an infant, leaving him with no memory of his birthplace. 'This little peculiarity,' Lévy speculates, 'may explain the philosophical obsession I developed about the need for free people to cut the ropes that link them to a national ground or ethnicity.'

If Lévy has an overarching message, it's that universal human rights exist and must be defended — once commonplaces of the Left that have now given ground to notions of 'tolerance' and 'cultural relativism'. Lévy, whose maternal grandfather was a rabbi, traces his universalist outlook to his Jewish heritage: 'To be a Jew means to be indebted to otherness,' says Lévy, echoing his 1978 work, *The Testament of God*. 'The masters of the Talmud teach that to be a Jew is to explore deeply what humanity is.'

In 1997, two years after his father's death, Lévy sold the family timber business for more than 750 million francs, funding the hideaway in Marrakech once owned by cultural philanthropist John Paul Getty. Lévy and Dombasle split their time between homes on the Left Bank of Paris, the French Riviera, and in Morocco. So, three houses in total? 'Yes, I think so,' Lévy nods, before adding: 'Maybe two in Morocco.' My reference to Morocco as a holiday destination prompts a salvo of 'No, no, no' — BHL cannot remember taking a holiday. The multiple homes, he says, help him and his wife to escape the public eye.

As a student at the École Normale Supérieure, he was taught by Jacques Derrida and Louis Althusser. The latter developed the philosophy of 'anti-humanism' that Lévy says influenced his distrust of revolution. Althusser would later distinguish himself by strangling his wife to death, but Lévy insists that 'craziness is not an argument against a thinker, and he was a very great thinker'. He suggests Althusser's madness was inextricable from his misanthropic philosophy. So is Lévy crazy, too? 'Frankly, I don't know,' he says with a dramatic Gallic shrug and no obvious embarrassment at being compared to his master.

The extent of Lévy's involvement in the student uprisings of 1968 remains disputed, but that year his brother, Philippe, was hit by a car and fell into a coma. BHL will say only that Philippe is now okay, though as recently as 2003 he told a reporter he was still comatose. In his autobiographical novel, *Comédie* (1997), Lévy recalls attending to a girlfriend in hospital during the May protests. A subtle allusion to his brother, perhaps? He stays close-lipped.

In 1971, civil war broke out over Bangladesh, setting the 22-year-old on his first reporting mission. After the country won independence from Pakistan, Lévy stayed on to serve briefly as a policy adviser to the country's first president, Mujibur Rahman. Lévy's daughter, now a bestselling novelist, was born shortly after his return. Fancying himself a libertine, Lévy named her Justine-Juliette in homage to the Marquis de Sade's best-known heroines: 'I thought that those two names would cover all possible destinies for the young woman she would be.'

Lévy's son from his second marriage, Antonin-Balthazar, is now a lawyer, but asked in what field, Lévy replies: 'I really don't know.' Aren't they close? 'Yes. But for lawyers there is a strict obligation of confidentiality.' When I point out that lawyers have no duty to hide their specialisation, Lévy adds with the trace of a sneer that he is 'probably a business lawyer'.

Legend has it that Dombasle, Lévy's third wife, fell in love upon seeing his photograph on a book-cover and being struck by his resemblance to Jesus Christ. After they met at a book-signing, Lévy hired a private detective to investigate her marital circumstances. For seven years, Lévy and his wasp-waisted mistress maintained a clandestine relationship, formalised in 1993. They address each other in public using the formal 'vous' — partly an attempt, says Lévy, to preserve their intimacy.

Aged 26, and with his father's financial backing, Lévy founded a newspaper, *L'Imprevu*. He aspired to revolutionise the press, but the daily lasted all of 11 issues. Of his flops, it is outstripped only by his 1997 feature-film debut, *Day and Night*, in which he directed Dombasle, alongside Lauren Bacall and Alain Delon. Critics slated it as a turkey. Not, Lévy says with a haughty twitch of his nose, that its failure would deter him from another cinematic venture.

There's no question that Lévy has enjoyed more success with documentaries. His films about the Bosnian conflict, *A Day in the Death of Sarajevo* (1992) and *Bosna!* (1994), were impassioned calls for Europe to intervene to stop the bloodletting. As the final words of *Bosna!* assert: 'Europe died at Sarajevo.' One of the first journalists to enter beseiged Sarajevo in 1992, he wanted 'to break what I predicted would be the indifference of Europe'. It would be more than three years before the West acted.

It's hard to imagine a writer in many other countries with Lévy's access to the political elite. Following the American military bombardment of Afghanistan, for example, Jacques Chirac sent him to Kabul on a diplomatic mission to report on the possibilities of reconstructing the country. Yet Lévy regularly turns down the state-bestowed *Legion d'Honneur*. 'I like to be honoured by my peers with literary prizes, but I don't want to be crowned or distinguished by Sarkozy or Chirac or Mitterrand,' he remarks. 'I don't respect them enough.'

Lévy was in Kabul when *The Wall Street Journal* reporter Daniel Pearl was beheaded by terrorists across the border in Pakistan. Lévy flew to Karachi and began the year-long investigation that became *Who Killed Daniel Pearl?* (2003). It's usual for BHL to be at the centre of his own books, but some felt he went too far by imagining the journalist's thoughts in the moments before his beheading. Pearl's widow, Mariane, called Lévy 'a man whose ego destroys his intelligence'. No doubt her eyebrows rose at lines such as: 'He thinks of Mariane, that last night, so desirable, so beautiful — what do women want, deep down? Passion? Eternity?'

For his part, Lévy makes no apologies about resorting to fiction when the facts are elusive. He coined the word 'roman quete' (investigative novel) for the genre, which he first experimented with two decades ago in *The Last Days of Charles Baudelaire* (1988). But he isn't advocating blurring fact and fancy, Lévy stresses. To the contrary, '*Roman quete* means precisely not mixing the two. There are three chapters in the Baudelaire book, and two in the Pearl, which are the work of imagination; the rest are strictly faithful to the available facts.'

Whether reporting from hotspots in Algeria, Burundi, Sri Lanka, Colombia, Sudan or, most recently, Georgia, Lévy maintains his trademark attire. I ask if it feels odd to travel through war-torn countries in designer suits. 'Are you suggesting that when you report on a war you should wear battledress? Or when you report in Africa you should wear a colonial suit?' Since the point is lost on him, I say it seems faintly absurd, tasteless even, to be so sartorially obsessed in the midst of carnage and poverty. 'I'm not concerned about my appearance,' he retorts. 'You might be concerned, but I am not.' His unvarying wardrobe is proof of that, Lévy says: 'I don't take time thinking, "Do I want a blue or red shirt?" This problem is solved forever!'

Some see a double standard between Lévy's crusade against anti-Semitism and his fighting words about the Muslim world. The veiling of women should be flatly condemned, he argues, whatever so-called multiculturalist feminists may hold: 'Veiling women means treating them as abnormal human beings, "disturbing elements" that have to be suppressed. Those who veil women believe that they are either just reproduction machines or like pornography that has to be hidden.'

Following the publication by a Danish newspaper of cartoons lampooning the Prophet Mohammed in 2005, Iran's Holocaust-denying President Mahmoud Ahmadinejad sponsored an exhibition of satirical cartoons about the Shoah. Lévy joined the rest of the intelligent world in protesting vehemently. But he'd also signed a manifesto, along with Ayaan Hirsi Ali and Salman Rushdie, denouncing Islamism as 'the new totalitarianism' and supporting the Danish paper's right to free expression.

The combative secularist sees no tension between his positions. 'Any Muslim, Christian, or Jew has the right to laugh about rabbis, God, Mohammed, and so on,' he says. 'Even for believers, mocking religion is a way to reinforce his own beliefs. If Ahmadinejad had put on an exhibition about the Old Testament, Moses, the Jewish God, and so on, this would have been a great thing.' The anti-Semitic drawings were different, however: 'Denying the Holocaust is an insult to humanity and the children of the dead. You cannot compare a mockery of dogmas and religions to the racist attacks against people that is the rise of anti-Semitism.'

Our chat has run to nearly 90 minutes when Lévy declares: 'Enough! You've harassed me.' His French publicist hastily intervenes to explain that the French verb *harasser* means to exhaust, not annoy. But could it be that the firebrand and public enemy is actually weary?

— *December 2008*

Janet Malcolm

Recently, the editor of *Bookforum* magazine travelled three hours to interview Janet Malcolm at her summer home in Massachusetts. Shortly into their conversation, she broke off one of her answers to paraphrase the dancer Isadora Duncan: 'If I could describe it, I wouldn't have to dance it.' Malcolm asked why he didn't forego the struggle to extract interesting answers from her, and review the book at issue, *Two Lives: Gertrude and Alice* (2007), instead. He closed his notebook, they had lunch, and he returned to New York to write a review.

Malcolm recounts this anecdote midway through our conversation in her Manhattan apartment, as a cautionary tale against expecting too much from her. Celebrated for her long, opinionated *New Yorker* profiles, she is understandably wary of the interview process. In *The Journalist and the Murderer* (1990), Malcolm described the inevitable betrayal involved in the journalist–subject encounter; the subject will regress like a patient in psychoanalysis, childishly trusting her questioner, only to discover that the journalist is not a compassionate listener but a professional with an agenda and a story to construct. Thus, according to the book's oft-quoted opening: 'Every journalist who is not too stupid or too full of himself to notice what is going on knows that what he does is morally indefensible.'

Malcolm, 75, is a small, fragile-looking woman, whose solicitous manner betrays nothing of her work's caustic tone. You can imagine her as an inconspicuous observer, fading into the background while her unsuspecting interview subjects, mistaking timorousness for sympathy, fill the silence and fall into her trap. The key to being a shrewd interviewer, Malcolm says, is 'to keep your mouth shut'. When I comment that reticence isn't much help interviewing her, she replies: 'The people I interview welcome the chance of self-expression, whereas I don't have anything to sell except my book.'

Her subjects generally regret being so voluble — most famously, Jeffrey Moussaieff Masson, the iconoclastic psychoanalyst who was anointed, then fired as, director of the sacred Freud archives. When Masson saw himself portrayed as a brash narcissist in the brace of *New Yorker* articles that became *In The Freud Archives* (1984), he sued for libel. Masson alleged that Malcolm fabricated quotations in which he reportedly described himself as 'an intellectual gigolo' who has bedded over 1000 women and planned to turn Freud's house into a place of 'sex, women, and fun'.

The decade-long, $US10 million lawsuit came to a close when the court ruled in Malcolm's favour, but not before Malcolm's colleagues questioned her claims that journalists should compress, rearrange, and smooth over quotations to remain faithful to the meaning, rather than the actuality, of speech. Malcolm now insists that I set aside my voice-recorder and take written notes instead. 'People talk in ungrammatical, unwriterly ways,' she says. 'I don't do good sound-bites. I think of myself as more of a maker than a thinker.'

When Malcolm started occasionally giving interviews several years ago, she was struck by the power of the question. 'People feel that they must answer them,' she says. 'Then I realised I can just say, "I can't."' She regrets not speaking to the press during the Masson affair, admitting 'you can't blame people for not understanding something when they've only heard one side'. The prestige of *The New Yorker* contributed to her naivety, since 'it was like an ivory tower where we assumed that everybody would know that what we did was ethical and correct'.

The libel lawsuit became the prism through which *The Journalist and the Murderer* was debated. In the book, Malcolm dissected the trial of Joe McGinniss, a non-fiction writer who was being sued by Jeffrey MacDonald, a former military doctor convicted of murdering his family. McGinniss befriended MacDonald and was given free access to his defence team, after leading MacDonald to believe that the book he was writing would prove his innocence. When McGinniss' *Fatal Vision* (1983) was published, revealing that he never doubted MacDonald's guilt, the murderer sued the journalist for fraud.

Although Malcolm condemned McGinniss' treachery, she controversially described it as an extreme instance of the double-crossing that results from any journalist–subject relationship. Many colleagues read the book as Malcolm's self-exculpation for her betrayal of Masson's trust. 'If I had sympathised with McGinniss, I wouldn't have written about the case because it would have been self-serving,' says Malcolm. 'By taking the other side, I didn't feel I had to rescue myself. What hurt me was that people used Masson's accusations as a weapon to hit me over the head with because they didn't like what I said about journalism.'

Controversy came late to Malcolm, who launched her career with *The New Yorker* in 1965, writing a column about home furnishings and design. 'The task of describing things in detail — there were no illustrations — and of going to shops and trying not to be seen while taking notes, turned out to be great preparation for journalistic work.' She made her first foray into extended reportage in the late 1970s, after quitting smoking and finding herself unable to write: 'Writing was so entwined with smoking for me, so I decided to do a piece that required reporting, to wean myself from that smoking–writing association.'

Following several years of psychoanalysis, she began reading Freud and speaking with other analysts, in order to understand what had taken place. One analyst, Aaron Green, was particularly garrulous and became the centrepin of *Psychoanalysis: the impossible profession* (1981). Despite Malcolm pointedly satirising the dogmatism of New York's psychoanalytic establishment, the book became assigned reading in many training seminars. 'They thought it was a very clear exposition of psychoanalytic theory, which is a measure of how murky their books must be if they have to take a popular text,' she says.

Malcolm's father was a Czech psychiatrist who had fled Prague with his family in 1939. So in *Two Lives*, Malcolm is understandably exercised by the question of how the charismatic modernist writer Gertrude Stein won enough friends for the Jewish lesbian ménage to survive in Nazi-occupied France. In her 1945 memoir of wartime life, *Wars I Have Seen*, the reactionary Stein neglects to mention her or Alice Toklas' Jewishness. 'I don't think I've ever been moved by anything Stein wrote,' says Malcolm, 'but an exception is the last part of *Wars I Have Seen*, where she writes about how the war is coming to an end, and the Resistance are coming out of hiding — where she's finally *gotten* it, where she finally understands how bad the Nazis are, and she keeps using the phrase *honneur aux maquis*.'

Malcolm's previous book, *Reading Chekhov* (2001), was a fusion of criticism, biography, and travelogue, in which she deprecates her mission as 'the absurdist farce of a literary pilgrim who leaves the magical pages of a work of genius and travels to an "original scene" that can only fall short of expectations'. As with *The Silent Woman* (1994), her study of Sylvia Plath's afterlife as the subject of biography, *Reading Chekhov* was less a work of literary biography than a deconstruction of it, examining the half-truths and omissions involved in stitching together the story of a life. Malcolm loved Chekhov's short stories, always crying in the same places when she reread them. But she did not feel that way about Stein, whose unintelligible, avant-garde prose has meant that her works have never attained a wide readership.

'I felt funny — Stein often used that phrase — about writing about a writer whose work I didn't enjoy,' says Malcolm. 'But I came to respect her achievement, mainly the originality and freshness of her language. One felt chastened by it, because it makes what we say seem so banal.' Malcolm shows me her mutilated copy of Stein's 925-page *The Making of Americans* (1925), which she cut up into six pieces in order to read on the subway and make the prospect of finishing it less daunting.

Malcolm identifies her younger self with the biographer Elizabeth Sprigge, who cast herself as the coquettish heroine of her 1955 study of Stein: 'She thought that everything she did was interesting,' says Malcolm. 'She had a very arch and feminine way of being, which evoked the cringe-making person I was.' Malcolm's sceptical, self-scrutinising voice pervades her books, but she says that her 'I' is a narrative construction and not an autobiographical 'I' like Sprigge's: 'It is an idealised version of myself, somebody who's more clever and certain and fluent than the "I" sitting with you, who has doubts and uncertainty.'

The themes of *Two Lives* are vintage Malcolm — the instability of knowledge, the partiality of biography, and the agendas that underlie interpretation. Just as Malcolm believes that real people must be fictionalised in order to insert them into non-fiction narratives, so too, as is often the case with novelists, do similar characters recur in her books. The sour Toklas, who devoted her final two decades to preserving Stein's posthumous legacy, compulsively writing letters and cagily deflecting the prying questions of biographers, seems a variation on Olwyn Hughes, Ted's sister and executor of the Plath estate, who looms large in *The Silent Woman*.

Equally uncanny is Leon Katz, the larger-than-life, maverick Stein scholar, who has outraged other Stein academics by sitting for decades on an unpublished interview with Toklas that may — or may not — unlock the secrets of *The Making of Americans*.

Katz recalls Jeffrey Masson, the charming, unconventional scholar who became the nemesis of Freudian analysts by arguing that the master's theories were based on his wilful distortion of evidence. 'Oh, that's interesting; it's as if writers have a kind of travelling cast,' remarks Malcolm, but she will hardly be prompted.

When Katz is scheduled to meet Malcolm for an interview, he deliberately bollixes up the appointment, arriving at the Los Angeles airport a day early, and then — presumably fearing that Malcolm would appropriate his story — declines to rearrange the interview. But Malcolm's inability to meet Katz doesn't perturb her; the veneer of a complete story isn't her aim. 'One of the things I've learned in doing this work is that you follow life as it occurs,' she says. 'I don't want to manipulate actuality; I want to record it.' Katz thereby becomes yet another Malcolm trope; like the absent Ted Hughes in *The Silent Woman*, a figure who doesn't appear.

Malcolm's scrupulously controlled, pellucid, cool style is the antithesis of Stein's often unreadable, hot-headed, unedited prose, which Malcolm at one point describes as 'a kind of nervous breakdown'. But the modernist master anticipated Malcolm's postmodern genius for exposing the limits of narrative. Malcolm describes Stein's *The Autobiography of Alice B. Toklas* (1933) as an 'anti-biography', in which Stein critiques the biographical enterprise through using Toklas' voice to write about herself in mock-aggrandising terms. Of Stein's 'anti-novel', *The Making of Americans*, Malcolm writes that: 'Stein keeps returning to the project it appears she has abandoned — that of writing fiction — and then berates herself for doing it badly.' Shortly after denying any affiliation with Stein, Malcolm comments: 'My scepticism of biography continues even though I keep doing it.'

— *October 2007*

Catherine Millet

Today, Catherine Millet is best known simply as 'Catherine M.', the Parisian nympho who made bookish types frisky with her 2002 memoir, *The Sexual Life of Catherine M.* But for three decades she was known only to the French chattering classes as a respected art critic and curator. Her matronly dress-sense and dumpy build betrayed none of her dissolute instincts.

'As a child,' reads the opening line, 'I thought about numbers a great deal.' And three pages later, Millet is recounting her first experience of group sex — aged 18, just weeks after losing her virginity. Though reticent in everyday interactions, she gained confidence through being the girl who never said 'No.' She didn't flirt, but was always available to men, regardless of their age, shape, or how many she'd already serviced in one night.

Of all her sexual partners, which must number in the thousands, Millet remembers just 49 names. For every orgy in a chic apartment, there was sex in railway stations, tractor-trailers, and cemeteries, in the bleachers of sporting stadiums, on park benches, and on car bonnets. But Millet — now 61, and with her swinging lifestyle long behind her — protests that there was nothing unusual about her experiences. 'There are millions of people in the world with the same sort of sexual practices,' she says in an email interview.

To foreign observers, the book was a typically Gallic mix of po-faced philosophy and *outré* sex from a tradition that produced the Marquis de Sade, Georges Bataille, and Pauline Réage's *Story of O* (1954). Gay novelist Edmund White praised it as 'one of the most explicit books about sex ever written by a woman'. But writing in *Liberation* newspaper, the late philosopher Jean Baudrillard carped: 'If one lifts one's skirt, it is to show one's self, not to show oneself naked like the truth.'

The sexual autobiography was translated into nearly 40 languages and sold 400,000 copies in France alone. Since then, two of Millet's books on art have appeared in English — *Contemporary Art in France* in 2006 and, in 2008, *Dalí and Me*, which focuses on the surrealist painter's little-known essays and autobiographical writings.

Born in Catalonia, Spain, Salvador Dalí lived in Paris for much of his adult life and mostly wrote in French. 'Dalí is still a taboo subject in France,' Millet says, 'French critics are attached to the notion of the cursed artist like Vincent van Gogh, and don't like successful artists.' Dalí's embrace of General Franco also taints his reputation, but Millet dismisses it as 'just another provocation'.

The bisexual Dalí was a trenchant critic of repression, and Millet considers him to be history's first painter of masturbation and buttocks. She pays particular attention to two of his paintings, *The Great Masturbator* (1929) and *Young Virgin Auto-Sodomised by the Horns of Her Own Chastity* (1954). Dalí was fascinated yet repulsed by sexuality, and generally abstained from carnal knowledge — hardly Millet's itinerary.

Yet as the title suggests, *Dalí and Me* is a very personal response to Dalí's work, with Millet digressing liberally into her own fantasy life. To Millet, 'Our first contact with a work is always subjective — a dimension which art critics usually stifle to analyse the work on a more rational level. I believe it can paradoxically contribute to an objective understanding.' Her interest in Dalí crystallised a decade ago while working on a study of faeces in contemporary art. 'For Freud and Dalí, who was a Freudian, excrement is the symbolic equivalent of gold,' she says. 'It's the reminder of our material condition — a representation of our destiny.'

In autobiographical works such as *The Secret Life of Salvador Dalí* (1942), Dalí detailed the state of his body while writing — the contents of his stomach, the way he is dressed, or the position of his body. 'A thought is necessarily produced by a body,' explains Millet, admiring his approach. 'The states of our body determine our thoughts.'

In the prologue to *Diary of a Genius* (1964), Dalí asserts that his book 'will prove that the daily life of a genius, his sleep, his digestion, his ecstasies, his nails, his cold, his blood, his life and death are essentially different from those of the rest of mankind'. But for Millet, his journals prove the contrary: 'When the TV cameras and the public were far away, Dalí had a very simple lifestyle.'

Dalí refused to prioritise events in his journals — to see the creation of his art as more important than his daily errands. For Millet, as much can be learned about great figures from the banal aspects of their lives as from their social and intellectual experiences.

The painter who once drove to a lecture in a Rolls Royce crammed with cauliflowers was a master at staging his public persona. He became famous at the beginning of the media era, recognising, before Andy Warhol did, the importance of being photographed. It's hardly surprising, then, that Millet felt her experience of celebrity after *The Sexual Life* enabled her to better understand Dalí.

She knows about using photographs for publicity — her husband, novelist Jacques Henric, published a book of nude photographs of his wife simultaneously with her memoir, fuelling the *succès de scandale*. Millet and Henric have been together for 26 years and married for 19. To the question of why a libertine might crave the conventional stamp of marriage, she retorts: 'Why should marriage, which is a consensual judicial act between two people, prevent their freedom?'

In France, the memoir was a throwback in a climate where Michel Houellebecq's bleak novels about society's sexual excesses reflected a backlash against the liberated mores of 1968. 'The sexual freedom of one generation is an inhibiting factor for the following generation,' Millet says. 'That's why absolute and universal sexual freedom is a utopia.'

She makes no apologies in *The Sexual Life* for her lifestyle. Nor is the book exactly a call for sexual liberation — in her matter-of-fact prose, Millet's experiences seem joyless and numbingly repetitive. 'It is a book written with some distance,' Millet concedes, stressing that she sought 'neither to move nor shock readers'. She avoided relating her experiences chronologically, because 'desire is unaware of the passing of time'. Instead, the book is organised into four themes: Numbers, Space, Confined Space, and Details.

Millet's emotional life was mostly absent from her memoir, though she hinted at some early traumas in her *petit bourgeois* childhood. Her parents disliked each other, and had affairs. Her brother died in a car accident when she was a teenager, leaving her alone to care for her chronically depressed mother, who finally took her own life. Aged 23, Millet entered psychoanalysis, but it was through professional recognition that she overcame her social awkwardness. 'I didn't need to assert myself as much through sexuality,' she says.

She continues to edit *Art Press*, a review of contemporary art that she co-founded in 1972. In France, Millet challenged Left Bank sensibilities again in 2008 with another memoir, *Jealousy: The Other Life of Catherine M*, in which she recounts the jealousy she experienced upon discovering that Monsieur Henric was being unfaithful.

After learning of Henric's infidelity, Millet was besieged by thoughts of him with his lovers, at once aroused and tormented. What anguished Millet most was that she felt no legitimate reason to be angry with her husband, given her promiscuity in the first years of their marriage. But her sexual morality remains unchanged. 'Jealousy is an impulse,' she says. 'Perfect sexual freedom — a libertarian morality — rids one of all jealousy.'

Millet barely mentioned her jealousy in *The Sexual Life*, as she feared that writing about it would give the impression that she was being punished from on high for her transgressions. She found the new memoir much more difficult to write — the memories were so painful that it sometimes took her hours to write one sentence.

Now we know that she played down her angst in *The Sexual Life*. How much was that book a fantasy or elaborate Dalíesque pose? 'I forced myself to avoid the traps that our subconscious places in our memories, especially when it concerns sexuality.' But she adds: 'Who can claim to completely master the subconcious? By definition, it is impossible.'

— October 2008

Adam Phillips

In his 150th birthday year, Freud's reputation is on the slide. His theories of penis envy and the Oedipus complex are widely ridiculed as saying more about his own priapic fixation than human nature. The so-called 'talking cure' of psychoanalysis has given ground to the quick-fix solutions of drug treatment and the 'think positive' slogans of cognitive-behavioural therapy. Meanwhile, psychoanalytic institutions cling anxiously to the image of Freud as a scientist.

In 1993, when Adam Phillips published his first book of psychoanalytic essays, *On Kissing, Tickling, and Being Bored: psychoanalytic essays on the unexamined life*, he was trumpeted as Freud's great white hope. Profiles in *Esquire*, *Vogue*, and *The New York Times* magazine followed, along with ten further books, which criticise psychoanalytic institutions as cults that refuse to accommodate developments in science. Phillips argues that the objective truth of Freud's theories is irrelevant and that their therapeutic power lies in their qualities as stories. Proposing that Freud be read alongside Pushkin and Dostoyevsky as a great literary writer, rather than as a scientist, Phillips baffles anti-Freudians who feel that he steals their ground. His colleagues either ignore him or upbraid him as a flighty postmodern stylist, seeking refuge in ambiguity, rather than drawing conclusions or committing to ideas.

Critics reach for desperately abstruse formulations to capture his paradoxical style, which has won comparisons with Emerson, Sontag, Trilling, and Barthes. The novelist Will Self, formerly an analysand of Phillips', praises his 'circumambulation tergiversation'. A Phillips essay presents less a linear argument than a playful interrogation of conventional assumptions about an idea. Even while ranging across innocuous-sounding themes — tickling, cross-dressing, flirtation, hinting, and being laughed at — the elusiveness of his essays makes a précis of them near-impossible.

'I don't want people to be able to repeat what I think,' says Phillips. 'I want them to have their own thoughts in the reading. The guru is the problem, not the solution here. So I'm very reassured that people often say: "I can't remember anything about that book, but I really enjoyed it." '

This slipperiness reflects the psychoanalytic process. In his 2006 book, *Side Effects*, Phillips describes digression as 'secular revelation'. 'With psychoanalysis, people come with a coherent narrative, and what turns up is an opportunity to speak up about their stray or nomadic thoughts,' he says.

Phillips' view of Freud as a literary titan is shared by Harold Bloom, and was recognised when Freud won the Goethe Prize in 1930. *Side Effects* explores Freud fear of his literary, unscientific instincts — what he saw as the similarity between a case history and a short story. Analysts Melanie Klein, Donald Winnicott, Jacques Lacan, and Sándor Ferenczi also tried to marry psychoanalysis with science. But Phillips sides with the anti-Freudian philosopher Bertrand Russell in disputing the scientific claims of psychoanalysis.

'You can't predict what's going to happen in psychoanalysis,' he says. 'You can't verify it or falsify it. The idea of doing psychoanalytic research seems to me to be a contradiction in terms, because each question is different.'

He traces Freud's loss of cachet to the insularity of contemporary psychoanalytic writing: 'Psychoanalysis needs to cease being a cult interested only in talking to its own members.' Phillips is not affiliated with any psychoanalytic organisations and he seems to relish being little read by other shrinks: 'If there is a thing called "psychology", it is about ordinary life. It's about how we all live as ourselves. So it shouldn't be a specialisation.'

That his detractors have him down as a subversive revisionist illustrates 'just how impoverished the reading of Freud has been. I'm a maverick because there's been so much dull, unimaginative consensus in the past.' Avoiding professional conferences, Phillips prefers to speak to university students, who are 'more alive, more engaged, more passionate, and more reckless'.

His recent editorship of the new Penguin translation of Freud didn't endear him further to the cognoscenti. James Strachey's definitive 24-volume edition was criticised — most famously by Bruno Bettelheim — for dressing Freud up with a scientific lingo, introducing jargon such as 'parapraxis' and 'cathexis' into his conversational German.

Phillips used a separate translator for each book, with 'no consensus about technical terms'. They were literary translators, rather than experts on Freud: 'As someone who can't read German, I was reading the translations for readability, not accuracy.' The introductions are written by literary critics who have 'no investment in psychoanalytic institutions'.

Phillips practises clinical psychoanalysis four days a week from his Notting Hill apartment, charging modest fees of up to fifty pounds per 45-minute session: 'I don't want to be part of the culture that believes that something is good if it's expensive.' Hanif Kureishi, Tim Lott, and Will Self are former patients but, contrary to hearsay, Phillips rarely takes on celebrities: 'That's just not the culture I want to be part of.'

His sole requirement for accepting a patient is that he is 'moved by what they're suffering from'. In place of the Freudian image of the detached analyst, Phillips suggests that the therapist–patient dynamic is 'a very intimately impersonal relationship. But that doesn't make it less intimate. It's not a laboratory.' He confines his writing to Wednesdays but works at a dizzying pace, producing enough lectures and essays for a book most years. 'I'm slightly fearful of giving myself more time to write,' he says. 'I'm fearful of what might happen if the writing ran out, because it comes from a part of me that I have no control over.'

Reading Jung's *Memories, Dreams, Reflections* (1963) at age 17 left him smitten by psychoanalysis: 'I was interested in what seemed like the depth. This looked to me like a great life.' Freud soon superseded Jung, who Phillips decided was 'a much more interesting man that Freud, but an infinitely less interesting writer'. He also found Freud's writings uncannily familiar: 'It felt like family life. There's something about Freud's work that feels — for want of a better word — very Jewish.'

Phillips' parents were secular second-generation Jews, born of refugees from the anti-Jewish pogroms in Russia and Poland. He experiences his Jewishness as a background white noise of threat, '… a feeling that the world can go very badly wrong. Our middle-class parents wanted us to integrate into culture; I've been to public school, I've been to Oxford, I've been to all the great British institutions. What it doesn't eradicate is the feeling of insecurity.'

At Oxford, Phillips studied English literature under a traditionalist faculty, which had not yet come to regard the poststructuralist and psychoanalytic theories he enjoyed as acceptable tools for literary analysis. He graduated with third-class honours: 'I believed that if I had the courage of my convictions I wouldn't take my degree, because I didn't believe that my interest in literature had anything to do with getting a qualification.'

After beginning — and abandoning — a PhD on the American poet Randall Jarrell, Phillips spent four years training to be a child psychoanalyst. His training analyst was Masud Khan — the charismatic Pakistani émigré, later disgraced for his sexual and emotional abuse of patients and his anti-Semitism. 'I don't mean that all the things that were said about him may not be true, but the man who I was in analysis with was really profoundly reliable, an extraordinarily powerful listener, and a very intuitive, intelligent man,' he says.

Khan helped him recognise his refusal to leave home emotionally, which was barring him from developing a satisfying sexual life: 'My passionate bonds with my parents made me more timid than I wanted to acknowledge about engaging with people outside my family.'

For almost two decades, Phillips worked as a child psychotherapist for the National Health Service. In 1995, frustrated with the bureaucracy, he shifted to private practice and began to treat mostly adult patients. Fatherhood reduced his desire to work with children: 'After I had my own children, I found it very difficult to listen to the things that people do to children and that children do to each other.'

He is adamant that psychoanalysis should be pleasurable, rather than the 'version of original sin secularised' he was schooled in. 'When I was in training, there was a very strong feeling that the people who were most authentically in touch with themselves were authentically in touch with their misery,' he says. 'Psychoanalysis at its worst makes people feel worse — makes them feel that they're very destructive, very inadequate, and very dependent. All those things may be true, but the opposites are equally true. People are as phobic of their strengths and talents as they are of their disabilities. There is a genuine pleasure in realistic acknowledgment.'

And if psychoanalysis is often caricatured as a bourgeois indulgence, Phillips sees himself as a facilitator of solidarity. 'When external reality becomes unbearable, people have symptoms,' he says. 'It seems no accident to me that psychoanalysis was "invented" during the rise of fascism and the breakdown of empire. The aim of psychoanalysis is to enable people to be less self-preoccupied, so that they can re-enter political, communal life.'

Moreover, with psychoanalysis long superseded by cognitive-behavioural therapy, Phillips regards it as no less than a 'counter-cultural' phenomenon. 'Cognitive therapy has got to be the therapy of choice in competitive capitalism, because people want to get people back to work as quickly as possible,' he explains. 'Psychoanalysis is wonderful because it doesn't do that. It doesn't easily and quickly turn you into a successful consumer and a reliable worker.'

— *August 2006*

Katie Roiphe

Katie Roiphe once needed bodyguards to give a book reading. In 1993, when she published *The Morning After: sex, fear, and feminism*, American campuses were awash with hysteria about the supposed date-rape epidemic. The 24-year-old doctoral candidate at Princeton attracted death threats for accusing anti-rape activists of conjuring a myth. Four years later, she drew more fire with *Last Night in Paradise: sex and morals at the century's end*, which argued that America's youth culture had been deadened by puritanism since the AIDS crisis. Roiphe (pronounced 'Roy-fee') claimed that the backlash against the sexual revolution and relentless sex-education campaigns were killing the mystery and excitement of sex.

But with her most recent book, *Uncommon Arrangements: seven portraits of married life in London literary circles 1910–1939*, critics raised the white flag. Upon its American release in 2007, *The New York Observer* announced that 'Katie haters will be sorry to hear that it's very absorbing.' A decade ago, Roiphe expected picketing whenever she spoke at a university. But since being hired in 2007 as a journalism professor at New York University, she's been an insider of the academy.

With a scholarly titled new book, on the bourgeois topic of marriage, Roiphe is mellowing as she approaches 40. 'I wrote my first book when I was 23, so I certainly like to think I've matured since then,' she reflects by phone in the honeyed voice of a sorority sister.

In *The Morning After*, Roiphe charged campus feminists

with depriving women of agency by encouraging them to view themselves as passive victims and see all men as potential aggressors. Rape-awareness lectures, sexual-conduct codes, Take-Back-the-Night rallies, key-chain alarms, and blue-lit emergency phones did not empower women, in her view, but infantilised them.

She regrets not having used a milder tone to protect herself from attacks, but feels that 'the brash adolescent way it was written was really effective in getting people to talk'. To her detractors, such as Naomi Wolf and Gloria Steinem, the book called for the return to a culture of blaming the victim, where women were ridiculed for speaking up about sexual abuse.

By the late 1990s, the culture of political correctness had shifted, and Wolf and Steinem were singing from a similar tunebook to Roiphe. Wolf styled herself as a 'pro-sex' feminist, and Steinem defended Bill Clinton against the charges of sexual assault from Kathleen Willey and Paula Jones. 'The idea that we shouldn't look at women as victims — and that it's insulting to say that men want to have sex and women don't — now seems very obvious,' says Roiphe.

Though *The Morning After* won accolades from hard-line conservatives such as Pat Buchanan, Roiphe votes Democrat and comes from fiercely liberal stock. Her mother, the writer Anne Roiphe, was a prominent 'second-wave' feminist, whose bestselling novel, *Up the Sandbox* (1970), explored the fantasy life of a bored housewife and became a film with Barbra Streisand in 1972. 'My mother has an instinctive liberal sensibility that I don't have,' she says, 'but I wouldn't call myself a conservative.'

Anne Roiphe supported her daughter throughout the kafuffle over *The Morning After*, causing her to fall out with several feminist allies. 'It's hard for me to tell whether she agreed with me or whether it was just unconditional love,' Roiphe says.

When Roiphe and her four sisters were children, Anne wouldn't let them play with Barbie dolls. She gave her daughters trucks instead, which they used as beds for their stuffed animals. Roiphe recalls feeling exasperated at hearing her mother repeat ad nauseum that, contrary to what fairytales suggest, a princess shouldn't await rescue by a prince. 'My generation absorbed these ideas of equality so instantly and so totally that it seemed superfluous to have this constant polemic being told to you.'

Roiphe makes a lesser attempt to shape the views of her six-year-old daughter, Violet. 'The feminists of the Seventies thought that they could create equality by just enforcing it,' she says. 'I don't think you can control those things.'

By the time Roiphe reached her mid-twenties, her mother was pressuring her to marry and have kids. 'A lot of women of her generation who were feminist in the Seventies all of a sudden were, like, "Wait, where are my grandchildren?"' But, in 1997, Roiphe horrified Anne Roiphe by publishing an article, 'The Independent Woman (and Other Lies)', in which she described her desire to be provided for by a man. 'She spent all these decades trying to crash down these stereotypes, so the enduring power of these old-fashioned ideas of men and women to exert a hold over our imagination is bewildering to her,' she says.

The idea of a dominant husband lost its allure, however. In 2005, Roiphe split with her husband of five years, lawyer Harry Chernoff. 'I didn't marry for money, but I had a fantasy of being taken care of. There is a cost in terms of your relationship and your identity in the world when you do that.' She since started dating a writer — 'definitely not a man in a grey-flannel suit' — who she implies is the opposite of Chernoff. Yet she still thinks that men should pay for dates.

As her marriage collapsed, Roiphe was inundated with condolence notes and offers to help out around the house. It felt like her friends were determined to imagine her cracking up. 'For people who are unhappily staying together, it's particularly troubling to see somebody leave a marriage and thrive. In Edith Wharton's New York, there was a different kind of moralism about divorce. Now we officially accept it as fine, but our moralistic attitude takes a different form — a worry that either the kids or the mother are falling apart.'

Her father, psychoanalyst Herman Roiphe, died during the year of her divorce. It was the worst period of her life, Roiphe says, but also the most productive. In an article for *New York* magazine, she wrote about 'the release of a strange jittery energy ... when you burn your entire life down', which made her more focused than ever.

Uncommon Arrangements is the fruit of that nervous energy. It examines seven complex literary relationships from between the two world wars, including Vanessa and Clive Bell, Radclyffe Hall and Una Troubridge, H. G. and Jane Wells, and Vera Brittain and George Gordon Catlin. Reacting against Victorian hypocrisy, the unions are governed by reason rather than convention — experiments in what Katherine Mansfield called 'marriage à la mode'.

Roiphe began reading about these couples to make sense of her own failed marriage. Though *Uncommon Arrangements* lacks the autobiographical anecdotes of her other books, Roiphe insists that 'its energy is the energy of someone trying to figure things out'. Reading the letters, diaries, and memoirs of these literary bohemians made her 'realise how much in a marriage can happen without you paying attention. One isn't aware of something falling apart until afterwards.'

Belonging to a period that long predated email meant that these writers' most private communications were preserved on paper: 'You can read their papers and get further into those marriages than you would your closest friends, who you see for dinner and you have no idea what really goes on in their house. Marriage is a mystery.'

Early-20th-century intellectuals often believed that by speaking rationally and openly about their extramarital affairs they could avoid inflicting emotional pain. 'I don't think that's a popular mode of thinking today,' Roiphe says. 'People give in to overwhelming feeling more easily.'

But she feels that the era's conflicts resonate with contemporary discussion about women. 'We're half-enchanted with these old-fashioned, traditional ideas of wifehood and motherhood, and half-enchanted with our legacy of absolute equality and women working. We're torn between these two ideas of what women are, in a way that mirrors this very peculiar period right after Edwardian England.'

Uncommon Arrangements reflects her aversion to conceiving of women as victims. She writes that 'where a man has been monstrous, the woman has almost always had some hand in creating her particular monster'. When Roiphe considers the marriage of Sydney-born novelist Elizabeth Von Arnim, and Bertrand Russell's older brother, Frank, she makes clear that Elizabeth desired a tyrannical husband. 'She was attracted to men who were overbearing and made her feel feminine, even though she herself was a strong, outspoken feminist figure,' she says.

The creativity of these relationships contrasts with the pettiness of contemporary discussion of marriage — dominated, as Roiphe sees it, by issues like whether husbands should share the duty of picking up Lego. 'Why,' she writes, 'when women have so many choices, are we still as angry as gloved suffragettes hurling bricks through windows?'

Still, the book's contemporary relevance is mostly implied rather than stated. Roiphe 'wanted to write a more complicated and rich portrait of these marriages than some sort of polemic would have been allowed'. But, Roiphe is quick to add, she still often writes contrarian journalism, and teaches a course on polemic at NYU. Her students rarely identify as feminists, which Roiphe sees as healthy.

She thinks the fact that they take feminism for granted means that the women's movement has achieved its goals. 'If feminism as a movement doesn't have much of a future, that's a testament of its success.'

When she began her PhD thesis on Freud and mid-20th century American writers, she wanted to be an academic. But convinced that no university would employ her following the *Morning After* controversy, she settled for journalism instead.

Now she has an academic job, but her appointment as one of two full-time professors in NYU's cultural journalism program was controversial. The post was vacated after the program's founder, feminist critic Ellen Willis, died from lung cancer in 2006. Some saw the choice of replacement as an affront to her legacy. But, counters Roiphe, 'Ellen was the person who, before she died, kind of selected me and really wanted me to have this job.'

Clearly, she still inspires fear and loathing from the sisterhood. But there's relish in her voice when she laughs and says: 'The Katie-haters still exist.'

— April 2008

Wole Soyinka

When the Nigerian writer Wole Soyinka was a student in Britain in the 1950s, he joined the army. The future Nobel laureate intended to exploit the colonial power's training resources to ready himself for a war of African liberation.

But after the Suez Crisis broke out in 1956 and he was called up to serve with the British forces, Soyinka realised his mistake. Having declined the call-up, he only narrowly escaped being court-martialled. He convinced his superiors that he couldn't possibly have sworn loyalty to Her Majesty by ensuring that no intelligible English emanated from his lips.

Those years were formative for the emerging playwright, poet, essayist, and activist who watched, appalled, as the first generation of African nationalists began visiting Britain regularly, more interested in bedding white women than with transforming the colonial order. His anticipation of pan-African freedom dimmed as he witnessed the lavish spending of the self-preening new leaders, who spoke with vicious condescension towards the societies they claimed to represent.

'The conviction of liberation ... made some of us feel that we could entrust the future of the continent to these first-generation leaders,' says Soyinka, 75, on the eve of publication of his memoir, *You Must Set Forth at Dawn* (2006). 'It was inconceivable that, coming out from under the yoke of external colonialism, any group of leaders would dare to treat their own people with the same contempt as the former colonial powers. Collectively, we failed to take the necessary actions to stop it.'

Soyinka fell out of favour with Nigeria's new political elite on his return from Britain in 1960. During a festival commemorating Nigeria's recent independence, he staged his play A *Dance of the Forests*, which cast doubt on the country's ability to shed the colonial culture of corruption. The play drew sharp criticism for metaphorically depicting Nigeria as a mythical half-child who is born old and must, therefore, die young.

He also attracted fire from intellectuals associated with the so-called Negritude movement, which endeavoured to define and promote an African spirit, and took exception to his use of European literary techniques. Soyinka cautioned his Negritude critics against promoting a stereotypical dichotomy between Western rationalism and African emotionalism. 'A tiger does not proclaim its tigritude,' he wrote. 'It acts.'

Yet Soyinka later came to accept 'that Negritude was an insurgent tool that was needed for the peculiar nature of French colonialism, which tried to make its colonials French and denigrated African values — unlike the British, who felt that the black man could not apprehend European civilisation, so left their colonials alone with their culture'.

Protesting against a rigged election in western Nigeria in 1965, Soyinka held up a radio station at gunpoint and switched the tape playing a speech by the self-declared winner with one proclaiming his illegitimacy. He was charged with armed robbery and detained for three months, before being acquitted on a technicality.

In 1967, he was imprisoned for 27 months, mostly in solitary confinement, for allegedly assisting the Biafran breakaway movement. That Soyinka was attempting to persuade the Biafran leadership of the recklessness of separation was irrelevant, as he was never charged.

What Soyinka feared most in prison was that he'd be killed while the outside world was fed lies about his activities. 'Once I was able to smuggle out the truth about my experience — once I got word back so that the wrong versions of events weren't believed — suddenly I felt like I could relax. What frightened me most was that I would have been made to die a lie.'

Initially, the deprivations of prison life made Soyinka hell-bent on spearheading prison reforms. He launched a hunger strike, even while he feared being blinded by the harsh desert wind that swept through his cell. Yet he came to realise the futility of seeing the prison system in isolation from the wider despotic regime. 'It doesn't take long to recognise that the immediate cesspit is only another facet of society itself, and you go back to what brought you there — the transformation of the entire society.'

After Nigeria fell under the rule of General Sani Abacha in 1993, Soyinka called for international sanctions in an effort to end the regime. The strongman retaliated by barring him from leaving the country. After Soyinka's friend, the writer Ken Saro-Wiwa was executed in 1995, Soyinka fled, riding a motorcycle for 12 hours to get across the Benin border.

He denies that his Nobel title gave him immunity. 'That concept, which especially the Western world has, is completely ill-founded. Abacha would have died a happy person if he could have put in his curriculum vitae that he hanged or shot a Nobel laureate.'

In 1997, Soyinka was sentenced to death in absentia, but returned to Nigeria the next year after Abacha's death. He accepted a post at Obafemi Awolowo University, after securing a guarantee than none of Abacha's former stooges would be made chancellor.

Soyinka also holds posts at the universities of Nevada and California, and in October 2005 was scheduled to come to Australia on a PEN lecture tour — but he cancelled in outrage at the visa requirements.

'Everything was set and then there was this "Pro Forma for Offshore Applicants Aged Seventy and Over". All my life I've fought against discrimination. So why should I accept becoming a subhuman being simply because I want to go to Australia? I don't care if I'm dying tomorrow and Australia has the cure for whatever illness afflicts me — if I have to fill out this form, I'd rather die.'

His sloganeering tone doesn't lift when discussing his family. Soyinka describes himself as an absentee father. His current wife, referring to his posts as a visiting professor at various universities, calls him a visiting husband. He refuses to say how many children he's sired, telling *The Guardian* in 2002: 'In our tradition we don't count our children. In my case the gods have been kind — maybe over-generous.'

Unlike Nelson Mandela, who regretted that politics stripped him of his capacity to be a father, Soyinka clearly feels no remorse about pouring his energies into activism and art. 'I always tell my family, "You have no choice. You didn't ask to be my relation. I didn't ask to be a member of your family." They can't deny enjoying people saying, "Oh, you're the child of Soyinka" or "You're the brother of Soyinka." So they have some compensations.'

'Of course,' Soyinka continues, 'there are moments when I'd like to sit with my family, to talk, eat together, go to theatre or opera or take a holiday together. But just like a doctor who's on call, who can be called out in the most private moment — who's he to complain? He chose his profession. I don't see the life of the activist as different.'

— November 2005

James Wood

It was the kind of meeting that even the most battle-hardened critics try to avoid. When James Wood started teaching part-time at Harvard in 2003, where Zadie Smith was a fellow, he knew that their paths would cross. 'I need to not know the writer I'm writing about negatively,' says Wood, 44, who is almost universally regarded as the finest book-critic of his generation, if not the world. 'Suddenly you meet the author and they say, "This was me you hurt", and they sort of break the terms of the review. It must remain abstract.'

In a devastating critique of Smith's *White Teeth* in 2000, Wood coined the phrase 'hysterical realism' to describe the trend for sprawling novels which mimic the chaos of contemporary reality through deliberately raucous prose and congested plots. He charged Smith, Jonathan Franzen, Salman Rushdie, Don DeLillo, and Thomas Pynchon with inaugurating a breed of novel, filled with social commentary and cultural trivia, in which 'the conventions of realism are not being abolished but, on the contrary, exhausted, and overworked'.

But when Smith and Wood finally met, their encounter was far from hostile: 'She takes on board everything you've said and wants to incorporate it. She's a serious artist in that she's perhaps too self-scrutinising.'

The same self-deprecating streak applies to Wood. When he became chief book critic of *The Guardian* at 26, he was already renowned in England for critical judgements of such erudition and brutality that you'd expect him to brook no self-doubt. But as

Wood leaves the Harvard seminar room where he's been lecturing undergraduates on *To The Lighthouse* (1927), and walks to a café through snow-covered streets sporting a professorial tweed coat, he reflects critically on his own work with all the rigour of his essays.

He's perplexed that 'hysterical realism' has entered the language of criticism and taken on a meaning that he never intended. 'It seems so imprecise to me,' says Wood. 'It just seems like journalistic phrase-making. It seems not to have the fleshed-out density of a proper critical term.'

What does he make of the idea that our rumbustious, media-saturated times call for similarly haphazard fiction? 'I don't have any problem with representing the weirdness of American reality — it's when it gets conflated with this idea that in our postmodern age the subject can't speak authentically because it's written over by so many discourses,' says Wood, who hunches low over the table throughout our chat. 'There are more discourses and it's more intense, but I don't think it's new. And fiction's job is not simply to say, "This is what it's like, I'll just go with it." It should excite in us a resistance.'

Wood's proselytising tone was sternest in his first book *The Broken Estate: essays on literature and belief* (1999) — a collection of essays with a moral seriousness not seen since F. R. Leavis and Lionel Trilling. It reflected Wood's preference for novels that enable the reader to believe in their fictional world, similar to the opportunity for unquestioning faith once provided by Christianity. His touchstones — among them, Anton Chekhov, Saul Bellow, Nikolai Gogol, D. H. Lawrence, and W. G. Sebald — are writers who quest after meaning and moral value, while creating an intimacy with the reader at odds with the alienating effects of much contemporary literature.

His 2004 collection, *The Irresponsible Self: on laughter and the novel*, struck a lighter note. Wood focused on 'the comedy of forgiveness' — a form of laughter inclined towards sympathy — rather than the tendentious satire of 'the comedy of correction'.

'*The Broken Estate* was a rather solemn, almost Eliotic, hallowed, quite harsh book,' he says. 'I wanted *The Irresponsible Self* to be more comic and praising.'

His newest book, *How Fiction Work* (2008), finds Wood at his most celebratory. In 123 numbered paragraphs, he examines the fundamentals of fiction — including detail, character, language, narrative, and dialogue — in the vein of E. M. Forster's *Aspects of the Novel* (1927) and Wayne Booth's *The Rhetoric of Fiction* (1961). '*How Fiction Works* is the fruit of a decision that I've done enough negating. Everyone knows what I don't like — so, "What do I like, and why do I like it?"'

It's a brilliant but also uncharacteristically restrained book, with few of the magisterial rhetorical flourishes of Wood's essays. 'The book comes out of the teaching that I've been doing since 2003. It's a more obviously pedagogical work than anything I've done before.'

The same genial and witty voice of *How Fiction Works* comes through in Wood's seminar. Although slightly stooped, he cuts a relaxed figure, sometimes massaging his right cheek as he speaks. Departing from the often ideological nature of university literary studies, he asks basic questions such as: 'What do you like about this book?'

Wood listens attentively, chewing on his pen, as a student comments that he felt Virginia Woolf was 'mean' by flippantly announcing a character's death between parentheses. That innocence, Wood later tells me without condescension, is why he finds teaching undergraduate students invigorating. 'I'm trying to keep alive some notion that there is this noble form of criticism that has nothing to do with the academy and that hugely predates the academy.'

In an event of major significance to that wider literary culture, in August 2007 Wood became a staff writer at *The New Yorker* (circulation: 1.1 million) after twelve years at the Washington-based *The New Republic* (circulation: 62,000). Wood felt that he was repeating himself at *The New Republic* and had also become lazy by writing less because of his friendship with its literary editor, Leon Wieseltier. (A keen musician, Wood played the trumpet at Wieseltier's wedding.)

But at *The New Yorker* his highbrow essays will have to contend with a more amorphous readership. 'The test will be — can a reasonably complex general literary criticism, that doesn't cede its sophistication to populism, go on in a mainstream magazine that's read by a million people a week?'

Wood's hiring surely displeased some *New Yorker* fixtures. The magazine was the career-long home of the late John Updike, about whom Wood once wrote: 'At his worst, his prose is a harmless, puffy lyricism, a seigneurial gratuity, as if language were just a meaningless bill to a very rich man and Updike adding a lazy 10 per cent tip to each sentence.'

The New Yorker has also been one of the elephantine critic George Steiner's main stamping grounds. Wood has likened Steiner's prose to 'the sweat of a statue that wishes to be a monument' with its 'platoon-like massing of its adjectives, its catheral hush around the great works'.

But taking down literary giants has lost its glamour for Wood. It's not that he's mellowed, Wood says, just grown bored with sounding similar. But he envisages occassionally surprising himself with 'a perfectly foul piece about something that needs to be prosecuted'.

Evangelism runs in Wood's blood. He was raised in a fundamentalist Christian household in Durham, England, the son of a zoology professor and a schoolteacher who spoke in tongues. By 15, he'd broken with God but come alive to the secular power of literature.

The pulpit-thumping zeal of Wood's criticism, with its unfashionable insistence on transcendent truths, suggests that perhaps his religiosity wasn't lost so much as redirected into literature. But Wood says that if his love of literature originated anywhere, it was in music. 'An ear for beauty, repetition, and patterns was trained in me early. I'm not sure I transferred the religious impulse wholesale onto literature, not least because I delight in the novel's secularism. The zeal is temperamental, so maybe I just have a religious zeal.'

After completing his undergraduate degree in English at Cambridge, Wood worked as a freelance book reviewer rather than pursuing a doctorate. At Cambridge he met his wife, the Canadian–American novelist Claire Messud, with whom he has two young children, Lucian and Livia. They moved to London, where Wood followed what he saw as the romantic idea of making a living from the pen.

Nostalgically, he recalls the pre-Internet days of delivering copy to newspapers. 'I was just at the tail end of this thing of finishing the piece and materially handling it — either faxing it through, or often just getting on a bike and taking it into *The Guardian* because it was late.' Still finding writing a chore, he typically waits until the day before an essay is due before starting it, then works through the night.

Wood's precocity as a critic was a double-edged scythe when it came to writing his own novel. 'The more I wrote about fiction, and the more I demanded from novels, the more other people — and, indeed, my own inner voice — would say, "Where's the beef?" I got into a funk.' At 35, he made a pledge: 'Either you do it now or you'll never do it.'

Published to mixed reviews, *The Book Against God* (2003) was, in some ways, a typical autobiographical first novel. Wood's anti-hero, Thomas Bunting, is the son of a parish priest, who has turned his back on his parents' values to write a mammoth debunking of religion titled *The Book Against God*.

But Wood's parents were more dogmatic than the Buntings. 'I wanted to take someone like me, but instead of saying, "Oh poor me, I had such religious parents", flip the question around and say, "Poor Thomas, his parents are all too genial, all too excellent. What the hell is he complaining about?"'

It was inevitable that the novel would be measured against Wood's critical standards. Indeed, the ferocity of some reviews suggested that Wood's detractors had been waiting for his novelistic debut to exact revenge.

Wood concedes that he broke his rules against being too essayistic and allegorical. As he wrote of Thomas Pynchon's *Mason & Dixon* (1997): 'Pynchon uses allegory to hide truth, and in so doing expands allegory into a fetish of itself.'

Above all, Wood thinks his novel suffered from over-writing. 'The stuff I write in *How Fiction Works* about detail, but also about writing over characters, relates to my tendency as a novelist to put in passages of fine writing which I should have kept out.'

Undeterred by the attacks, Wood is writing another novel — albeit, he says, 'with a lot less God stuff in it this time'. He muses about the possibility of issuing it under a pseudonym, then outing himself as its author after the reviews — if only he could get his editor to agree. He plans to bring out a third collection of criticism, but thinks that three books of essays might be enough. 'Will it be more impressive when I'm 60 and I've published seven of these identical collections?'

Instead, he hopes *The New Yorker* will allow him to try other forms of writing. Like his teenage hero George Orwell, who was as eloquent describing a Leo Tolstoy novel as the shooting of an elephant, Wood is eager to venture out into less bookish terrain. 'It would mean giving up an anxiety to seem intellectually in charge, and just following the world, just letting the real come to you.'

Meanwhile, we can look forward to his second novel. But it might be a while until we know it's by James Wood.

— *January 2008*

Acknowledgements

I am indebted to my editors at the various newspapers and magazines, Australian and international, who either commissioned or republished versions of the interviews included in this collection. I credit *The Financial Times* with first publication of my essays on Haruki Murakami, Elfriede Jelinek, Ismail Kadare, and José Saramago.

Thanks to my indefatigable agent Lyn Tranter and also to Henry Rosenbloom, Michael Campbell, and Emma Morris at Scribe for their commitment to this book. Above all, thanks to Bron Sibree and Jennifer Moran — two immensely generous people who launched a career for me back in 2001 and made this book possible.